Changing Human Behavior

CHANGING HUMAN BEHAVIOR

John Mann

CHARLES SCRIBNER'S SONS
New York

To
A. R.

Contents

CONTENTS

LIST OF TABLES

Changing Human Behavior

Introduction

I T is one of the ironies of our age that while there have been numerous fundamental advances in scientific knowledge and technology, one of mankind's oldest and most crucial problems has been left
almost untouched by scientists—the need to improve man's utilization
of his own positive capabilities. Little more is known today about how
to foster the development of constructive behavior than was known
two thousand years ago. Man's inability to consciously evolve the creative aspects of his own nature tends to dilute and divert his most
earnest social efforts and turns recent scientific breakthroughs, which
should set man free from social and economic bondage, into sources of
greater anxiety.

Throughout the ages mankind has recognized the importance of
understanding and guiding human development. The philosophers of
ancient Greece and the sages of India and China sought tirelessly to
clarify this problem and to develop practical solutions. During the
Dark Ages men sought self-improvement in a theological, rather than a
philosophical or scientific, framework. The search for salvation was,
and always has been, an attempt to find personal completion and as
such must be classified as a search for a means of human development.

In our own day the quest continues. Endless books are written for
professional and lay audiences about mental health, self-development,

and human understanding. Some are good, others not, but most tend either to philosophize or to present merely practical guides to living. They contain little that has been objectively validated.

Scientists for the most part are mute on this issue. They prefer to pursue the more comfortable and traditional approach of accumulating knowledge for its own sake, with a central emphasis on the precise description, prediction, and control of objects, events, and people in their normal conditions. When scientists stray toward research into the abnormal, as clinical psychologists or psychiatrists do, the emphasis is on helping the patient return to normality. This habitual conservatism of scientific investigation is understandable and useful, but one must pay a price for it. In this case, the price is the separation of science from certain areas of human experience that urgently require exploration. In social and behavioral studies—those disciplines that concern us most directly here—a number of subjects are traditionally avoided, including sex, suicide, parapsychology, homosexuality, and death. They are outside the pale of scientific acceptability for various reasons, but in general they threaten the fabric of society or certain individuals within it. This is as true of the study of death as it is of the study of behavior change. Whenever scientists begin to examine behavior in order to control it, the public reacts very strongly in the misguided belief that behavior really can be altered in some important manner. Usually it cannot, but the power of science always seems to threaten that a small demonstration, such as the use of hypnosis to produce antisocial acts for experimental purposes, will become a fundamental means of regimenting or manipulating human beings.

These reactions to potential breakthroughs help to explain why scientists have so seldom studied the problem of behavior change. The public does not support or sustain such research. Moreover, those scientists engaged in basic research, those who express their work in abstract, but precise, terms and deal with the theoretical aspect of the problems they are investigating, are viewed as performing more valuable research than those who seek answers in the less objective realm of human behavior. Scientists who focus their attention on issues of immediate, practical importance, without attempting to formulate abstract principles from their conclusions, are engaged in what is called applied research. While they may receive acclaim from the public, they are usually viewed by their colleagues as making a relatively minor contribution to their science. Since the sociologists and psychologists

2

studying behavior change typically devote their research to practical problems, the area has been regarded as less valuable than other scientific fields.

This hierarchy is actually quite reasonable. Applied researchers often are not as analytic, careful, or searching in their work. They do not take the broad view. Their investigations are often technically deficient because of the conditions produced by the direct contact they have with society in an environment they cannot control and the modest funds that are available to them. Basic research usually is protected from such sources of "contamination" and conducted in a laboratory with elaborate equipment and dedicated scientists, associates, and assistants. Everything is at hand to encourage well-controlled and carefully conceived studies. The results are naturally more satisfactory.

Further, science is by tradition amoral; that is, it does not take an ethical stand but limits itself to the discovery and verification of objective facts and relationships. It is not surprising in view of this tradition that many scientist have avoided those topics that seem to have moral implications. In fact, the more distant these implications are from the subject, the greater the scientific effort tends to be. On the surface, at least, there is nothing less related to morality than atoms and molecules, and it is the scientific disciplines of physics and chemistry that have advanced most markedly. Of course, this very progress has created some searching moral questions, but nothing could have been farther from the minds of the scientists responsible for these developments at the time they began their work.

Behavioral and social scientists of whatever type—anthropologists, sociologists, psychologists, psychiatrists—have not behaved any differently than physicists. They have tried to uncover basic facts about human behavior, but they have been influenced in their selection of what to investigate by the traditional viewpoint of what the most valuable type of research is. For the most part, they have been blind to the fact that the alteration of human behavior and the development of human potential are basic problems as much as are the description of personality and the development of a new learning theory.

On the surface, it may seem that a theoretically oriented scientific approach to the problem of consciously produced behavior change would be a contradiction in terms, that these investigations, by their nature, must be looked upon as applied research; but this contradiction is apparent, not inherent. The fact that most behavior-change studies have been motivated by practical ends does not mean that such research cannot be conceived of in terms of a general theoretical system. Knowledge about the ways to modify human behavior tells nothing about their ultimate application. The dictator needs such information as much as a senator; the psychotherapist must base his actions upon it as well as the communist engaged in brain washing. All are joined in their common dependence on verified information and principles of behavior change, which each uses to attain quite different goals.

In spite of the need for reliable knowledge of this kind, there seems to have been an unconscious conspiracy to delay substantial scientific exploration in this area. No general body of information has been built up. In most areas, findings are sparse and usually unrelated to one another rather than cumulative. In recent years, there has been an indication of a new trend, and in certain limited and fairly superficial areas, clear and well-conceived attacks have been launched on subjects bearing upon behavior change. However, reports of these studies have appeared in many unrelated literatures and have been dispersed throughout the outpouring of information that currently characterizes most sciences.

Findings are further obscured by the fact that each specialty develops its own techniques, vocabulary, and, ultimately, its own training programs and traditions. This tendency of disciplines to insulate themselves from their conceptual associates has reduced intercommunication of relevant findings to a bare minimum. This, in turn, has further slowed the assimilation of the little applicable basic research on the subject that does exist. In this manner, the natural growth of a science eventually interferes with its progress, producing a situation in which scientists in adjacent areas developing along parallel paths are in ignorance of each other's findings.

These developmental patterns fortunately are counteracted in time by the equally natural formation of new scientific areas that span the gap that has been created. Thus, the biochemist, the physiological psychologist, and the social psychologist are now attempting to work in areas left obscure by previous specialization. The creation of such new integrative scientific disciplines seems to be required if the study of behavior change is to be pursued fruitfully. To establish a groundwork for such development, it is necessary to clarify what is meant by behavior change.

4

There are at least three ways to approach the study of human change. First, it can be attributed to uncontrolled short-term variations in the social environment or the individual. Depending on their nature, they may produce violent behavioral alterations, as in the case of a sudden earthquake or a heart attack. In other situations, the effects may be quite mild, such as those produced by bodily fatigue or elevated atmospheric temperature. These variations occur continually and affect human behavior either singly or in interaction with other, simultaneously changing, external or internal conditions. From the viewpoint of predicting human behavior these changes are of interest, but they do not fall within the scope of the present work because they are not intentionally produced.

The second form of change in the social, cultural, and physical environments occurs over a long period of time. Sociologists study this aspect of variation as "social change." Geologists study a related problem by examining the strata of the earth to see how its surface has been altered over the centuries. Biologists view animal and plant life in terms of evolution, relating the modification of species to changing environmental conditions. In principle, behavior change resulting from slowly evolving social and physical conditions is the same as that produced by a sudden alteration. In both, the new behavior is due to forces that are not consciously controlled.

The third type of behavior alteration is created by man for certain specific reasons. It can be classified as consciously induced change. Into this category must be placed such diverse activities as advertising, psychotherapy, human-relations training, and hypnotism. The present volume is devoted to studies of this type of change. Research in these areas has not developed comprehensively and coherently. At best, one finds fertile areas of knowledge in a desert of ignorance, but little communication among the oases of information.

This inspection of the goals of the behavioral sciences has suggested that the study of intentionally produced change is not about to be altered in any dramatic or systematic manner in the near future. Therefore, the initiative must be taken by interested individuals if the current diverse and rather disorganized forays into experimental investigation and the irregular attempts at integration of findings are to be coordinated into some more complete picture. The problem of developing human potential and altering human behavior is a crucial issue in our day, and we cannot afford to wait until the social and cultural forces that influence the direction of current scientific interest finally assimilate the present historical situation.

The first step in producing any widespread realization of the need for a reorganization of our commitments and scientific strategy in this area logically ought to be the compilation and analysis of the findings that have already been obtained. Such an exploration forms the natural foundation upon which future work should be built. It is the central purpose of this book to provide this groundwork and also to document the present state of knowledge about the enhancement and alteration of human behavior.

Two major approaches have been adopted by scientists interested in behavior change. The first seeks to document the ascribed effects of currently applied methods, such as psychoanalysis or human-relations training. These results usually are weakened by a variety of technical and social problems, and, for the most part, the conclusions have been ambiguous. Because of its technical nature, the general aspects of this form of research, its peculiar problems, and its lack of productivity are discussed at length in the Appendixes.

The second approach, on which this volume concentrates, utilizes experimental methods to study specific aspects, or *components,* of behavior-change processes under controlled conditions. The results of this research have on the whole been more satisfactory and constitute the objective foundation for more fruitful developments. Yet reliance on published reports places definite limitations on the subject matter that can be covered.

A number of topics have received widespread attention in the popular press—brainwashing, subliminal perception, glandular injections, and the like. These subjects never fail to arouse interest because of the stimulating and possibly sinister possibilities they seem to suggest. However, they will not be discussed in this work for two reasons. Either no substantial experimental evidence has yet accumulated, or these techniques are simply not as effective as was originally supposed. Several of these topics have been discussed by the author in a previous volume, and the interested reader is referred to that source.*

Similarly, certain complex social experiences said to develop the personal or social adjustment of those who participate in them have

* John Mann, *Frontiers of Psychology* (New York: The Macmillan Company, 1963).

not been dealt with here. For example, the famous English school known as Summerhill, which specializes in the use of affection and love as motivating forces for education and personal growth, has been described eloquently, but it has not been scientifically assessed, so that nothing objective is actually known of its actual value. In America, the Encampment for Citizenship, a summer training school for the development of youthful leaders, has been subjected to evaluation that tends to support the effectiveness of the program; but there is little or no precise information about just what aspects of the Camp's program have the greatest impact on the youths. Again, therefore, little can be said about the cause of any positive change that takes place.

By limiting this book to topics about which clear, scientific evidence is available, it is hoped that an insightful and objective picture of our present state of knowledge about modes of changing human behavior will emerge. If it causes the reader to question, disagree with, and reassess his own views, it will have served its function. If it further serves, even indirectly, to renew professional interest in a vital area too long neglected by the orthodox citadels of scientific thought, it will have fulfilled its potential.

CHAPTER ONE

The Evaluation of
Behavior-Change Processes

THERE are many ways to induce a constructive behavior change in individuals. The *practitioner,* or change agent, the man who tries to bring about such change, is not a researcher; he devotes himself to working directly with people on problems of immediate, practical importance. Among the practitioners who devote themselves to treating the mentally ill are the *clinical psychologist* and the *psychotherapist,* who usually have Ph.D. degrees and who use certain techniques of psychological therapy on their patients; the *psychiatrist,* a medical doctor whose specialty is mental illness; and the *psychoanalyst,* usually a psychiatrist who has taken further training in a particular kind of psychological therapy at a psychoanalytic institute. Other practitioners are more interested in attempting to bring about more overt kinds of behavior change related to one's social environment, the *social worker,* for example, or the *human-relations trainer,* who works with psychologically normal persons to help them improve their skills in relating to others. All practitioners share the same general aim of trying to improve the social and psychological performances of the people with whom they are working.

For many years it has been believed that the most natural and fruitful way to study behavior change is to evaluate the effects of those methods that are believed by the practitioners who use them to have the most power. A wide range of processes, of course, is utilized, including counseling, psychotherapy, and leadership training. They are applied in a variety of settings, such as schoolrooms, doctors' offices, mental-hygiene clinics, and industrial training centers. By focusing directly on the effects of these processes as they are applied in their natural setting, scientists thought that important information about the general process of behavior change would be obtained. Such reasoning has been based on the notion that all these processes contain certain common components that collectively determine their impact. By evaluating the effectiveness of various behavior-change methods, it was believed that the nature and contribution of the components would be clarified. In addition, those who sponsored and conducted such research hoped that a sober scientific light would be generated, removing behavior change once and for all from the darkness of untested theories and personal belief.

Such a redefinition seemed about to occur. Behavioral scientists, administrators, politicians, therapists, and educators watched the horizon eagerly for signs of the coming dawn. However, with the passage of time, their vigil has been unrewarded; the sky has remained murky. The accumulation of findings has resulted only in the compounding of confusion, and the scientists who are closest to the situation have long since been disillusioned.

Some Problems of Evaluative Research

Because of the apparent logic of the evaluative approach, its lack of efficiency is not readily understandable. Its explanation lies in an analysis of the social and methodological problems haunting such efforts, as well as in the interpretive problems that must be faced when analyzing the deceptively simple conclusions such studies provide. A detailed, more technical discussion of these various elements appears in Appendixes A and B, where readers particularly interested in evaluative research can review the material. Some summary statement is necessary here, however, so that the chapters that follow can be viewed in the proper frame of reference.

The first major point that must be made is that it is relatively easy to perform an evaluative study. It is only necessary to administer the treatment undergoing evaluation to a given set of subjects and to compare changes in their behavior with those noted in an equivalent group not receiving the particular treatment. Because of the directness and

10

simplicity of this approach, many unwary investigators have been attracted to conducting such studies, hoping for answers to such controversial questions as whether psychoanalysis cures neuroses or whether group therapy administered to several patients simultaneously is more effective than therapy of persons treated individually.

The passage of time has revealed what those familiar with the scientific method have known from the start: evaluative research is much harder to conduct than the basic model, described above, would suggest. It is beset with a swarm of methodological and social difficulties that try the patience and intelligence of even the experienced investigator. These problems do not prevent such research from being undertaken. Their effects are more insidious; they undermine the results that are obtained. This is dangerous because it is not readily evident and can be covered up to some extent by the original investigator if he is so motivated or if he is willing to comply with biased administrative directives.

The social difficulties of such studies are generally easier to understand and, therefore, provide a convenient point of departure. One recurrent obstacle is the reluctance of the practitioner to participate in the evaluative study. Whatever the initial interest that may stimulate such research, the man whose work is being evaluated soon realizes that he has little to gain from the experience. Most practitioners are fully convinced of the efficiency of their methods and do not require objective validation. Further, it is difficult for a practitioner to distinguish between the method under evaluation and his ability as a practitioner, or even as a human being. Thus he may be threatened by the evaluative process and seek to subvert it or at least to alter the results so that they will be favorable to him. This tendency is quite human and natural, but it makes evaluation difficult since the researcher and the subject of his study are working at cross purposes.

Parallel technical difficulties exist. Most of this evaluative research is conducted with only one or two practitioners who themselves work with a variety of subjects. When the study is limited to a sample of only one or two, it is extremely difficult to draw any conclusions. Another difficulty produced by the use of a small sample of practitioners is that one cannot distinguish between the effectiveness of the method under evaluation and the impact of the unique personality of the man applying the method, irrespective of the particular approach he employs. Since it is well known that personal relations are an important aspect of the change process, it is vital that such an influence be controlled if the method itself is to be assessed. Usually, however, the refinements of technique that are required to make this distinction are not employed. Such social and methodological difficulties accumulate and contaminate the obtained results with various sources of error that may be difficult to control or even to identify; and the conclusions, however precise, are cast into doubt.

That these errors do, in fact, often occur, does not indicate any intrinsic flaw in evaluative research, but it does document the inherent difficulties. If one is willing to take the necessary steps to counter such errors, then clear conclusions can be obtained. Unfortunately, most evaluators have not taken the trouble to do so and have, therefore, produced conclusions that are difficult to interpret.

However, the basic source of difficulty in evaluative studies is more profound. It cannot be corrected by technical excellence or careful control of social conditions; rather, it requires a redefinition of the area of inquiry. The most that any evaluation can provide is a simple and clear answer to the question, "Does method x produce demonstrable effects?" Generally, the answer to such a question is either known beforehand or is intrinsically unrewarding. Usually, we are not interested in whether a method works, but rather in how it works and why. Evaluative research is dumb on both of these issues. It can document the method's effect but not explain it. The reason for this failing lies not so much in the nature of the research procedure as in the nature of the material under analysis. Because of the inherent complexity of the vast majority of the processes used to induce behavior change, it is almost impossible to describe their nature precisely. Most methods are simply not that clearly formulated; as a result, one is at a loss to know what happened, and, therefore, the cause of any demonstrated effect cannot be determined.

A positive change in behavior may be found. Assuming that the study itself was carefully designed and executed, this finding may be accurate. But to what is it to be attributed? When the method is carefully examined, it is quickly seen to be an amalgam of components of unknown or partially uncontrolled proportions. One cannot evaluate, for example, whether the success of a nondirective counselor is to be attributed to the way in which he speaks, what he says, what he does not say, the nature of the client's problem, the length of time he is seen, the amount he is charged, or any of a hundred other uncontrolled, and perhaps unknown, variables.

Many investigators have argued that such conditions must be tolerated if one is to conduct behavior-change research under realistic conditions. In a sense they are right. If evaluative studies are to assess the effectiveness of the methods in which we currently place our greatest belief, and if the conclusions are to have general validity, the research must surely be conducted under natural conditions. However, this decision presupposes a more basic assumption: namely, that such studies should in fact be conducted. At the present time, because of the doubts noted above, there is good reason to question whether evaluative studies ought to be performed except for highly specific and limited purposes, such as an immediate administrative decision about whether or not to employ a particular procedure.

All may not agree with this estimate, but those who have directly studied the process of the therapeutic interchange between patient and practitioner rather than its ultimate effects know very clearly how complex and subtle it really is. If the process cannot be described with precision, any attempt to evaluate its effectiveness is not likely to be helpful.

Nevertheless, there is an inevitable tendency to perpetuate evaluative research on the theory that it is better to have some studies, even if they are not satisfactory, rather than none at all. Moreover, as long as the nature of an alternate approach is not clarified, the existing procedure seems preferable.

Components of Behavior-Change Processes

In the case of evaluative research, however, reasonable alternatives are available. As has been stated, the major difficulty that haunts evaluative studies is the imprecision of the methods that are subject to investigation. The solution is to reduce these methods to simpler and more controllable forms. An analogy can be drawn here with the science of chemistry. As long as men studied substances in their natural form, they understood little about them, regardless of the precision of their observations. However, when the molecular theory was devised it became possible to view all complex substances as made up of combinations of the known elements. By analyzing the nature of the elements and how they combined in various proportions to make compounds, it was possible not only to understand the structure of the more complex substances, but in many cases actually to synthesize them.

While behavior-change processes are not composed of elements in the same material sense as are chemical compounds, there is little difficulty in isolating a number of components that some or all share in varying degrees. These components lend themselves to precise description and measurement and can therefore be employed in experimental designs with rigor and control to attain cumulative, interpretable, scientific conclusions.

One example of such a component of behavior change is "selective social approval." The practitioner may indicate such approval by smiling, saying some encouraging words, giving money to the patient, allowing special privileges and the like, but he always uses such selective approval in relation to specific kinds of action. Another component is the utilization of *feedback mechanisms,* that is, social arrangements by means of which the practitioner provides—feeds back to the subject—a systematic reaction to his behavior. This feedback may be a psychoanalytic interpretation of his behavior or it may consist of the discussion of scores obtained by the subject on an objective personality test. In each instance, however, the practitioner provides the subject with observations on his own behavior in such a way as to facilitate the change that has already been instituted.

By studying such individual components, the social problems involved in studying complex methods under natural conditions can be eliminated and the methodological ones more easily controlled, even though the generality of the conclusions is more limited. It is even more important that, because components of behavior change are common to many or all such processes, by studying one component, something is learned about the efficacy of a wide range of processes.

Moreover, the components lend themselves to the most powerful form of scientific study: experimental investigation. Most of the recent important methodological developments in the behavioral sciences require the use of an experimental model of data collection in which all factors are carefully controlled and manipulated at will by the experimenter. When such conditions can be approximated, the efficiency and generality of the investigation can be enormously enhanced. That is, more precise information can be obtained for a given effort than by any other approach. It is, therefore, of crucial importance that the study of behavior change be redefined so that these technical developments can be employed fully. This can be done only, as has been indicated, by reducing behavior-change processes to their components and subjecting them in that form to experimental research of increasing complexity, so that in time actual behavior-change processes will be approximated.

Although this fundamental strategy has already been applied to limited areas, it has not yet been accepted as the natural mode of attack for a general study of the alteration and enhancement of human functions. The preceding analysis of evaluative research clearly suggests that an experimental approach is the appropriate orientation from which to study behavior change, and it is toward this end that the following chapters are directed.

CHAPTER TWO

Models of
Behavior-Change Systems

THE experimental investigation of behavior-change components cannot be considered a comprehensive approach to the development of a science of human modification since behavior change is not studied in its total complexity as it functions in its natural habitat. As has been pointed out, the nature of experimental technique requires that the system, or set of relationships under investigation, be broken down into simple elements so that each can be varied and controlled at will by the experimenter.

Many practitioners object to this approach, feeling that the results of any limited experiment are so far removed from behavior in normal circumstances that they cannot be taken seriously or readily generalized to other situations. The experimenter usually counters with the argument that the elements he studies are related to each other by a *model*, an abstract set of conceptual relationships, that does have a direct, though abstract, relationship to normal social situations.

In this argument, the conceptual model provides the vital link between the admittedly artificial and restricted environment of an experiment and the complex set of interlocking, overlapping, generally uncontrolled events that constitute the real world in which behavior change takes place and must be stabilized. It is important, then, that such models be examined before the more specific and limited evi-

16

dence supplied by experimental research is studied, since the implications of these investigations must ultimately be interpreted in terms of some such model.

At the present time, there appears to be a renewed interest in the formulation of models of behavior-change processes. This development may be symptomatic of a maturation in behavior-change studies; whatever its cause, the interest itself is of use because it helps to clarify whether these efforts at abstraction can be successful. Many scientists and practitioners are skeptical about the possibilities of developing such a generalized model of behavior change. They emphasize the incredible diversity of theoretical background, technique, and training of the practitioner, the variations in populations served by him and in the goals of treatment that characterize different behavior-change processes. They point out that for every approach emphasizing the need to accept the subject's behavior, whatever it may be, there is another requiring that the practitioner make direct suggestions about changing it. For every method emphasizing the interpretation of repressed material, there is another that avoids such a confrontation and emphasizes the use of reward, punishment, and other relatively superficial procedures. Where, then, is the communality?

Rosenzweig's Components of Behavior Change

One answer has already been suggested. The idea that all behavior-change techniques are composed of a relatively small number of components common to many of them is not new. As early as 1938, the psychologist Saul Rosenzweig* discussed in an article six factors that he felt made important contributions to a wide variety of behavior-change techniques.[1] Some of these, such as the faith of the subject in the practitioner and the influence of the practitioner's personality, have already been mentioned. Others are somewhat more general. One important aspect common to many procedures is the use of psychotherapy for the redefinition and reformulation of social relationships. From this viewpoint, the behavior-change process provides an example of healthy interpersonal dealings that can serve as a model for the patient in the redefinition of other relationships.

Another interesting common aspect among different techniques of changing human behavior is the utilization of some logically consistent

* All individuals whose contributions have been referred to in this volume are American unless otherwise stated.

theoretical system. Rosenzweig made the iconoclastic suggestion that the truth of the theory is not as important as is its solidity and generality. It provides both the therapist and the client with articles of faith upon which both can depend. Whether or not they are realistic is less important than the fact that they provide assurance and security.

A final and related shared element is the use of interpretation by practitioners. Rosenzweig suggests that human behavior is so variously motivated and complex in origin and performance that almost any consistent explanation or interpretation must be at least partially correct. It does not matter so much, therefore, what the practitioner says or does; as long as the interpretation is consistent within itself, it cannot be too wrong. Or to put it differently, all approaches will meet with some success, a statement that is supported by available evidence.

Rosenzweig also supplies a parallel explanation of another puzzling aspect of all behavior-change processes, namely, what is changed? What do counseling, therapy, training, and so on, really do for the client, assuming that they do something? In the same discussion, Rosenzweig draws a suggestive analogy between immunology and behavior change. He believes that the major kind of change produced by emotional reeducation techniques, such as psychotherapy, is an increase in the ability to tolerate frustration. The healthier the person, the more frustration he can withstand without reacting in a destructive, or self-defeating manner. From this viewpoint behavior-change techniques can be divided into two major categories: (a) those that, through a long and gradual process, attempt to increase frustration tolerance in the individual—this is analogous to creating permanent immunization on the physiological level; (b) those processes that aim at providing an immediate temporary effect in terms of certain specific problems and situations—this sort of behavior change is analogous to a gamma-globulin injection for the prevention of measles, which has a strong, but limited effect. In the first case, the protection is built up within the person. In the second, the protection is built up elsewhere and injected into the patient to provide limited relief. The more basic nondirective therapies, including psychoanalysis, are of the first type. The more directive, such as the use of suggestion and hypnotism, characterize the latter approach.

This classificatory scheme is intriguing in its simplicity. Its importance is that it highlights an area of common concern that all processes attempting to induce behavior change share—namely, the nature of the effect they seek to produce. If this effect can be described as an increase in the ability to tolerate frustration, there is reason to suppose that the methods producing such a general effect cannot be as different from one another as they may appear on the surface.

Frank's Common Features of Behavior Change

A similar line of inquiry has been followed more recently by the psychologist and psychiatrist Jerome D. Frank. In recent years, Dr. Frank has been pursuing the elusive common core of behavior-change techniques with persistence and ingenuity. Some of his research studies will be described in Chapter Six. His central ideas have recently been brought together in the book *Persuasion and Healing*.[2] In this volume, Frank attempts to relate not only different types of psychotherapy, but also such activities as Chinese thought reform (brainwashing), the actions of the shaman, or medicine man, in primitive cultures, religious revivalists, and Christian Scientists, all of whom share the same general goals of producing beneficial behavior changes, though they define the terms somewhat differently.

Frank concludes that all of these forms of healing and persuasion share three common features. First, the practitioner attempting to induce the change is given a certain degree of authority, which helps him to inspire faith in the patient. He is viewed as a potent figure in his own right, capable of producing important influences and changes. This authority is created through elaborate symbolic paraphernalia, special systems of training, social expectation, the use of special treatment settings, payment of fees, and the like.

The second major common element is the practitioner's wish really to help the person who has sought him out. The process is not routine or perfunctory, but implies a definite personal commitment to aid the subject. Because it is so obvious, this aspect of the behavior-change situation is often overlooked. However, even the Chinese thought reform interrogator, who has the subject under complete external domination, must transmit this feeling if he is to be truly effective.

Finally, the practitioner acts as a mediator between the suffering individual and the larger society. In part, he protects the patient from the effects of society by creating a situation in which greater freedom without punishment is possible. Moreover, he becomes society's representative and attempts to lead the person in emotional difficulty back to a mode of expected social behavior. Thus the change agent, whether he likes it or not, is charged by society to normalize the behavior of deviant individuals. Society, at the same time, allows him certain privileges in the process, including the right to suspend traditional mores, such as the need to react with moral indignation or the obligation to report criminal acts to the police if the client tells him about them in confidence.

These are by no means all of the common elements that seem to occur in rather diverse behavior-change processes. Frank discusses a number of others, some of which were touched upon earlier in the discussion of Rosenzweig's ideas. These components include the acceptance and forgiveness offered by the practitioner for whatever the person may have done in the past; the confession by the client of past errors; repeated meetings during which the behavior-change process occurs; the application of some theoretical system that helps to explain why the patient is suffering, the validity of which is less important than its impressiveness and consistency; and finally, the active involvement of both the therapist and the patient in the change process.

Of course, the adherents of different techniques of behavior change generally do not believe that all methods are basically similar; unlike Frank, they emphasize the differences. This may be useful for training purposes, but from the scientific viewpoint the identification of common components is of vital importance as a guide to the formulation of effective research strategy in this area.

The interest in reanalyzing behavior-change processes in a search for unity amid obvious diversity is further evidenced in the recent volume, *Psychotherapy: The Purchase of Friendship*, by the psychologist William Schofield.[3] In that book he considers psychotherapy to be a remarkable social relationship. The person attempting to bring about change in another is someone who wants to help. However, because he is a professional consultant rather than a personal friend, the therapy process takes on the peculiar and unique characteristics that must characterize any relationship that is intimate, temporary, and paid for with money. This analysis reveals a slightly embarrassing aspect of attempts to alter behavior that is often tactfully ignored.

Shared Factors of Psychotherapy Systems

A similar wide-ranging attempt to bring various theories of psychotherapy within a common frame of reference has been recently undertaken by the psychologist Perry London in *The Modes and Morals of Psychotherapy*.[4] While his intent is partially didactic, the trend toward unification that he illustrates is significant.

A somewhat different approach has been taken by the psychologist Carl Rogers, who has drawn heavily upon his own experience and that of his followers.[5] He believes that most therapy, if it is successful, tends to follow a certain pattern, just as all body wounds go through various well-defined stages of healing, regardless of the particular biological or surgical circumstances, and Rogers has tried to describe this normal course of therapy.

Rogers has described a seven-phase model that he believes can account for many of the observed behavioral changes brought about by psychotherapy and other similar processes. This model, interesting in itself, is also of particular value because it was devised to act as the basis for a research program. It is too early to determine how correct Rogers' model is, but it should at least serve as a stimulus for others to formulate testable counterproposals.

Very roughly, the stages described and measured by Rogers can be summarized as follows. In the first stage, the individual talks only about external, impersonal events, avoids recognition of his own problems, and has little desire for change. Next, he begins to talk about himself, but he attributes his problems to external causes; his insight into himself is minimal, and he tends to disown his own emotions even when he expresses them. In the third and fourth stages, a gradual loosening of inhibitions occurs. In the fifth phase, the patient, recognizing his feelings as they arise, begins to experience spontaneous reactions that surprise but by no means delight him. Further, he is able to face more realistically the contradictions and incongruencies of his experience. Next, the patient tends to live more and more in the present, experiencing himself, his hopes and fears as they occur without being unduly threatened or upset. He is no longer an object or a subject but participates in experience directly. Finally, in successful psychotherapy, the patient stabilizes the modes of experience described in the fifth and sixth stages and develops them more fully. He looks upon himself and his life as process rather than structure. Communication pathways are open internally and on the interpersonal level.

Not all therapists would characterize the stages of psychotherapy in this manner, but that is not the real issue. What Rogers has done is to formulate a testable version of the process and make it possible to rescue it from the realm of personal speculation by translating it into terms that are amenable to scientific investigation.

Common Factors in Individual and Group Change Processes

A rather different, and even more relevant, attempt to reformulate behavior-change processes within a common framework was undertaken by the psychologists Ronald Lippitt, Jeanne Watson, and Bruce Westley. In their book, *The Dynamics of Planned Change—a Comparative Study of Principles and Techniques*,[6] they attempt to create a conceptual scheme that can be applied, not only to different types of practitioners, but also to different scales of behavior change, ranging from efforts to alter the individual to attempts to influence institutions and whole communities. Their orientation is comparative, theoretical, and integrative, and the basic approach is to view any behavior-change process as a system whose elements are defined differently as one moves up the ladder of social complexities. Thus, in psychotherapy, the individual views all aspects of his normal social life as external to the therapeutic interaction. In group therapy, the group is viewed as internal and the social structure within which it exists as external. On the level of the community, surrounding communities are external, but all members of the given one are internal. Thus, the external and internal aspects of any system can be defined, but the elements change with the scale of the system.

In *The Dynamics of Planned Change*, the authors seek to demonstrate the proposition that problems arising in any system of behavior change take general forms and that, consequently, a limited array of techniques is sufficient to handle these problems, whether they arise from the nature of the system itself or from particular types of imbalance that have arisen within it. If such an approach is actually appropriate, it would certainly be highly economical and aid in the structuring of one general model of the behavior-change process.

It is difficult to do justice to the complexities involved in such a comparative analysis, but certain conclusions presented by the authors should be noted. First, all change agents, regardless of their professional affiliations, tend to work through certain channels and to utilize certain classes of procedure. When working directly on the internal structure of the person or group, they attempt to reorganize the distribution of power, either by encouraging the development of new sources of influence or by making old power centers more representative of the structure as a whole.

Another vital task is to increase the efficiency with which energy is mobilized to produce useful behavior. This can be done first by ceasing to utilize inefficient techniques and then by developing new patterns of task distribution and organization to increase the efficiency of performance. The third major internal mode of attack is through *communication networks*. The practitioner opens up channels of communication that were previously closed or "noise ridden" due to interference of some sort that was wholly or partially obstructing the transmission of information. He does this by acting as a temporary go-between, interpreting and transmitting the messages when there is no direct communication at the time. If he is successful, he can eventually withdraw, and the new communication channels will continue to function. A rather different alternative is to give information to the client that has been obtained and analyzed externally, such as research data. Such objective findings may "clear" channels of communication.

The second large class of client problems involves his relations to others outside the immediate social unit—that is, other individuals, groups, or societies. One such difficulty involves a lack of congruence between the subject's perception of external reality and the environment as it really is. This faulty perception may be due to the influence of the subject's motivation, lack of information, uncertainty of expectations, and a variety of other factors. The general approach of the practitioner to this problem is to create an artificial intermediate situation or setting that the client can explore in order to better understand the nature of external reality. This setting may vary from the analyst's office to a human-relations workshop.

In another basic approach to the creation of new behavior patterns, certain actions are forced by the use of strong external sanctions in the belief that, if the client goes through the motions under duress, the new patterns will tend to gain a certain functional autonomy and remain a permanent part of his behavior. This is part of the rationale behind recent decisions relating to the integration of public schools, equal use of the same public facilities, and so on.

In a third, rather different procedure, the practitioner acts as an educator transmitting problem-solving skills to the subject, so that in the future he can resolve his own problems without resorting to the services of a professional practitioner. In psychotherapy, the patient learns eventually how to handle his own anxieties by understanding where they originate and by facing them in a realistic manner. In industry, the board of directors may be taught to use self-evaluative procedures to work out problems through appropriate democratic machinery, seeking group decision on matters of general concern. The means will be relative to the setting, but the concept of transferring certain kinds of problem-solving abilities is general.

These types of approach characterize a vast number of processes affecting various levels of behavior. They are of particular interest as a frame of reference in terms of which to organize material that otherwise remains fragmentary; and, presumably, they offer a basis for the systematization of research into behavior alteration. It is, therefore, strange that in the years since *The Dynamics of Planned Change* was published no body of research has been stimulated by it. The authors may have been in advance of the behavioral sciences, or they may have failed to recognize that individual practitioners do not really want to be envisioned as participating in a broader framework of which they are only a small part. At present, this work, while extremely broad and comprehensive in scope, remains a lonely landmark, patiently awaiting some more exact redefinition by means of experimental research to make its descriptive analysis the basis of a realignment of scientific strategy in this area.

Systems of Psychotherapy

An attempt to study behavior-change methods in psychotherapy, *Systems of Psychotherapy: a Comparative Study,* has recently been written by the psychologists Donald Ford and Hugh Urban.[7] This pioneer work compares ten diverse psychotherapeutic systems within the same general framework to clarify points of underlying similarity and difference. Most of the book is concerned with an analysis of the different theories of personality propagated by the schools discussed, which is interesting in itself, but irrelevant to an assessment of behavior-change processes. Different theories may lead to the same processes, and similar theories may be associated with quite varied approaches in practice.

However, Ford and Urban derive a number of suggestive conclusions from their comparisons of the traditions associated with practitioners adhering to various therapeutic schools, including the psychoanalysts, ego analysts, learning theorists, conditioning therapists, individual psychologists, will therapists, client-centered therapists, existential analysts, character analysts, and adherents of Sullivan's theory of interpersonal relations. The importance of these conclusions lies not so much in their content, which is, in general, fairly obvious, but rather in the fact that they were systematically derived from a carefully designed comparative survey of most of the leading contemporary positions in psychotherapy.

In brief, the following conclusions were drawn. First, the goals of behavior change are considered in one of three general ways by the different schools. The therapist is viewed as an expert who knows what to do and how the patient should solve his problems, or the patient himself determines the goals of treatment, or the goals are jointly worked out by patient and therapist in a democratic manner.

As to therapeutic goals, two central distinctions are made. Either primary attention is given to the elimination of undesirable behavior, or the development of new behavior is stressed as the primary task.

There is some degree of unanimity as to the purpose of psychotherapy. It is agreed that the treatment should eliminate reactions, behavior, or attitudes that interfere with the effective and productive functioning of the individual. This view bypasses the question of how one decides which aspects of the person's life are functional, but when one is mentally ill, the answer is often rather simple. In addition, many schools emphasize the importance of developing alternate kinds of behavior patterns to increase the general flexibility of the individual in responding to the situations and problems that arise.

In relation to questions about what psychotherapists really do in treatment, Ford and Urban report a strange silence. Little is written about how therapy is to take place or what the therapist actually should do, though in each case it is implied that certain types of behavior are practiced and others avoided. This remarkable oversight indicates that these theories are not really intended to explain what to do or why to do it, but rather to provide a general theoretical framework within which the therapist can operate. As Rosenzweig and Frank have suggested, the conceptual scheme serves the function of giving security to patient and therapist rather than offering a precise road map of the therapeutic process.

Further, psychotherapeutic theorists have not had too much to say about general principles of behavior change, though certain guides have been mentioned frequently, such as the principle that people should learn to behave so as to avoid unnecessary anxiety. This guide holds on all levels, from the physiological to the social. Major emphasis is also placed by therapists on the importance of understanding and insight in the production of behavior change. Insight, or self-understanding, is viewed as a necessary condition for effective behavior change by adherents of the major schools of therapy, though it is by no means universally accepted.

There is some disagreement about the extent to which the therapist must be informed about the patient in order to treat him. At one extreme is the belief that he should work in ignorance, letting the problems emerge during the course of treatment; at the other is a desire for a detailed, careful preliminary diagnosis—the taking of the patient's medical and psychological history followed by an exact planning of the full course of treatment. Most schools take a middle position, utilizing some diagnostic interviewing and the formulation of a preliminary plan of action.

Another level of conclusions in Ford and Urban's study is more germane to this review of behavior-change research. It concerns the conduct of the therapeutic interchange.

One controversial issue in this area has to do with the extent to which the therapist should lead the patient. Procedures vary from the nondirective following of the patient's lead to an expectation that the therapist should control the situation, setting the goals and standards. This general issue is translated ultimately into what the therapist does or does not say, what he notices, and what he ignores. It is at this level of response that his behavior seems to reach a degree of specificity that helps to clarify whether the ten psychotherapeutic schools are talking about similar or different processes.

All schools generally agree that evaluative statements are to be avoided; the patient is not to be praised or blamed for his behavior. There is some agreement on the importance of summarizing the meeting as a method of giving the patient some perspective on what he has been saying and doing. This summary may be objective and factual, or it may be interpretative. The use to be made of the therapist's own reactions is debatable. There are those who would bring them into the open as a realistic situational element; the general tendency, however, is to avoid their expression and to handle them in another way if necessary, since it is the patient and not the therapist who is supposed to be treated.

The therapeutic relationship, regardless of how it is defined, is usually held to be the heart of the behavior-change process and typically involves the patient's development of a friendly feeling toward the therapist as well as a willingness to confide personal information to him. All schools regard the therapist's verbal reactions as of particular importance. They represent his tools.

Most therapeutic systems seem to ignore the problem of maintaining any improvement of behavior attained during the course of therapy outside the treatment situation as well as the description of the sequences of change that is to be expected. It is not surprising that, in this context, little specific is said about the training of practitioners and the evaluation of therapy itself. What Ford and Urban's comparative study shows is that the persons who have been theorizing about psychotherapy have not really addressed themselves to the problem of behavior change in any specific and detailed manner.

Strategies of Psychotherapy

As a refreshing contrast to this material, one can turn to an original and intriguing book, *Strategies of Psychotherapy,* by communications scientist Jay Hayley.[8] Behavior change is examined within the framework of normal social interaction, of which it forms a special, and, in a sense, a limiting case. More specifically, psychotherapy is viewed as a social situation in which the patient is forced to change because he literally has no alternative. The therapist does not typically employ force, but he relies on a subtler and probably far more effective strategy—the use of paradox. In this context, the term "paradox" implies the simultaneous presentation of two conflicting alternatives. If the choices are truly opposed, the individual is trapped by them. His only alternative is to leave. Having once begun, according to Hayley's analysis, the patient cannot win. He is involved in a gambling situation in which the cards are clearly stacked against him. The therapist has at his disposal countermoves for anything the patient may do. In reality this is his therapeutic technique. It is usual in social behavior to have some degree of conflict and ambiguity between the competitive goals of people who come in contact with one another. What is unique about the behavior-change situation is that this degree of conflict and uncertainty is heightened and becomes the chief tool of control of social behavior and the eventual cause of emotional growth.

This conflict occurs at all phases of treatment. In the beginning, the

27

behavior-change process usually is entered into voluntarily, but it becomes compulsory as it proceeds. Further, it is generally not clear who determines the outcome of the therapy. As long as it remains unclear, the therapist controls the situation. If the patient says he wishes to terminate the relationship suddenly, he will be told that he does so at his own risk, a clear indication that he is going against expert judgment. However, if he asks what he should do, he is told that it is up to him; he should say whatever comes to his mind. Whichever way he moves, he cannot be in control.

Further, the patient finds himself in the confusing position of revealing intimate personal material without being either rejected or forgiven. The psychotherapist, like the priest, accepts whatever is told him, but unlike the priest he does not grant absolution. A similar procedure is used in brainwashing. No matter what the captive says, he never satisfies the interrogator. Thus he goes on and on, looking for some statement that will win him final approval and offer some guide to correct behavior.

In a similar vein, the therapist dominates the interaction by being permissive. He gives the patient permission to express himself. However, since he has given the permission, it is he who dominates. If the patient does not present useful material, the therapist will indicate that he should continue to talk about himself, but that he is avoiding the deeper aspects of the issues. In other words, he should continue what he is doing, but do it in an entirely different manner.

To the observer, therapeutic interaction is unique. It is at one time a deadly serious enterprise and a game. The serious aspect of the activity is obvious, but the artificiality is not. Consider the spectacle of the therapist telling the patient to be spontaneous and say whatever comes into his mind while he, the therapist, proceeds to sink into a silent lethargy that could not be less spontaneous. In addition, the patient is supposed to tell the truth, while the individual who faces him is equally obligated never to do so. That is, the therapist does not express his own subjective feelings.

Another strange aspect of the therapeutic situation is the notion that the patient must go through an ordeal in order to be cured. The experience is inherently difficult for the patient, since it forces him to do things that he would not do normally. He is forced to face situations, memories, and emotions that he would rather avoid and forget.

In short, he is made to suffer while he is told that this suffering will help him. Like the surgeon, the psychotherapist must hurt to help.

Beyond any of these specifics, the therapist and the patient are part of a social system that is *homeostatic;* that is, it seeks balance, always attempting to return to it from any disturbance. The fundamental law of such systems is that when an element changes in one direction, a move must be made in the opposite direction to compensate for it. This law creates the therapist's major stumbling block, and it helps to explain why he must resort to the manipulation of paradoxes rather than saying to the patient as a friend might, "Why don't you pull yourself together?" If the therapist simply told the patient how to get better, he would counter by getting worse, just as a child resists whatever is suggested to him. The therapist, therefore, does not request or dictate change while, at the same time, he puts the patient in an intolerable position in which he can do no right and for which nobody appears to be to blame. When this situation becomes sufficiently difficult for the patient, he may change simply because it is less painful to change than it is to stay in the environment that the therapist has created. Thus the therapist maneuvers the patient into health, taking the precaution to make any increase in the severity of his symptoms even more intolerable than his present state. This is done by maintaining the paradoxical nature of the therapeutic situation, regardless of what the patient chooses to do. If he allows himself to get worse, he has to put up, not only with his illness, but also with the therapy, and he is worse off than before. His only real alternatives are to flee the therapist if he can or to get well.

This, in brief, is the original and very provocative view taken by Hayley. It is of particular interest because, while it is so general, it is at the same time capable of experimental verification, though this has yet to be attempted seriously.

Three Behavior-Change Models

An appropriate conclusion to the present discussion is supplied by the writings of the psychologist Charles Slack, who, though trained as a clinician, has preferred to discard his role as professional therapist in his work with antisocial adolescents.[9] Dr. Slack has been responsible for a number of startling innovations in the realm of technique, such as paying the patient to come for treatment or using patients as advisors

29

to professional practitioners. His practical approaches are intriguing, debatable, and sometimes shocking, but his basic conceptual framework is simple and extremely provocative.

Slack describes three basic models of behavior change that are commonly employed. These are exemplified by three types of persons who may relate to the client: the scientist, the professional, and the friend. A scientific relationship is characterized by the objective search for truth. In a professional relationship, one person, the professional, is paid to help another, the client or patient. The third model is characterized by a friendly interchange among equals engaged in pursuits of common interest. All three situations may be employed in the production of behavior change. The objective study of a situation may lead to direct changes within it. The professional approach has such change as its prime objective. Friends and acquaintances often produce change, not always intentionally, but rather in their role as upholders of the norms and standards of society.

It is certainly helpful to view behavior change within a larger framework than that provided by the professional and his activities. Slack, however, goes further, stating that the professional is less likely to produce change than anyone else. His argument is very simple. Most persons and groups in need of change are, for one reason or another, unable to accomplish it with their own resources. If they are forced to seek professional help, they must tacitly admit that they are partially incompetent in managing their own affairs. Slack believes that for many people such an admission is extremely difficult and potentially destructive since it leads to dependence on professional authority rather than to greater personal autonomy. In contrast, such a problem does not exist in either the friendly or the scientific approach.

The scientist is not interested in changing anybody. He is interested in understanding the truth about people, situations, and events. If one becomes part of such an investigation, it is not with an a priori admission of incapacity and guilt. Rather, one joins in an adventure, a concerted attack on the unknown. In such a context, the individual makes a positive contribution to science and society by giving something of himself for the common good. The traditional form of psychoanalysis came very near to this model. Freud was less interested in curing than in understanding the mechanisms that produced the disease. His early patients were really his co-workers, exposing their psyches in a common research endeavor.

Similarly, equals working in a friendly manner toward common goals can be a powerful force for change. The success of Alcoholics Anonymous and Synanon, which applies similar techniques to the problems of drug addicts, indicates the power of nonprofessional organizations to change behavior that has proved resistant to the professional. In part, the democratic political system is based on just this concept of social change induced by group action among equals.

Slack has used these models to develop a number of unorthodox approaches to treatment, such as the use of hardened criminals to help combat juvenile delinquency. Both his viewpoint and Hayley's are refreshing and challenging. They serve to document the climate of interest that has been created, not only in traditional, but also in unusual channels for the integration of hitherto separated materials and the formulation of new generalizations that may aid the simplification of an area that is adrift in a sea of terminologies, confusion, and misguided identifications.

In summary, the preceding discussion substantiates the belief that behavior-change processes do share common underlying assumptions and general models of them can be constructed. Therefore, an experimental approach is appropriate. Experimental techniques are most fruitful when components of a generalized model can be tested. If this model exists, the results of the experiments can be cumulative and powerful. Without it, experiments may only compound the confusion that already exists. The analyses that have been described do not prove in a scientific sense that such models are valid, but they do indicate a clear interest in and various degrees of success with the design of such guides to experimentation. This type of scientific speculation forms the necessary and natural prelude to more specific and precise experimental investigations.

It is now appropriate to examine the experimental evidence that has been accumulated to date to ascertain its character and ultimately to determine whether it relates directly or indirectly to some general formulation or theory upon which a systematic approach to the change of human behavior can be constructed.

CHAPTER THREE

The Psychopharmacology Revolution

BEFORE entering directly into a discussion of the psychological and social methods of altering and enhancing human behavior, it will be helpful to review briefly changes of another sort—those that are induced by intervention with normal physiological processes, with particular emphasis upon the use of drugs. These behavioral alterations attract a great deal of attention because they are so sudden and dramatic. The way in which these agents produce their effects is often puzzling to the layman and the professional scientist, since such intervention depends on chemical and biological processes with which they may be unfamiliar. In fact, frequently the effects of methods such as brain surgery, chemical or electric shock treatment, or drugs are not well understood by the research workers and clinicians who use them. In spite of this, if they achieve satisfactory results, their use is apparently justified; if not, they are abandoned.

For example, in the course of an operation a brain surgeon may apply a weak electric current to various portions of the brain of a patient, who remains conscious during the procedure. As is expected, when the *visual cortex*, the portion of the brain specializing in the interpretation of visual stimuli, is stimulated, the patient reports seeing flashes of light. When the auditory center is stimulated, the patient hears sounds. However, to everyone's great surprise, when certain locations in the cerebral cortex on the outer layer of the forebrain are electrically stimulated, the patient reexperiences certain past events with striking vividness. These memories recur only when the stimulation is administered, with or without the patient's awareness. The stimulation of different points in the same area elicits different memories. The patient may hear his mother's voice calling to him. When another location is stimulated, he relives the performance of a play seen many years ago. Every time the same point is restimulated, the same memory is reexperienced. Further details of the incident may be recalled.

This discovery is of great interest to a neurologist, a doctor who specializes in the study of the nervous system, since it casts some intriguing, though indirect, light on the mechanism of memory. As far as behavior change is concerned, however, the implications are of a different nature. This technique offers the possibility of directly altering subjective experience by forcing the patient to go through an event again with all the impact and details of its original occurrence rather than as he remembers it. Surely, there could be no more pervasive and intimate form of behavior control.

As a second illustration, let us picture a withdrawn patient in a mental hospital who is being given an injection of the drug sodium pentathol by a psychiatrist. The patient relaxes visibly, and then somewhat disconnectedly begins to talk. The doctor asks him questions about certain incidents in his life. The patient is anxious, unwilling, but in spite of himself begins to describe and relive the traumatic events that have reduced him to his withdrawn and anxious state. All of the memories he had repressed come flooding back to be shared with the psychiatrist.

Finally, in another experiment, an apparently normal individual takes a pill and after a relatively short time begins to report a series of exceedingly strange phenomena. He sees visions. He feels detached from his body. Colors are suddenly extremely intense. His perceptions of the outer world and his subjective sense of himself are both radically altered.

Such illustrations are not surprising in light of the recent advances in the use of physiological intervention to alter perceptions of the real world as well as behavior. They have been described in the popular press and in a variety of professional publications. It is, in fact, the general uncritical acceptance of such techniques that is striking. In each case there appears to be a remarkable demonstration of the ability to control and, to some extent, enhance normal psychological functioning. It is true that the drama of these methods may not be proportional to their lasting value. Nevertheless, physiological mechanisms have been demonstrated to be effective in producing psychological and social change.

As with any new force released by scientific exploration, the social use of these agents is not predetermined. The physiological techniques for behavior alteration may be used to reduce human beings to docile automatons or to help them through emotional crises. They may open to them new realms of experience, or cause them to become addicts of a new breed, who though they are not physiologically addicted, seek out these drugs in the compulsive search for new sensations.

In discussing these agents it is necessary to establish one fundamental axiom: no intervention—physiological, psychological, or social—can add anything new to already existing human behavioral patterns and predispositions. They cannot make the person different than he is. What they can do is to restrict certain aspects of behavior and release others that were previously inhibited.

Thus, drugs will not make a man into a monster or a genius unless he is one already. They will, however, produce remarkable alterations in behavior simply because the social face that most men wear is but a small fragment of the undisclosed area of conflicting desires and aspirations that lie unexpressed and dormant within him.

The ease of administration and the dramatic impact of many forms of physiological intervention may in the long run be self-defeating and dangerous to those who use them. The danger is in proportion to their effect on the individual under treatment. This conclusion is drastically supported by the recent experience of the psychologist Dr. Timothy Leary, whose story is worth recounting as an illustrative history of the pitfalls that can trap those who loosen scientific standards to obtain greater freedom in the pursuit for truth.

The LSD Controversy

During the time Dr. Leary was director of Psychological Research at the Kaiser Foundation Hospital, he wrote the influential book *The Interpersonal Diagnosis of Personality*.[1] This work provided a comprehensive multilevel approach to the study of personality that marked a significant departure from more limited theories characterizing the

34

field at the time. Soon after its publication, Dr. Leary moved to Harvard University's Center for Research in Personality. It was while on vacation in Mexico that he first came into contact with the effects of hallucenogenic drugs found in a particular form of cactus and certain mushrooms. In a spirit of scientific curiosity Leary ate a number of the so-called sacred mushrooms, supplied to him by a friendly anthropologist who had been studying the Indian tribes that used them as part of their religious rites. The impact on Leary was remarkable. At first, he felt that he had died. Then, in a short period, he relived his whole life. This experience was followed by a reversal of the evolutionary cycle until he felt he had reached the stage of a one-celled animal.

This experience changed the course of Dr. Leary's life, though it took some time for the scope of this alteration to become fully visible. At first, he simply was enthusiastic about performing research on the remarkable effects of another hallucenogenic, *LSD*, the abbreviated name for a type of lysergic acid. He was soon joined by another colleague, Dr. Richard Alpert, who had conducted several studies in the area of child development. Both men were overwhelmed by the immediate and prodigious nature of the impact of the drug on subjective human experience. Each person who ingested LSD seemed to have unique reactions and sensations. Leary slowly came to the conclusion that a new way had been found to explore the unknown heights and depths of the human psyche.

Under the influence of LSD subjects would stare at a single tree for hours, convinced that it was somehow the platonic ideal tree. Mystical experiences were not uncommon. An overwhelming aesthetic impact was received from simple objects, such as pebbles. On the other hand, some who took the drug felt that they were being subjected to horrifying ordeals that made Dante's "Inferno" seem lacking in imagination.

There was no doubt that these experiences were real, since the subjects who described them were thoroughly shaken. But they were subjective, and they were unpredictable. It was just this characteristic that led Leary and the group of student converts with whom he slowly surrounded himself, gradually to begin emphasizing the experience at the expense of objectively verifiable truth. Slowly, the nature of his drug sessions with students became more widely known; the university grew concerned. Hostilities toward Leary's work mounted, though they were much slower in gathering than might have been expected because of the traditionally high level of academic freedom at Harvard and Dr.

Leary's own reputation. Finally, however, the ultimate confrontation occurred. Dr. Leary left Harvard at the request of the University, but this did not discourage him. Rather, his conviction about the importance of his work was enhanced. The organization he had formed, the "International Federation for Inner Freedom," became the center of a group who sought new experiences of various kinds. The concept of "multifamily transcendental living" was evolved. Eventually, the group was forced to move; soon their relocation became habitual. Finally, they left the United States when it appeared that their drug sources would be cut off, and went to Mexico. Here, too, protests were made to the authorities, investigations were conducted, and the group was expelled. The end of the story has not yet been enacted, but in a sense it no longer really matters. The tragic pattern, if it be viewed as such, is sufficiently complete.

Nothing that Dr. Leary has done has undermined the actual effects of the drugs he has studied, or suggested that its actions are other than described; but his case does suggest the need for external constraint, a set of rules and objective standards that are abandoned only at the scientist's peril. Ordinarily, researchers are rarely tempted in this sense, since the nature of their work is less dramatic and immediate, and certainly less personal. The more compelling the experience, the stronger the safeguards must be to prevent scientific study from becoming a vehicle for personal expression. However, it would be truly tragic if the experiences of Dr. Leary were taken to imply that the study of LSD and similar drugs should be discouraged or abandoned. On the contrary, the very power of these drugs demands that they be investigated for our own protection, if for no other reason. But these investigations must be dignified, controlled, and open to the full scrutiny of scientific evaluation.

Evaluating Drug Effects

A serious inquiry into the substantiated, experimentally demonstrated effects of physiological intervention will reveal a situation reminiscent of the previous discussion of evaluative research. There is no difference between evaluating the effects of a drug on behavior and evaluating the effects of a new counseling procedure. Drugs are perhaps a little simpler to judge, in that one can specify exactly the amount to be administered, its purity, strength, and frequency of dosage. Analogous aspects are extremely difficult to control in psychotherapy. Further, one can allow for the influence of the practitioners' beliefs concerning the drug by using "double blind" techniques in which neither the patient nor the doctor knows whether the active drug or a *placebo*, a chemically inert substance, is being administered. For these reasons, evaluations of drugs are often technically superior to those of psychotherapy. However, the results are just as confusing in the long run, since the evaluation of the effectiveness of drugs and other physiological action does nothing to explain the actions themselves.

While the use of physiological interventions to alter and enhance human behavior exists in virtually all cultures of which we have extensive records, it is only comparatively recently that these activities have been subjected to serious scientific scrutiny. The effect of drugs on animal behavior was examined in the late nineteenth century, and studies of the influence of caffeine on human behavior were conducted in the first decade of this century by the psychologist H. B. Hallingworth. However, major interest in psychopharmacology is recent, dating from the development of tranquilizers for the treatment of mentally ill patients. Lately, activities have been divided between the development of new and more potent drugs and studies designed to demonstrate and ultimately explain the mechanisms by which they exert their effects.

The current rate of psychopharmacological research is very high. The National Institute of Mental Health, a federal agency located in Bethesda, Maryland, has recognized this development by establishing a Psychopharmacology Service Center to encourage and support such research, to foster conferences, and to provide physical facilities and direct consultation to investigators.

As in most scientific situations of this type, a great deal of activity leads to the rapid accumulation of partially contradictory findings and often the generation of more questions than answers. It becomes apparent that it is more difficult to measure the relevant effects than had been supposed and that there are sources of measurement contamination of which there was no initial awareness. More basically, it becomes evident that, because how these physiological interventions operate is not known, it is difficult to classify them properly. The chemical structure of the drug is not in itself important, but the impact it has on the body is. At the present time, either the research findings are grossly simplified or they become lost in a maze of highly technical studies that are somewhat contradictory in their results.

Drugs are currently classified in terms of their clinical usefulness in the following terms: minor tranquilizers, major tranquilizers, antidepressants, nonbarbiturate sedatives, and finally, psychotomimetic agents.

Major and minor tranquilizers are used to calm psychiatric patients. Antidepressants are used to stimulate activity. Nonbarbiturate sedatives are used to reduce activity and encourage sleep. The psychotomimetic agents, such as LSD, produce striking alterations in the psychological state of the patient. While these distinctions are of practical utility, still needed are the behavioral profiles attributed to different drugs or classes of drugs.

This, however, is not the only difficulty. It is also necessary to isolate the intervening mechanisms by which the drug translates physiological activity into behavior change. One important step toward this is the use of anatomical localization in the placement of drugs. By carefully developed surgical techniques, minute quantities of a drug can be placed in virtually any location in the body and its effects on the surrounding tissue observed. Such localized activity characterizes these drugs, since stimulation of a given area has certain specific effects. Different drugs have also been demonstrated to have varying effects on the same physiological site, so that certain actions are specific to the drug rather than the area on which it acts. Most research of this type has been concerned, at times almost obsessed, with methodological issues. The need to study several different dosage levels of any given medication has been stressed, since the strength of the dosage may be more important than the drug that is used.

Using the same subjects for more than one drug study presents still another problem. Since most research of this type is carried out in certain typical locations, such as mental hospitals, there is a tendency to employ the same subjects in more than one study. This may inadvertently result in the interaction of drug effects and make the findings difficult to interpret. Finally, the need to define and measure carefully the behavior that is to be influenced by the drug has been increasingly emphasized, since the results can be no better than the measures employed to detect them.

Each new drug has to be evaluated experimentally on appropriate subjects before it is used for psychiatric purposes. The fertility of drug companies in creating likely medication for clinical application has forced a searching reevaluation of the process by which such drugs are tested. This assessment has been intensified, because of past studies that indicated certain drugs were much more effective than they were later found to be.

While the discussion of this evaluative problem has been extensive, it has been obscured by specifics. The ultimate objective, however, is simple: to determine the effectiveness of particular drugs in reducing mental illness or correcting other psychological conditions. Though these studies have practical utility, they do little to clarify the importance of other factors, such as the social environment, training, or subject motivation that may exert a strong influence on the effect the drug has in a given case.

Conclusions about Drug-Induced Behavior Change

There are, however, a number of well-established conclusions about the use of drugs to influence and alter human behavior. First, it has been unequivocally demonstrated that the subject's belief that he is receiving a supposedly active drug will in itself produce noticeable effects, which will be discussed in Chapter Six. It is presently estimated that from 30 to 50 per cent of normal subjects are reactors; that is, they have symptomatic relief after the administration of a pill they believe effective, but that actually is physiologically inert. Such a pervasive and important aspect of psychopharmacology must clearly be controlled if behavior change is to be attributed to the specific physiological agent and not to the process of administration.

The converse situation, in which a drug is given to the subject without his knowledge, has also been investigated. In such an approach, there can be no possibility of a placebo reducing physiological change, since the subject does not know he has received anything. However, this advantage may be more real than apparent, unless other conditions of drug administration are carefully specified. If the subject, for example, is in a prison, he may be on his guard, whether or not he is aware that he has been given a particular drug. This underlying reaction will certainly color the effect of the drug, particularly if the subject realizes that he has begun to act strangely and does not know why.

A similar issue involves the effect of the administrator's motivation on the subject. Patients who receive identical doses of the same drug under different circumstances have quite different reactions, depending on the setting in which the drug is administered. If it is relaxed, the patients are at ease; but they immediately become tense when the conversation is directed toward disturbing topics. In either case, the effect on the patient is stronger with some drugs than without them, but their direction is unspecified—the patient is either more relaxed or more tense. In a similar vein, it has been found that younger, friendly practitioners administering a drug obtain a greater percentage of pain relief than do older and more remote scientists who give the same dose. Further, it has been demonstrated that the actions of given drugs can be reversed or suspended, depending on the rewards that are offered in conjunction with their administration. All of these observations are eloquent testimony to the impact of social factors in drug studies.

There are, of course, a variety of other personal characteristics that alter and influence the basic effect of a medication. Differences in drug reactions attributable to the subject's sex, age, and intelligence have been demonstrated. Personality is undoubtedly a vital intervening variable. Studies of several drugs have clearly demonstrated that physically normal volunteers, chronically hospitalized patients, and narcotics addicts react in quite different ways. Since drugs are physiological in their function, it is natural that their effects are also modified by other concomitant physiological conditions, such as fatigue, sensory deprivation, and other abnormal conditions.

Perhaps the strongest test of the influence of a given drug is its use in a situation such as criminal investigation in which the subject resists its effects for his own protection. If the drug is effective in such instances, its impact under other less resistant circumstances can be reasonably assumed. As one would anticipate, studies of the so-called truth serum drugs administered under such conditions result in mixed, though intriguing, findings. Interestingly enough, psychologically healthy subjects are found to be more resistant, that is, they are better able to lie than neurotic subjects, when both groups attempt resistance. Unfortunately, the observer has no simple guide to indicate how much of the truth is being told or how distorted the version is when suppressed or repressed material is released under the influence of the drug.

The necessary conclusion is that, in spite of the direct and observable effects of drugs and other procedures of physiological intervention, the interpretation and isolation of specific effects is a subtle matter requiring rigorous controls and a high degree of methodological sophistication.

As a partial antidote to this complex situation, it may be useful to outline the general course of behavioral alterations and disturbances produced by agents of physiological change. By disturbance, what is generally implied is the disruption of functioning of the brain and spinal cord, since these are most easily disturbed by any variation of the body's internal equilibrium. Such imbalance can have many causes, from elevated body temperature, shock, or poisoning, to starvation, dehydration, or physical immobility. These conditions have certain underlying similarities to the effects of drugs, electric shock treatment, hormone injections, and other physiological interventions that have been studied in the past. The general stress syndrome that can result from any of these influences tends to follow a pattern of progressive deterioration characterized by a set of standard symptoms or reactions.

In an early stage, the only overt symptoms of such disturbance may be a slight deterioration of appearance and speech. A minimal performance deficit may be noted on standard tasks, but the whole set of symptoms may easily be overlooked, particularly if the onset is gradual. As the stress increases or grows chronic, further disturbances of mental functioning are noted. Memory for detail is obscured, and unnoticed partial amnesia may take place. In this state, the judgment of the individual is affected, and his sense of proportion is disturbed.

As the syndrome progresses further, the subject's appearance continues to deteriorate. Becoming aware of his mental deterioration, he may grow extremely frightened, or, if the development is more gradual, he is more likely to be depressed and indifferent. It is at this point that sensory illusions are likely to occur. Suggestibility is also heightened. Consequently, he may manufacture fantastic stories, which he may actually believe. Finally, he passes into a state of clouded awareness from which he emerges, if at all, only when his body's homeostatic balance is restored.

While all of these changes can be created by physiological imbalances, they can also be produced by factors such as isolation, sleep deprivation, and general fatigue. To a certain extent, they may also be created by certain drugs that, regardless of their specific action, upset the general equilibrium of the body.

The individual is rendered more suggestible and easier to influence but less reliable in his statements and reactions. This may help to explain why the action of drugs has been reversed or counteracted by surroundings and concomitant circumstances relating to their administration, since the condition created by the drug in part renders the person more open to other sources of influence and less able to order his responses in a consistent manner.

The use of drugs in medical practice has always been joined to the practitioner's personal effect, commonly described as "the bedside manner." Scientific studies of physiological interventions with behavior have isolated and documented those aspects of the social-psychological situation that influenced the impact of the drugs and clarified how these mechanisms might be maximized or eliminated to meet the needs of different situations. The study of the most tangible ways to induce altered behavior thus leads us inevitably back to the less tangible, but no less potent, social-physiological influences.

CHAPTER FOUR

Hypnotic Suggestion

B OTH drugs and hypnotism have been used to influence many aspects of human behavior for thousands of years in a variety of cultures. Both are able to produce a sudden and dramatic alteration of behavior with little apparent effort on the part of the practitioner. In some ways, hypnotism is the more impressive agent, since no direct physiological intervention is involved. The hypnotist simply talks to the subject, who then may see hallucinations, believe that he is eating a hearty meal or talking to an absent friend, act as if he were once again seven years old, develop various physiological symptoms, ignore pain and fatigue, and, in general, behave in startling contrast to his normal waking state.

Hypnosis can be induced by a variety of technical means, from a series of monotonous suggestions given by the hypnotist to the use of mechanical stimuli, such as a metronome or a moving light. All of these procedures have in common a certain soothing monotony.

If the hypnotic induction is successful the subject enters a trance-like state, which varies in depth from person to person and in the same person at different times during the session. The depth of the trance is judged primarily from the willingness and ability of the subject to carry out commands. Under light hypnosis, he may act like a dog if requested to do so, but a deeper trance is required if he is to ignore a painful stimulus, such as a needle. The hypnotist usually seeks to make the trance as deep as possible in order to maximize the effects of his suggestion, but regardless of his success in any particular case, the contrast in behavior during the waking and the hypnotized state is usually quite startling, and the kinds of behavior that the hypnotized subject manifests at the suggestion or command of the hypnotist are remarkable.

The dramatic nature of these changes in behavior encourages the use of hypnotism for sensational theatrics rather than as a focus of scientific investigation. Moreover, hypnotism has been used by persons of dubious professional affiliation in an unwarranted and irresponsible manner with resulting discredit to the procedure itself. However, in the last few decades the study of the effects of hypnotism has been brought within the field of respectable psychological investigation, and many of its characteristics, known for centuries, have been subjected to scientific verification and redefinition. As in most such instances, the general result of objectifying an area that was rank with superstition is to reduce its stature. Much of the mystery is removed, and what remains seems rather commonplace.

Ways in Which Hypnotism Affects Behavior

It has now been established that hypnotism can produce a number of well-documented changes in human behavior.

1. The hypnotized individual exhibits greater muscular strength and resistance to fatigue than he has in the waking state; he can perform such feats as acting as a rigid bridge between two chairs, supporting weights for a long time, and so on. Generally, these enlarged abilities are greater for muscles under conscious control in the waking state than for those, such as the muscles in the intestinal wall or those that contract the pupil of the eye, which are not.

2. The subject can behave as if he were anaesthetized, either in a specific area or over his whole body. This psychological anaesthetic is sufficiently powerful to be used while a patient is under surgery without ill effects and without anaesthetic hangover. Such an application depends, of course, on the individual being a suitable hypnotic subject.

3. Hypnotism can be used to produce physiological changes ordinarily completely beyond the conscious control of the individual. These include the creation of cold sores, the reduction of warts, and the pro-

44

duction of small burned areas or blisters. While these reactions have been clearly documented, they are by no means present in all subjects. However, the very fact that they can be created at all is of considerable significance, since they serve as dramatic evidence of the power of psychological influences on the formation of strictly physical symptoms.

4. Persons who are hypnotized usually will have hallucinations if they are instructed to do so by the hypnotist. They will see things that are not there, such as scenes, persons, or objects or, even more remarkably, fail to see what is present, such as the audience, the hypnotist, chairs, or colors.

5. Not only can hypnosis lead to a misperception of the present world, it can be used to change the individual's perception of himself in time; that is, the hypnotized person can be regressed to an earlier stage of life. He will then recall long-forgotten incidents and act as he did at that age. This phenomenon has been of great interest to scientists trying to formulate a theory of personality as well as to psychotherapists, since both are concerned with the formation of personality structure, which can be directly studied and experimentally manipulated through hypnotic regression.

6. Hypnotized persons will perform a variety of actions after coming out of the hypnotic trance, if they are told to do so while still in it. For example, the subject may be told that after he awakens, he will have an intense desire to leave the room if anyone mentions chewing gum. When, in fact, this does occur, he becomes uncomfortable and finds some excuse to depart without any conscious knowledge that he is following the hypnotist's instructions. This phenomenon is particularly interesting since it provides us with an experimental equivalent of the process by which unconscious influences are translated into behavior under normal social conditions.

7. Perhaps the most sinister application of hypnotism is its use to make subjects perform acts that are criminal or dangerous to themselves and others. For many years it was believed that no person would do anything under hypnosis that violated his own moral code. For example, if a hypnotized subject were told to undress, he or she would refuse to do so and awaken feeling somewhat angry, though unaware of just what had happened.

Recently, however, this optimistic belief in moral sanctions over behavior while under hypnotic suggestion has been seriously challenged by experimental evidence. Subjects have been made to steal, place their hands in a box containing, they are told, a rattlesnake, throw what they believe to be acid in the hypnotist's face, and carry out a variety of antisocial and unconventional acts that they presumably would not engage in normally.

A careful reanalysis of these studies suggests, however, that subjects performed these acts only when they were partially misled about their nature. They behaved in ignorance or in the belief that no real harm could occur, since the hypnotist was in control of the situation. Thus, the subject instructed to throw acid in the hypnotist's face knew that he must have protected himself before making such a request; the person who was stealing did not fully realize that the coat he took was not his own, and so on. While this conclusion is comforting in that hypnotism does not turn men into criminals, it also suggests what history so well confirms—that people will perform antisocial acts if they are led to misperceive the consequences through the use of suggestion, conscious or otherwise.

Hypnosis, then, produces two kinds of behavior change, physiological and psychosocial. Most of these effects are dramatic and impressive to the onlooker. They certainly earn for hypnotism a legitimate place in any enumeration of methods for changing human behavior.

Modern Research in Hypnotic Influence

Virtually all of these effects were described before behavioral scientists began to scrutinize hypnotism more carefully. Their explanation, however, was not known, and it was to this problem that scientists addressed themselves.

Research into the nature of hypnosis has been conducted for several decades, but as yet no definite answers have emerged. It is strange that a phenomenon so easily reproducible seems to elude explanation. A number of facts have been established, nevertheless. Individuals vary as to how hypnotizable they are. The *brain waves,* waves produced by the electrical activity of the brain, of persons in a hypnotic trance can be distinguished from normal wave patterns of states of wakefulness and sleep, though they more nearly resemble those of the waking state. But none of these findings, however useful, really explains the nature of hypnosis or the reasons why persons in this state can perform apparently abnormal feats.

46

Research has centered particularly on the physiological, as distinct from the psychological, effects of hypnosis, since the former are harder to produce consciously and easier to measure objectively. In general, these investigations have examined whether physiological changes can be produced only through the mediation of hypnotism or whether a direct suggestion made to a person in the waking state, who has not been hypnotized, is sufficient.

One easily measured physiological change is the induction of color blindness through hypnotic suggestion. Various degrees of color blindness have been induced. However, when nonhypnotized subjects are given the same instructions; that is, when they are told to ignore certain colors as they look at the test cards used to measure color blindness, their responses tend to duplicate those of the hypnotized subjects, indicating that hypnosis is not a necessary condition for the manifestation of this particular reaction.

Related to these studies are those of a more striking phenomenon, hypnotic blindness. Subjects who are in a deep hypnotic state are told that they are experiencing certain degrees of blindness, including a total lack of sight. Under such instructions, susceptible individuals appear to be blind; they fall over objects and fail to respond to visual stimuli. In the attempt to uncover the physiological correlates of this temporary condition, perhaps the most striking finding has been that, under hypnotically induced blindness, the subject manifests the same type of brain-wave patterns as found in physiologically blind persons. One normal brain-wave pattern, the *alpha pattern,* is a fluctuation of waves at approximately 10 times a second. When sighted persons receive the stimulus of a sudden light, it interferes with their alpha pattern. The blind, however, do not respond to such stimuli. It is impressive to find a similar lack of response to light occurring under conditions of hypnotic blindness. However, further studies have demonstrated that control of this reaction can be attained even without hypnotic inducement, simply by concentrating one's attention on something other than the flashing light.

Further studies of hypnotically blind subjects have shown that they avoid looking at objects they are not supposed to see. Consciously or unconsciously they attempt to simulate conditions approximating blindness in order to create the illusion that they are blind. Here again, a striking phenomenon can be reproduced without the necessity of hypnosis.

A similar pattern of evidence characterizes the phenomenon of hypnotic deafness. When subjects who have not been hypnotized are instructed to pay no attention to auditory stimuli, they perform in the same manner as those experiencing hypnotically induced deafness.

Another physiological phenomenon that has been investigated involves the influence of hypnotic suggestion on blood flow and involuntary muscle action. In one test, it was suggested to the subject that a given part of his body was immersed in warm water. Under such conditions, he tended to manifest increased blood flow and elevated skin temperature in the given portion of the body. Other studies have demonstrated that noxious stimuli, such as mild acids, were less able to be tolerated if applied to areas the hypnotized subject had been told are sensitive and tender rather than to equivalent places that it was suggested were without feeling. Thus, the suggestions in these cases appear to lead to direct physiological responses. However, as in the previous examples, somewhat similar reactions have occurred after suggestions made to nonhypnotized subjects, so that hypnosis does not seem to be necessary to induce the reaction.

A good deal of work stimulated by research on heart disease has been devoted to the study of effects of hypnotic suggestion on heart action. This represents a direct test of the power of hypnotism on a vital physiological function. Three general avenues of investigation have been pursued: variation of normal heart beat, alteration of the body's electrical activity associated with the stimulation of the heart, and temporary suspension of the heart's activity altogether.

Altered heartbeat of a subject under hypnosis has been clearly demonstrated. Unfortunately, most of the studies in which such demonstrations were achieved failed to control for two vital elements: the respiratory rate of the subject and his general level of activity. If he breathes faster or slower than usual, or if he imagines himself in intensive activity or extreme lethargy, he can alter the pace of his heart beat. In only one study do these conditions seem to have been controlled by observing breathing rate and emotional arousal during the hypnotic session.[1] But, unfortunately, the subject was not asked to attempt to alter his heartbeat when not in a hypnotic trance, so no information is available on this possibility. Since other research has shown that certain individuals can consciously alter their heartbeat, the evidence for the hypnotic state as the vital intervening factor appears slight.

48

In other studies, subjects under hypnosis were told that they were anxious and afraid. As a result, their heartbeats became abnormal. This evidence was very impressive until it was shown that similar abnormalities occurred in the patterns of persons with otherwise normal heart action under conditions of great emotional stress, such as those directly preceding surgery. Thus, hypnotic commands to simulate emotion were effective, but there is no evidence of direct physiological change as a result of hypnosis.

Perhaps the most dramatic action attempted by hypnotic intervention is the elimination of the heartbeat altogether. Naturally, this particular kind of research is not widely employed. In one case, however, in which heart trouble had led to previous surgery, a physician was able to induce a very temporary suspension of heart activity by suggesting to the patient under hypnosis that he was having a severe fainting attack.[2] However, others have demonstrated similar phenomena in subjects not under hypnosis who were able to produce heart stoppage through complete relaxation.[3]

Using a somewhat different approach, investigators have explored the influence of hypnotic suggestion on the amount of sugar in the blood and the concentration of digestive secretions in the intestinal tract with similar results. Hypnotized persons were able to alter these levels when suggestions were given that aroused emotion or stimulated hunger, but these effects have also been obtained by suggestion to subjects not in the hypnotic trance.

A quite different area of hypnotic influence that has been intensively investigated has already been mentioned. It involves the alteration of skin tissues through the formation of blisters and other irritations and, conversely, the cure of existing growths such as warts. Cold blisters on the lip have been created successfully under hypnotic instruction, but only when an indirect approach is used. A suggestion that the subject form such blisters has no effect. However, a suggestion that arouses emotions and a simulation of the physical conditions that would, in turn, lead to the formation of blisters, has been successful, which indicates that the instructions were effective because of the emotions they aroused rather than because of any induced direct physiological change.

When the hypnotic suggestion of tissue injury is involved, more interesting findings have been produced. Subjects in a hypnotic trance receive strong suggestions that they have been burned by an iron or received an injury in a specified area; the physiological effects are then observed. In a number of reported cases, burn blisters have occurred, suggesting that the body has responded in the absence of any real physical injury. However, once again, further studies have tended to undermine the preliminary conclusion. Dermatologists distinguish among different degrees of skin injury. Some mild forms occur in sensitive persons in response to nothing more than pressure applied to the areas in question. Since the subjects in all these studies were admittedly an atypical group, because of their skin sensitivity, the effects may in part be due to physical pressure, which was typically a part of the hypnotic suggestion, rather than to any direct impact of suggestion itself.

Finally, medical studies of the treatment of warts by hypnosis have produced clear evidence that such an approach might be useful. In one study, patients under deep hypnosis were told that warts on one side of their body would vanish.[4] In nine out of ten patients, the warts on the specified side disappeared. The warts on the other side of their bodies were unaffected. These impressive findings, however, held only for patients capable of a deep hypnotic trance.

Unfortunately, equally impressive results have been attained by the use of a placebo presented to the patients as a new and powerful drug. Thus, suggestion without hypnosis seems once again as effective as suggestion with it.

Clearly, the physiological changes that have been demonstrated in subjects under hypnotic suggestion can be duplicated in persons who have not received this inducement. Thus, hypnotism apparently is effective through an enhancement of the subject's emotional suggestibility rather than through any direct influence on his physiological activity.

In view of this conclusion, research into hypnotic behavior without hypnotic trance is of particular interpretive interest since in these cases the effects are produced when the presumed cause is eliminated. In one study, a female research assistant who knew nothing about hypnotism gave a psychology class of over two hundred freshmen direct instruction, lasting from one-half to three quarters of a minute, to manifest some particular kind of hypnotic behavior, such as hallucination, body rigidity, or amnesia.[5] About a fifth of the class promptly responded. Their later comments were like those of people who have been in a deep hypnotic trance, in spite of the fact that no effort to induce such a state had been made. These findings suggest that the so-called hypnotic phenomena, however dramatic, are the direct outcome of another person's influence and do not require the induction of the hypnotic trance. This conclusion does nothing to mitigate the known effects attributed to hypnotism but rather suggests that the trance itself does not cause them. Thus, behavior under hypnosis, which seems to lie so far out of the ordinary repertoire, is found to be related to one of the more normal and pervasive aspects of everyday life.

Hypnotic Regression

As a partial antidote to the physiological emphasis of the preceding material, it is of interest to review briefly one of the more intriguing psychological effects of hypnotism—hypnotic regression. Subjects under hypnotic instructions will relive with realism and authenticity situations that occurred when they were young children. Their intelligence will function at an appropriately lower level. Their interests and desires will change. Experiences not consciously remembered are easily recovered. Even more impressive, behavior reflects not only the age to which the subject has regressed, but also the environmental conditions at that time. Thus the individual does not act like any three year old but like a three year old who lives in the world as it was when *he* was three.

These studies quite clearly demonstrate that earlier behavior patterns and memory are not destroyed but are integrated into more complex networks and associations. For example, certain subjects spontaneously evince various impediments, such as stuttering, that characterized their earlier behavior but from which they had apparently recovered. Their adult recovery did not eliminate the childhood impairment; rather, it was superimposed upon it. When they regressed to the state of children, the old difficulty was reactivated.

Further studies of regression demonstrate that here, too, the hypnotic trance is not a necessary condition. Using certain evidence, such as a subject's drawings, it was demonstrated that regression could be stimulated in both a nonhypnotized and a hypnotized state, though the trance appears to facilitate it. Thus, even on the purely psychological level, there is some question as to the interpretive importance of the trance. It might be said that the creation of a trance reduces the inhibitions of the subject, and it is this that releases his role-playing abilities, allowing him to portray himself as he once was. This, in fact, is one of the theories that has been advanced to explain the phenomenon, but it is by no means the only one. Other explanations have emphasized the reactivation of earlier memory patterns. Still others have suggested that the hypnotic state inhibits the manifestation of a stronger, mature response, so that the earlier, generally inhibited response is allowed to manifest itself. All of these explanations are at best only partially satisfactory, and none of them has clear experimental support at the present time.

How Hypnotism Affects Behavior

The net impact of research into the effects of hypnosis on behavior change has been to suggest that it is an appearance, not an actuality. The phenomena attributed to it, other than the trance state itself, can be reproduced by other means. Its power is, therefore, more apparent than real. These findings are not entirely satisfying. On the one hand, the impact of hypnotic phenomena on behavior is clear. Hypnosis seems to be exceeded in dependability only by direct physiological intervention, such as the use of drugs. Further, certain hypnotically induced psychological changes, such as age regression, are not readily duplicated by other means. Still, none of hypnotism's so-called effects are uniquely associated with the trance. One thing is clear, however; hypnotism demonstrates that human behavior can be altered startlingly with very little effort, even if this change is limited to the duration of the trance. Its nature is various, and its importance is not so much in its particular form, but that it can occur.

It is understandable that the way in which some kinds of physiological intervention change behavior may not be understood because of the elaborate biochemical reactions involved. No such mechanisms are involved in hypnosis; no drugs, electric shock, or surgery are necessary. One person simply talks to another. Nothing could be more natural, and nothing could be simpler. The process therefore ought to be readily understandable. Certainly, there is no dearth of explanation. Hypnosis has been ascribed to physiological, neurological, psychological, and psychosocial causes, but none of these has yet received clear experimental documentation.

Hypnotism as an Example of Interpersonal Influence

Jay Hayley's view is of particular cogency in this area because he uses the hypnotic session as a model for the social interaction that occurs in many change processes and not just as a unique and isolated phenomenon. Hayley believes that hypnotism is the behavior-change situation in which the practitioner takes the most direct approach possible. Nevertheless, just as in Hayley's theory of psychotherapy, the practitioner is viewed as maintaining control, not through the direct imposition of his authority, but through the manipulation of paradoxes that give his subject no choice but to obey.

It is clear that hypnotism can be characterized as an interpersonal influence situation. In all cases at least two persons are involved, the hypnotist and the subject. The former is doing something to the latter that results in marked changes in his behavior. What is not so obvious is how this can be interpreted as the imposition of paradoxes and a battle of wits between hypnotist and subject during which they seek to outmaneuver each other. However, this becomes clearer when the process of hypnotism is examined. Regardless of the specific method employed, several characteristics are always found. First, the subject is forced to concentrate his attention on some single stimulus; thus, he cannot mobilize himself to fight the hypnotist. Second, the hypnotist initiates all commands, which gives him the advantage. Finally, he makes a series of tests ostensibly to determine the depth of hypnosis. The subject is told he cannot blink his eyes or move his hands and then is challenged to do so. This command places him in a paradoxical situation. He is being told he cannot do something that ordinarily he can do. If he successfully passes this test, he is told that he can now do certain things and experience phenomena, such as hallucinations, that ordinarily would not be a part of his experience—again, a stronger but even more difficult paradox.

The social process involved in the induction of hypnosis is extremely limited. In fact, the only thing the hypnotist does is give the subject instructions about what to do. There is no small talk and no democratic decision-making involved. The subject has two choices. He can accept the situation for what it is and play an essentially subservient role, or he can resist the suggestions of the hypnotist. If he resists, the hypnotist is forced to outmaneuver him on a higher level, by

53

ostensibly letting him control the way things are to be done while still maintaining command or by actively suggesting to him that he increase his resistance. When this struggle, which characterizes the induction of hypnosis, has been resolved, the individual is prepared to manifest various hypnotic phenomena. If no resolution is attained, he is dismissed as a poor subject.

A successful trance usually is described in terms of its physical characteristics, since these are its most obvious attributes. However, there is one characteristic that is even more encompassing and certainly more important. In the waking state, people generally are aware of and feel responsible for their actions. In the hypnotic trance, however, the individual is in the continuous process of denying responsibility for what he is doing. Things happen to him. His arm lifts. His memory is lost. He cannot see. He regresses to an earlier age. Regardless of what he does, he denies that he himself is doing anything. He does not know what is happening, or it is the hypnotist who is responsible. However, to the observer, this behavior seems paradoxical, because in the last analysis it is only the subject who determines what happens. He does not have to obey the commands he receives.

The subject's behavior becomes clearer when we examine in greater detail the situation he faces when the hypnotist confronts him with demands that he is unable to perform an act, such as raising his hand, which he can ordinarily perform without difficulty. When this request is made, the subject can do one of three things. He can refuse to cooperate by not responding to the hypnotist's suggestion, which will end the session and antagonize the hypnotist. He can lift his arm consciously; and, if he does, the hypnotist will simply carry on with more suggestions. Finally, he can attempt to raise his arm but find that this is impossible. This last alternative is often the most preferable from the subject's viewpoint; it pleases the hypnotist and also allows the subject to feel that he is in no way responsible for what is happening so that his own behavior can be ignored or excused. Having once arrived at this solution to the paradoxical situation in which he is placed, the subject continues with the same sort of responses to the hypnotist's suggestions. The hypnotist aids him in this interpretation by inferentially accepting the responsibility for the subject's actions, which he is ostensibly directing. The consequences are the feats of suggestibility, upon which most investigators have focused their experimental attention. But, as Hayley has made explicit, these manifestations are, in a sense, a smoke screen for the elaborate interpersonal game that is being played. This analysis is particularly interesting because, as has been shown previously, it can be generalized to psychotherapeutic situations and even more generally to any method by means of which one person attempts to influence and alter the behavior and attitude of another.

In this sense, hypnotism is the most direct example of a behavior-change process. Far from being a strange and unique phenomenon, it provides us with a convenient model for the study of the more socially acceptable processes of altering behavior.

CHAPTER FIVE

Learning and Conditioning

Perhaps one of the most natural of the behavior-change processes is learning, and a central interest of modern psychologists has been the study of how learning is most efficiently achieved. For the most part, this research has been conducted on that noble and pure-bred animal, the laboratory rat. From this work has emerged a set of principles that applies to a wide variety of learning situations, including those designed to change human behavior and not simply to teach information.

Much of this research is built around the concept of *conditioning*, which can be defined as a specialized form of learning that occurs due to the systematic association of events in space and time. Extremely elaborate experiments have been devoted to clarifying the circumstances under which conditioning is most and least likely to occur and to determining those conditions that will encourage or discourage the permanence of the conditioning once it has been formed.

The Two Types of Conditioning

In general, two types of conditioning have been distinguished. The first, which is associated with the famous Russian physiologist Ivan Pavlov, whose work extended into the twentieth century, is called *classical conditioning* and is related to the temporal association of events. When a bell is rung consistently before a dog receives food, the dog comes to relate the sound of the bell with the food. After sufficient association with the food, the sound of the bell alone will cause the dog to salivate. In this type of conditioning, the originally neutral stimulus that comes to be associated with the normal action, such as receiving food, is called the *conditioned stimulus,* in this case the bell. The food is called the *unconditioned stimulus.* Generally, conditioning is most efficient if the conditioned stimulus occurs shortly before the unconditioned stimulus; that is, the bell should be rung just before the dog sees the food. However, conditioning can occur with simultaneous presentation or even if the bell is rung after the food is shown. This process of association appears to be automatic and can happen without the conscious awareness of the individual who is being conditioned. If the conditioned stimulus is repeated a number of times by itself, without the occurrence of the related unconditioned stimulus, the conditioning slowly loses its power and is extinguished. In this way the association that has been created can be broken.

Although this type of conditioning has a certain interest, it appears to be limited in application. There are, however, certain general features of classical conditioning of more general interest. For example, when conditioning has once been established, it tends to generalize. Thus, not only a bell may elicit the response, but also a gong. As the conditioned stimulus becomes more generalized, it becomes harder to isolate in order to eliminate it. For example, if a child generalizes a rifle shot that frightened him to a fear of all sudden noises, it may be more difficult to cure him of this reaction than if the attempt had been made soon after the original fear was formed. This is one reason why it is important to decondition anxiety-producing situations by facing them immediately. Thus, the pilot who has crashed is sent up to fly another plane almost at once so that his fear does not have a chance to generalize to other events associated with the experience. On the other hand, it is possible through training to create conditioned stimuli of high discrimination. Animals can be taught to respond to a certain sound frequency but to no other. Such discriminations are clearly an important part of the learning experience. However, they can occur only through conscious intent on the part of a trainer or experimenter, whereas classical conditioning occurs continually in the laboratory and in society.

The second major form of conditioning, and the one upon which increasing emphasis is being placed, is called *instrumental conditioning*. This is the learning of new behavior patterns by associating them with systematically applied rewards and punishments. More simply, if a subject is rewarded for performing a certain act, he will tend to repeat it. If the reward is not provided as the act is repeated over a period of time, the conditioning will be extinguished.

Effects of Reward and Punishment

What is of interest in this form of conditioning is not so much the basic process itself, as the types of arrangement that favor its rapid development or extinction. Studies that vary the amount of reward used to produce instrumental conditioning have shown some fairly surprising results. For example, while the best way to condition a response is to reward it whenever it occurs, such conditioned responses are also the most easily extinguished. Conversely, the best way to extinguish a conditioned response is to punish the individual whenever he makes it, but the effects of this deconditioning tend to be reversed after the punishment is stopped. It is perhaps for this reason that revolts occur in oppressed countries almost immediately after the degree of punishment associated with forbidden activities is reduced. Constant punishment has not effectively deconditioned the kinds of behavior it is intended to prevent. The effect of constant reward may help to explain why overabundance is often a source of potential social decay. If all activities are immediately rewarded, they cease to have any autonomy and are easily undermined and extinguished when the reward system is disturbed due to outside interference, internal economic adjustment, overpopulation, or other normal processes of social change.

While high rates of reward are necessary in order to establish instrumental conditioning, once it has occurred partial reinforcement leads to much stronger conditioning than continuous reward. In fact, within certain limits, the less often the conditioning is rewarded or reinforced, the more resistant to extinction is the response. Similarly, punishment is a more effective deconditioner if used only intermittently. Normally, rewards are not provided continuously for approved behavior. The student is not praised for every right answer; the worker does not benefit from every productive act; the child does not receive candy or a smile for every correct performance or a shout for every disapproved act.

This empirically confirmed fact helps to explain the extraordinary persistence that human behavior often exhibits in the face of minimal reward. A mother will expend great energy and emotion for occasional smiles and appreciation from her family. A graduate student will endure considerable delay, discomfort, anxiety, and difficult preparatory labor for examinations and theses for infrequent commendation from his teachers and the ultimate reinforcement of a degree. Many important creative efforts seem to be made in the context of such a reward system. Artists may be harshly criticized and ignored, but the occasional reward of success and critical acclaim produces incredible endurance and persistence in the face of long-term hardships.

Conversely, as has been noted, though punishment inhibits the expression of instrumental conditioning, if it is removed, the response tends to reassert itself. A number of implications for child rearing and other change processes more limited in time can be drawn from this fact. For example, most parents believe that they are failing in their duty if they do not punish reprehensible acts, such as fighting, stealing, or telling lies. However, learning experiments suggest that it is better to punish these acts only occasionally. The relative inefficiency of our legal reinforcement system is, from this point of view, a superior arrangement. If every speeder were caught immediately, it would not as efficiently extinguish this behavior as the occasional conviction that more typically occurs. An absolute enforcement of the laws against it would temporarily eliminate speeding, but removal of this punishment would occasion a rampage of speeding. However, after occasional punishment, most individuals learn to drive at a reasonable speed whether or not a police car is immediately evident.

It is, however, important to note that intermittent punishment and reward should not be applied to the same behavior. If one kind of activity is rewarded and punished on different occasions, the child may become confused, and a neurotic conflict may be created. For this reason, parents who inconsistently reward and punish the same kinds of behavior often produce children who have emotional difficulties. Consistency is essential in the type of reinforcement employed for the greatest permanence of the desired behavior patterns, but reward and punishment need not and should not be applied regularly.

When learning theorists discovered the impact of intermittent rewards on human behavior, they began to devote a good deal of effort to testing the relative effects of different reward schedules. From this research emerged the general conclusion that variation in rate and interval of reward is associated with greatest strength of conditioning, or rather greatest resistance to extinction. More specifically, it was demonstrated that it is not only the intermittent character of the reinforcement, but the random nature of its appearance that adds to the impact. Here again, the peculiar potency of natural conditions is confirmed. We normally do not know when occasional rewards will come. Many persons look for mail each morning hoping for a kind word or indications of external success. Usually, bills and advertisements arrive. This does not stop them from anticipating good news but increases its intensity. An even stronger case is the behavior of the gambler, who literally lives for his occasionally received random reinforcement.

While this general conclusion has been established, it, by no means, completely covers the available data. An infinite number of reward schedules can be generated, and each presumably has a somewhat different effect on the conditioned response's resistance to extinction. The only way to establish their relative effectiveness or efficiency is to subject them to empirical test. The most rigorous and impressive demonstration was performed by the psychologists Charles Ferster and Burrhus Skinner. In a monumental effort, *Schedules of Reinforcement,* the effects of varying reinforcement patterns on the pecking response of pigeons was investigated.[1] Many hundreds of pages are devoted to presenting the effects of a large number of slightly different reinforcement schedules. While this overwhelming mass of raw data is difficult to digest, it clearly indicates that relatively minor variations in reinforcement can have an important influence on pigeons' behavior. Since such schedules are virtually infinitely variable, even a lengthy report can only touch upon some of the highlights; no simple conclusions emerge, except that a large body of experimental data must be collected before the full implications of reinforcement patterns on human behavior are fully appreciated.

Conditioning as a Behavior-Change Technique

The simplicity and universality of conditioning processes have naturally led to a number of attempts to use them more or less directly as techniques of behavior change. Particularly in the area of psychotherapy, a vocal minority of experimentally oriented therapists have applied various modifications of conditioning processes to neurotic and psychotic patients suffering from many different symptomatic conditions, varying from bedwetting to feelings of anxiety. In this endeavor, numerous conditioning techniques have been employed; they vary in character and in sophistication. For convenience, they can be classed in five types. The first utilizes punishment to eliminate undesirable behavior. This approach is direct; that is, undesirable behavior is punished whenever it occurs, and punishment is systematically reduced when the undesirable behavior is reduced.

The second major technique utilizes practice without reward or punishment. It is essentially an extinction procedure. The undesirable behavior is consciously repeated until it slowly extinguishes itself. The stutterer, for example, is made to stutter more, and the alcoholic is forced to get drunk.

The third process involves the direct use of instrumental conditioning. Desired behavior patterns are rewarded until they are firmly established. Then intermittent reinforcement is applied.

The fourth type of attempted behavior change involves an extension of instrumental conditioning. If after it has taken place an undesirable response occurs, the reward is reduced or eliminated.

The final technique involves progressive desensitization to stimuli that evoke undesirable responses. For example, a woman who is afraid to enter an elevator is first instructed to think of an elevator. Later she may be asked to push the button to summon one. If these experiences do not evoke too much anxiety, she may next walk into the elevator and then right out. Then she enters it and stands there for ten seconds. At the end of this graduated series of steps, she will be able to ride in an elevator, presumably without fear.

The main appeal of these processes of behavior change is their simplicity and the direct relation they bear to learning-theory research. The usefulness of conditioning techniques has recently been evaluated by the psychologist John M. Grossberg, who examined over 130 reports of such therapeutic approaches.[2] He states that one or another method of conditioning has been used as a treatment for a wide variety of psychotic or neurotic states. Not all approaches have been equally successful, either in general or with specific types of disorders, but the degree of success reported is high.

The findings of so many studies are necessarily complex and need not be considered definitive, since they are for the most part reports of individual cases, not controlled research in which persons were treated or not treated on a matched or random basis. Therefore, these conclusions cannot be taken as demonstrative, except when their research

61

deals with patients who had already been shown to be resistant to more traditional forms of psychotherapy or where an attempt was made to treat conditions not usually helped by customary approaches. Some positive evidence of this type is offered, but a great deal of work is required before confident statements can be made about the efficacy of conditioning processes as opposed to insight-oriented techniques emphasizing self-understanding. The evidence is clear enough to indicate, however, that conditioning is more than a tool of the experimental psychologist. It is a phenomenon of comprehensive scope and considerable power in determining the resistance to change of most of our well-established behavior patterns. Further, it provides us with a simple guide to the creation of new patterns and the elimination of nonfunctional reactions that cause emotional anguish or behavioral dysfunction. In general, therefore, while most of these studies were uncontrolled, they collectively suggest that rather simple adaptations of conditioning processes are, indeed, strikingly effective in changing behavior patterns in mature adults.

Such direct translation from learning theory to behavior-change principles has really just begun. A major breakthrough in education is the use of the *teaching machine*. Its basic principle is to reduce any learning situation to a set of discrete steps, each of which is reinforced as it is mastered. These often complex machines, employing programs of instruction that require half a year to write, are based on the fact that new behavior is most quickly learned if it is immediately and consistently reinforced. However, in this respect the machine cannot be duplicated by any human teacher who does not divide up his subject matter into small units and who cannot practically reinforce all learning by each member of the class as soon as it is accomplished.

Social Conditioning

Another development closely related to laboratory studies of conditioning is the *socialization* of the young; that is, the process by which children are trained to become members of society. Most descriptions of socialization emphasize normal needs, developmental sequences, and strategies employed by parents and society to mold the behavior of the child. Relatively little attention is given to the systematic use of conditioning to teach desired behavior patterns. Perhaps it all seems a little mechanical and inhuman. Nevertheless, if conditioning works, it is necessary to ask whether some of our relatively fuzzy socialization processes need to be classified along the lines suggested by learning theory.

Some studies of socialization have come close to evaluating the direct effects of conditioning by studying them as a means of determining the impact of reward and punishment on the actions of children, an issue of great concern to parents and psychologists alike.

Any research of this type runs into a variety of practical difficulties not encountered in laboratory work with animals. Either specific children must be studied as they grow up, which necessitates long periods of data collection, or dependence must be placed on the recollected experience of adults, which is likely to be faulty. Further, over long periods of time, the effects of punishment and reward tend to become contaminated, diluted, and otherwise transformed by other variables that also influence the child. There are theoretical problems as well. Rewards and punishments vary in their mode of administration and in their intensity. Parents may use physical means, psychological influence, or combinations of the two with varying degrees of consistency.

There are relatively few studies of the systematic use of rewards and punishments in socialization in spite of the important practical issues involved and the closeness of the experimental questions to those raised in the context of learning theory. Currently available research indicates that overdependence on punishment rather than intermittent reward as the mode of socialization tends to produce anxiety in the child. If the punishment is severe, the anxiety tends to generalize to other types of behavior that were not punished. On the other hand, the use of reward for parentally desired activities makes it easier for the child to identify with his parents, since they are not seen as personal threats but rather as sources of satisfaction.

These conclusions do not bear directly on the relative effects of reward and punishment on the behavior toward which they are directed. Presumably, those effects would follow the principles of conditioning that have already been described. However, the findings are of particular significance in that they suggest other relevant aspects of the conditioning process that need to be considered, such as what effect rewards and punishments have on the child's attitude toward the parents. Conditioning is thus viewed as an interpersonal event, a significant step that removes it from the laboratory and places it in a more accessible social context.

In a related area, the psychologists Wallace Kennedy and Herman

Willcutt have recently reviewed 33 studies of the effect of praise and blame on the performance of school children.[3] In general, these studies, conducted over a period of 50 years, indicated that praise facilitated performance whereas blame inhibited it. However, some interesting exceptions to this general trend are noted. Praise decreased the performance of one group of underachievers, whereas blame increased their performance as well as that of very bright adolescents and Negro children working with Negro testers. Thus, while the basic relationship is simple, some of its more specialized aspects are far from obvious.

Quite a different approach can be taken in relation to the significance of conditioning in the production of behavior change. It is possible to interpret more natural, complex processes as rather subtle instances of simple conditioning. For example, a salesman talking to a prospect attempts to reward those responses that he thinks may lead to a purchase by the use of social reinforcement, that is, by a smile or a friendly word. He may extinguish undesirable responses by letting the person talk himself out of other possible purchases. He may attempt to utilize mild negative threats toward nonpurchasing tendencies, such as suggesting that the price may increase at a later time.

The generality of conditions in normal social intercourse has been clearly characterized by the psychologist William Verplanck in a study involving the social reinforcement of spontaneous opinions given in a variety of social circumstances.[4] To perform the research, he enlisted the aid of seventeen of his students at Harvard University, who were enrolled in a course studying the psychology of learning. These students were instructed to reinforce any statement made to them by people with whom they usually came into contact that began with the words "I think," "I believe," "it seems to me," or "I feel." They did this by saying "You're right," smiling, or paraphrasing the statement and expressing agreement with it. Those conditioned in this manner included uncles, friends, total strangers, roommates, and boy or girl friends. The settings in which the conditioning took place included a dormitory, a hospital ward, telephone conversations, a public lounge, a restaurant, and a private home. The results were remarkable. In every case, the subject increased the rate at which he verbalized the reinforced opinion, regardless of its nature. Even more disturbing was the fact that in no case were the subjects aware that they had been conditioned.

As the climax to this striking study, Verplanck had the sobering experience of describing the results of his work to an associate who proceeded to condition him during the conversation by the same process Verplanck's students used. Verplanck did not know that he had been conditioned until he was told about it. This study clearly demonstrates that conditioning can exert a pervasive influence on general social behavior and is not just a laboratory curiosity.

The evidence to support such a view has recently been examined by the psychologist Leonard Krasner.[5] In a review of 31 research investigations, he was able to demonstrate conclusively that mere verbal approval or disapproval could produce conditioned effects that determined the nature and rate of verbal expression. Even such neutral expressions as "mm-hmm" have been proved capable of altering verbal behavior. A flasher, a buzzer, or an electric light will do as well. Awareness on the part of the subject is unrelated to the conditioning.

Since we are constantly reacting in one way or another to everything that is said to us, the implication is that we are engaged in a vast conditioning experience in which each person unconsciously encourages in others the attitudes and responses he is seeking from them. Fortunately, individuals work at cross-purposes to each other so that these conditioning effects are partially neutralized. If one person reinforces another when he makes a liberal statement, and a second does so when he makes a conservative statement, the two influences tend to counteract and negate each other. However, when social influences are controlled and move clearly in only one direction, as in a totalitarian state, the effect can be very difficult to counteract.

Krasner, in his discussion of these studies, points out that they suggest that traditional psychotherapy, with its emphasis on a nondirective approach, may actually be a subtle conditioning process in which the therapist's slightest reaction acts to condition the remarks of the patient, encouraging those that are reinforced and reducing or extinguishing those that are not. Thus, the patient unconsciously gives the therapist the kind of material and reactions of which he approves. The effect is so subtle that neither is aware of what is happening. In this way the therapist can use the material from his patients to justify any theory he happens to hold, since the conditioning produces the sort of data required to confirm the theory.

In summary, conditioning procedures have been demonstrated to have a number of general implications for behavior change. They are powerful determinants in their own right, supporting already acquired behavior patterns and aiding in the establishment of new ones. Negative, positive, and deconditioning procedures each represent experimental analogues of naturalistic situations that collectively are responsible for an important segment of the social and personal change that occurs with and without conscious intent.

Even more generally, research into the mechanisms of learning theory provides a graphic illustration of the utility of experimental studies in the development of basic principles that have widespread, practical implications. This scientific precedent lends additional support to the belief that orthodox scientific procedures can be applied to a wide range of behavior-change processes with every likelihood of achieving important results.

CHAPTER SIX

Components of Psychotherapy

AT the conclusion of Chapter One, it was suggested that change processes must be reduced to their component parts if they are to be studied effectively by scientific methods. This theme has now been approached from several different vantage points. The types of model that might be developed from the interrelation of such components have been examined and the separate effects of physiological, hypnotic, and learning variables assessed. The problem has not, however, been directly attacked. The evidence relating to major components of behavior-change processes has not been evaluated.

The present chapter seeks to determine the extent to which it is practical and meaningful to conceive of behavior-change processes, such as psychotherapy, as a synthesis of clearly differentiated components that can be tested separately and in combination. The purpose here is not to summarize all that is known about such components, but to indicate the qualitative nature of the evidence so that a more seasoned and realistic estimate of the success to be expected from this approach can be made.

Before embarking on a direct assessment of the evidence, it may be helpful to clarify the function of various forms of psychotherapy. In all cases one or more clients consult a practitioner about various psychological difficulties and seek solutions to these problems with him. The ways in which the client is helped differ greatly, but in general they can be classified as either directive or nondirective. In *directive therapy,* the therapist tells the patient what he should do, taking an active role in leading the course of treatment. In contrast, the therapist using *nondirective* techniques does not tell the patient how to behave and leaves the course of the treatment sessions up to him. The nondirective approach characterizes many different forms of *insight therapy,* all of which emphasize the need for greater self-understanding as a prerequisite to permanent and fundamental personality change. These therapies require a long period of work, often years, on the part of both patient and therapist. The more directive approaches require less time, since their objectives are usually related to specific overt change, and the results are more readily obtained and evaluated.

In recent years, all forms of therapy have been adapted to groups of patients meeting together with promising results and with increasing economy of effort. The general goals of *group psychotherapy* are the same as those of individual therapy. However, the sessions take quite a different form. Usually, small groups of patients discuss their personal problems and analyze the problems of others during regular meetings with a group therapist, who guides the group interaction and facilitates the therapeutic process by encouraging quiet members to speak or offering interpretations of the behavior of participants.

Regardless of these distinctions, it is still possible to view psychotherapy or any behavior-change process as a complex pattern of basic components that can be separated and evaluated in terms of normal standards of experimental control.

When psychotherapy is dissected, some of its vital aspects must be reassigned to other disciplines. Variables such as discussion and feedback are more logically discussed under the heading of small-group research. Conditioning effects are more usefully dealt with in relation to learning theory. This chapter will treat the components that are left after an appropriate reorganization and redistribution has been made.

Further, this discussion must be clearly separated from that of Chapter Two in which models for interrelating specific components were described. The power of the components must be established independent of any model, and such verification must precede the testing of the model or the decision as to which components ought to be included.

Three general approaches will be employed. First, some of the experimental literature relating to specific components will be reviewed, both for its own sake and to gain some sense of the character and fruitfulness of this approach. Second, the relationship between the therapist and the patient will be explored in the belief that it forms a crucial aspect of most, if not all, change processes in psychotherapy. Finally, the integrating of the various components of psychotherapy will be discussed as it relates to the problem of programming an electronic computer with sufficient and properly organized data, in order to use the computer to simulate human behavior-change processes.

Selected Components

Perhaps the most striking and influential of the components that constitute the psychotherapeutic situation is the faith of the client in the practitioner who seeks to help him. Faith was discussed in Chapters One and Two as a source of error in the evaluation of behavior-change processes and as a basic element in a model of such change. Here, the experimental evidence relating to the power of faith as a change agent in its own right will be examined.

Perhaps the easiest way to understand the influence of the client's faith is through a study of the effectiveness of placebos. They are often given as controls in tests of medically active substances in order to determine the actual physiological efficiency of the drug under question. From these studies it has become clear that the pharmacologically inert control substances also have a powerful effect. Placebos have dramatically relieved serious medical conditions such as bleeding peptic ulcers. A group of patients with peptic ulcer received nothing but sterile water, which they were told was a new medicine that would relieve them. Over 70% of the cases improved and maintained improvement for more than a year. Only 25% of the cases in a *control group*, who also received the sterile water but who were told it was a medicine of undetermined effect, experienced improvement.[1]

More pertinent to evaluating the influence of faith in psychotherapy is a recent study of placebos conducted at the Henry Phipps Psychiatric Clinic.[2] In this instance, the effects of medically inactive pills were compared with those of short-term psychotherapy on outpatients. The pattern and extent of symptom reduction was found to be the same for each approach on scales designed to measure "ineffectiveness" and "discomfort." Short-term therapy was no more helpful than the inert pill. Change was produced by faith and not by the psycho-therapeutic method itself.

Another important component of any psychotherapeutic process is often described as the degree of direction, or lead, supplied by the practitioner. An ambitious series of studies has been carried on at the University of Pennsylvania to investigate this component of the psychotherapeutic process.[3] In these studies, the directive approach involved interpretation, suggestion, advice, and persuasion. The following type of therapy was modeled after the nondirective approach as developed by psychologist Carl Rogers. In this approach the practitioner allows the client to talk about whatever he likes and attempts to transmit to the client the feeling that he accepts, understands, and respects him. In this way he seeks to encourage the client to have the strength and courage to slowly resolve his own difficulties without becoming unduly dependent on the practitioner in the process. In the primary studies, the comparative effects of the two approaches were determined on twenty-four clients who were seen by one of six therapists. Each therapist treated two patients by leading and two by following. Each therapeutic method was used for an average of thirteen sessions. Twenty-one measures of change were obtained from a personality test, a client interview, and standardized ratings made by the client and the therapist. Of the twenty-one possible changes that might have occurred, only two were actually obtained. First, the therapists, as shown by their ratings of success, favored leading therapy. However, the authors point out that all but one therapist personally favored the leading method before the experiment began. Second, reluctance to discuss sensitive material was greater in leading therapy. In general, relatively little support is given to the conclusion that one approach is better than the other.

The distinction between leading and following has also been utilized by the psychologist Jesse Gorden in an unusually fine experiment.[4] In this study, eighteen male college students were treated by nine graduate-student therapists. Each subject was randomly assigned one type of treatment and each therapist treated two persons, one in each way. Since all subjects were normal, it was necessary to create a problem that therapy could solve. This was accomplished by exposing the subjects to a standardized, hypnotically induced conflict: namely, that they had been unjustly accused of having tripped the gym teacher.

The degree of intensity of the conflict was controlled by producing the same one to the same degree in each subject. The therapists were unaware that the conflict had been induced; they were simply instructed as to the different strategies they were to adopt in therapy. That their behavior actually varied in the two types of treatment was verified by analysis of the content of the treatment interview. Judges who rated transcripts of the sessions were ignorant of the hypnotic preparation of the subjects. The effect of therapy was measured by the amount of recall of the hypnotically repressed incident, the time taken for recall and recognition of the conflict, as well as ratings of degree of hostility manifested by the client toward the therapist. The results indicated that there was no significant difference between the methods in terms of these criteria, though special statistical analysis suggested that leading was more helpful in facilitating recall to the limit of native ability than following.

The two previous studies point toward somewhat equivocal conclusions. They suggest that either leading and following are not really important components in determining the outcome of psychotherapy or that their influence is somehow obscured by the concurrent action of other components to which they are related. In view of the latter possibility some interest has centered around a similar, though perhaps more influential, set of components that can be called insight as opposed to effective social functioning. Most following types of therapy emphasize the importance of attaining insight into the causes of one's own behavior, whereas most leading therapies place greater emphasis on the ability to function effectively in social situations. A number of relevant experimental comparisons have been made of the relative importance of insight and effective social functioning. The first two of these to be dealt with here involve varying degrees of interpretation designed to produce insight rather than a direct comparison of the effect of insight as opposed to that of social interaction.

The psychologist C. D. Keet has compared an expressive technique with an interpretive approach.[5] The expressive technique emphasized the acceptance of the client's feelings and attitudes without offering explicit interpretation. The interpretive technique included these elements in addition to making use of interpretive comments designed to facilitate the client's self-understanding. Thirty students were randomly assigned to one or the other of these therapeutic situations, both of which were conducted by the experimenter.

Process analysis, performed by observing how frequently certain kinds of behavior occurred during the interview, confirmed the distinction between the two methods. Inability to recall disturbing key words previously learned was used as the measure of change. The results of the study indicated that the interpretive method was superior to the expressive in producing recall.

A similar study was made by the psychologist David Grossman.[6] Two groups of ten undergraduates were selected from a sample of six hundred. They were matched on personality characteristics, intelligence, estimated future adjustment, motivation for therapy, and degree of insight. Each subject had three sessions involving either minor or extensive use of interpretation. Unfortunately, in spite of the matching procedure, the more resistant subjects were by chance assigned to the group receiving extensive interpretation. Three measures of insight obtained from a personality test, a projective test, and the ratings of the client and his therapist were used to compare the effects of different amounts of interpretation. An analysis of these measures did not indicate that the extent of interpretation was related to an increase in insight.

A direct comparison of insight and effective social behavior has been made in several investigations. One interesting and carefully designed study was conducted by the Canadian psychologist Wesley Coons in order to compare the effect of these components in group therapy.[7] Two experimental conditions were used in the study. In the groups receiving therapy that emphasized social behavior, stress was placed on interpersonal interaction in a warm permissive climate where no reference was made to personal difficulties of the subject. The second type of therapy stressed intellectual understanding of personal difficulties in a benignly authoritarian climate and was modeled to some extent after psychoanalytic group therapy. Process analysis confirmed that these differences of emphasis were maintained in practice. Each group held three sessions a week, over a fifteen-month period, with an average of thirty therapy hours per person. Two therapists conducted the sessions, each using both methods with different groups. The subjects consisted of sixty hospitalized patients assigned to groups matched on economic status, occupational class, diagnosis, educational level, *I.Q.,* age, duration of illness, and duration of hospitalization. The *Wechsler-Bellevue intelligence test* and the *Rorschach ink blot test* for measuring personality characteristics were used as measures of change. The Rorschach test consists of standardized ink blots that are presented to the subject one at a time. He is asked to tell what he thinks each blot looks like. Since the blots are accidentally formed, it is assumed that whatever the subject sees reflects in large part his own personality. All of the responses of the subject to the ink blots are recorded and collectively constitute what is called the *Rorschach protocol.*

In spite of the unlikelihood of finding large changes in the level of intelligence, which is usually assumed to be stable, a significant improvement of intelligence occurred in the groups stressing interpersonal interaction. Ratings of Rorschach protocols on the criterion of level of adjustment by a person unacquainted with any of the group members also favored the groups that emphasized effective behavior rather than self-understanding.

A somewhat similar study was conducted by the psychologists N. Charles Bourestom and W. Lynn Smith.[8] In their study, a comparison was made between a group receiving therapy emphasizing an understanding of how people felt about each other and one in which the emphasis was placed on how people behaved toward one another. The first procedure emphasized insight, the second social effectiveness. The treatment of both groups was conducted by the same therapist, and each met for fifty minutes, three times a week, for a total of twenty meetings. The sample was relatively small, consisting of only twelve male psychology students, divided into two groups of six each. The relative effects of the two methods were measured by a projective test, and an analysis of tape recordings of the sessions. No differences were noted between the two groups on the projective test. However, certain behavioral changes noted in tape recordings suggested that focusing the group's attention on feelings was more anxiety-producing than focusing its attention on behavior. These studies somewhat surprisingly seem to favor social interaction over insight as an agent of change, but the results are sufficiently limited to suggest that no firm conclusions should be drawn.

The above findings, relating to only a few of the components that might be discussed, suggest several tentative conclusions. First, there are no basic obstacles to performing studies of components of psychotherapy. Second, results of such research are not necessarily in accord with current belief. The confirmation of the influence of faith is almost greater than one would have anticipated, and insight certainly seems to have less impact than is generally believed. Third, as with any experimental work of this type, partially contradictory results are obtained when conditions are not comparable from one study to another. This kind of discontinuity is not unnatural but merely points to the need for a systematic series of investigations in order to clarify all relevant aspects of the influence of any given component.

The Relationship between Therapist and Patient

As practitioners became aware that any process of behavior change was essentially a social interchange between at least two people, it was recognized that the relationship between therapist and patient was the crucial element in altering behavior. The manipulation of this relationship forms the psychotherapist's central tool, and it is, therefore, natural to make this interaction the focal point of study. This orientation on the part of clinical research workers has led to a new kind of study in which some measures of the psychotherapeutic relationship are related to other background, process, or outcome variables.

Before presenting some of the findings of these studies, it will be useful to examine the psychotherapeutic relationship itself. However, most researchers have been more interested in what the relationship ought to be than in its actual nature, because it helps to establish a convenient frame of reference for other investigations.

A wide variety of subjects with different professional affiliations, degrees of training, and experience have been asked their conception of the ideal psychotherapeutic relationship. In general, it has been found that certain qualities of the therapist, such as warmth, permissiveness, respect, understanding, and liking of the patient, are universally recognized as desirable. In fact, the interested layman has approximately the same view as the expert. Such differences as do exist seem to stem from the individual's degree of commitment to and interest in helping others rather than from any particular training or professional affiliation itself. This degree of conceptual communality is interesting and helps to justify the concept of psychotherapy as a unified activity.

Having established a definition of a good therapeutic relationship, it is logical to inquire whether its existence in particular cases does, in fact, tend to produce constructive changes in the patient. A number of studies bear on this issue. However, virtually all of them have methodological deficiencies, and the results themselves are varied. They generally indicate that a good relationship does have some connection with a successful outcome, a finding that should surprise no one.

A number of other studies relate the nature of the psychotherapeutic relationship to such variables as the initial diagnosis of the patient, his motivation for treatment, friendliness, ethical values, degree of dependency, social class, and expectations of therapy.

Therapists seem to prefer, and feel they can be most helpful to, patients who are not too maladjusted and who display ability to relate to others in an energetic and uninhibited manner. These patients have strong motivation to change, are friendly, moderately dependent, somewhat altruistic, of the same social class as the practitioner, and expect a moderate degree of warmth from him. This is not surprising, but it does serve to limit the effectiveness of psychotherapy as it is ordinarily practiced.

A number of studies have also been made of various characteristics of the therapist that affect the therapy process, including his personality, familiarity with the patient, and the degree of his previous experience. It has been found that most such characteristics do not have any simple effect on the success of the relationship. They may be irrelevant, or extremes of any characteristics may be undesirable, while a midrange is helpful. While therapists generally like patients better when they know something about them, there is no evidence to suggest that they can predict the patient's behavior better than anyone else. What is important is that the patient believe he is understood, not whether, in fact, the therapist does really understand him. Finally, experienced therapists are better able to attain an approximation of the ideal relationship than inexperienced practitioners. This distinction is of particular importance in the treatment of more difficult patients.

In a more socially oriented approach, one can relate the real or assumed similarity between therapist and patient to the quality of their relationship. While there is some evidence that the degree to which the therapist assumes he is similar to the client may relate to his liking for him, the situation involving actual similarity is more complex. Certain trait similarities seem to produce conflict, others, friendliness and progress. It is necessary to specify the nature of the trait in order to accurately determine and predict its effect.

Finally, one can examine the relative importance of the type of psychotherapeutic technique and the relationship between practitioner and patient to the ultimate outcome of therapy. While these aspects

75

have been investigated for fifteen years, no clear conclusion has been reached. Both factors have demonstrable effects, but their relative importance has not been defined clearly. Such studies are complicated by the fact that the same type of therapist usually chooses to utilize the same kind of technique, which differs from that used by another type, so that one cannot separate the personality and experience of the therapist from the method, since one tends to determine the other. A similar relationship between the personality of the patient and the method of therapy he chooses also exists but to a lesser extent, since he may not be aware of the nature of the therapist's technique until it is too late. Even if he has some awareness of the differences among approaches, he may choose to seek out a therapist he finds personally congenial regardless of his techniques, which further complicates the problem of determining the effect of the separate components.

The Simulation of Psychotherapy

The ultimate test of an understanding of any behavior-change process is the ability to synthesize the process from a specified set of components. This is analogous to the work of the organic chemist who artificially creates a substance normally found only in nature. His understanding is most complete when he can build the substance out of its constituent elements.

In many ways, the task of the behavioral scientist is far more difficult than that of the chemist. No one knows what the elements of psychotherapy really are, so that all attempts to reconstitute it from its separate components are premature. Nevertheless, a *simulation*, that is, an abstract working model of the process, is extremely revealing.

Most therapists and patients are repelled by the notion of a simulated psychotherapy, though for somewhat different reasons. The psychotherapist feels automation threatening his livelihood and reducing his science-art to mechanistic formulas. The patient may resent the idea that his unique life experience can be treated as a set of variables that are somehow related to one another.

Any attempt to simulate a behavior-change process must be guided by a decision as to which aspect of experience the simulation is to reproduce. Psychotherapists are attracted to models that focus on the patients' defenses against anxiety. A simulation of this process would emphasize the various defenses that might be employed by the patient in the kinds of anxiety-provoking situations that might occur during the normal course of psychotherapy. A rather different approach might be employed by the social scientist who views therapy only as a specialized form of social experience. In this instance, primary attention might be given to the relations among patterns of communication between therapist and client rather than to any attempt to infer the motivation lying behind them. Ultimately, of course, all components must be utilized in any successful simulation of the whole process of psychotherapy, but, because of its complexity, it would be foolish to begin this way.

The first approach has been taken by the psychologist Kenneth Colby, who has programmed a neurotic process on an electronic computer.[9] He attempts to have the computer re-create and predict what a neurotic individual will do when faced with different kinds of threatening or attractive situations. While this is not a direct imitation of psychotherapy, there is no doubt that the kinds of maneuvers that Colby seeks to re-create on a machine constitute an important aspect of the field. The specificity of the program has helped in achieving an understanding of neurotic behavior and suggested further research needed to provide vital information for increasing the accuracy of the simulation.

The previously discussed components of therapy could also be used as a basis for a simulation that would characterize typical kinds of effect on patient behavior produced by the variation of these specific components by the therapist. For example, certain kinds of evasion by the patient might evoke an insight-producing comment from the therapist, or a skeptical statement might be met with a faith-producing action.

The second approach is more superficial, but it is also more comprehensive in scope. The complex, but obscure, nature of the dynamics underlying the psychotherapeutic situation is totally ignored, and the focus is placed on observable behavior. When this is done the scientist can then utilize a number of powerful methods developed by social scientists to analyze observed behavior. Perhaps the most general and widely used of these methods is *interaction process analysis,* a method of observation that is used to place each act of behavior in one of twelve description categories such as "asking for opinion" or "showing antagonism." The advantage of such a procedure is that all observed behavior can be translated into one general framework consisting of only twelve categories. The computer's task in the simulation process is thus greatly simplified from having to simulate an infinite number of events to having to simulate only twelve basic events, each of which is then combined in a mathematically determined number of combinations.

In order to simulate the therapeutic process, the machine must know what kind of action will probably follow an action that has occurred. Phrased another way, the computer needs to know the statistical probability of each of the twelve categories of action following the occurrence of each other category of activity. Such information can be obtained from direct observation of a large number of psychotherapy sessions, or it can be created on the computer by trying all possible combinations of probabilities until the best match is achieved with a sample of real behavior. No one would claim that a simple understanding of the relative likelihood of different sequences of behavior would, in itself, enable one to predict the course of psychotherapy. But it should help to provide a framework within which such a simulation could slowly be approximated.

There are actually four different ways in which one can approach the simulation of psychotherapy as a process of interaction, each of which provides different kinds of information. The first alternative is the limiting case in which neither the practitioner nor the client is simulated. They are simply observed, and their patterns of interaction are transformed into a *matrix of probabilities,* which expresses the relative likelihood that any particular act will be followed by any of the twelve categories of action. In other words, the identifiable patterns of normal social behavior are quantitatively determined. Such information then provides a standard for assessing the adequacy of subsequent simulations.

In the second type of approach, the client is simulated, but the therapist is not. This might be done by supplying the therapist with written statements in response to his own actions. Thus, he might inquire: "Do you think what you said is totally accurate?" This response would be translated into its appropriate category, which might be "asking a question." The machine would then determine the relative probability of each class of patient response. Having selected the most likely class on the basis of known probabilities, it could select replies at random from the examples of the category stored in its memory, and this selection is the statement the therapist would receive from the machine. Thus, whatever move the clinician made, the computer would respond, though not always with the most probable class of response since this would not be entirely realistic. If these patterns of behavior were compared to known standards of excellence, that is, if norms were obtained from expert clinicians, this approach would provide a useful training device for therapists. It would be as if all practitioners were treating the same patient, even though the interaction sequences would be unique in each case.

The third approach would be to simulate the therapist but not the patient. This involves the creation of a therapy machine. The patient's comments are programmed into the machine by category, and the computer selects a statement at random from the responses that would be likely. If these comments have been tape-recorded by a therapist and stored, the patient might be unaware that he is not talking to a human. However, this might not be an important factor; an answer from a computer might be more impressive than a human response.

The fascinating aspect of this approach is that one can evaluate the success of a treatment whose nature is objectively determined. Further, every element of this treatment can be altered in a specified manner; that is, the category of each action can be determined even though the particular action may be randomly selected. Thus, one is provided with a situation in which psychotherapy becomes truly manipulable. The advantages for research could be great. Further, if such therapy were effective, even only in part, it could have an impact on the treatment of mental illness, since there is little prospect that enough human practitioners will ever be trained to meet the expanding need for services of this kind.

Whatever the level and complexity of the simulation, the automation of attempts to alter behavior strikes a cruel blow at an intimate and artistic aspect of human experience. Nevertheless, it is only an extension of the objectivity and specificity that characterizes all scientific investigation, since knowledge obtained from scientific study is the prerequisite of any successful simulation. It represents the natural outcome of psychotherapeutic research, whether one likes it or not.

The fourth approach to simulation has already been briefly described. It involves the simultaneous simulation of the therapist and the patient, and the total psychotherapeutic process would take place within the computer, or rather a model of it would be programmed into the machine with instructions on ways to choose responses of both patient and therapist. When the machine can approximate an abstract description of the therapeutic process, it can be said that therapy is fully understood. Naturally, such a development lies far in the future, but even at the present time, it is fair to conclude that the general strategies to be employed in future simulations of behavior-change processes are already clear. Further, a number of the components of these processes have already been subjected to preliminary investigation. As the components are identified and investigated, both singly and in combination with each other, the goal of successful simulation becomes closer. It must be emphasized that it is not the simulation itself that forms the goal, but rather the thorough understanding of the basic process of behavior change that the successful simulation implies. Further, in this quest the partial failure of any simulation provides us with valuable clues about the value and extent of our present knowledge and thus helps to direct the course of future investigations.

CHAPTER SEVEN

The Small Group as a
Behavior-Change Medium

T HE previous chapters have examined behavior-change processes occurring in various kinds of social situations, but little direct attention has been given to the influence that the situation has on these processes. This problem has most directly been examined by sociologists and psychologists studying groups of humans. The small group is usually defined as being composed of from two to twenty-five or thirty persons; it is difficult to establish a precise upper limit. Generally, such a limit is considered to be the size that still allows all group members to be aware of each other's presence.

As early as 1904, the well-known American psychologist Lewis Terman was performing studies of leadership in small groups that favorably compare with current work.[1] But for the most part small-group research is a relatively recent phenomenon; starting with the work of the German-American psychologist Kurt Lewin in the late 1940's, it developed explosively.

Scientists with a variety of special interests explore this area. One type of small-group research closely allied to our present interests uses the group as an arena in which permanent changes in individual members might be produced. In a second approach these groups are studied as models of large-scale social influences. The small group offers a flexible setting within which it is possible to explore significant aspects of larger social structures under carefully controlled conditions. A third line of investigation utilizes the small group as a vehicle for the study of the way in which particular individuals form interpersonal relationships. In these studies the small group becomes a sort of social background that throws individual performance into prominent relief. A fourth type of study utilizes behavior change within small groups to alter behavior of larger aggregates of people. Thus reorganization of small groups of workers within a factory might increase over-all productivity, regardless of whether the individual group members undergo personal change or not. Finally, small groups are studied simply in order to understand how they operate; that is, the area is investigated as a subject in its own right rather than for any practical end.

When, in the late 1940's, individuals with these various interests came to the realization that techniques were available to make small-group investigations practical and even relatively simple, it is not surprising that interest in them increased and, indeed, still has not ceased to grow.

When the small group is used as a means of altering the behavior of its members, certain of its aspects became important. These include its size, the nature of its membership, task efficiency, power structure, reward systems, natural detrimental processes, the effects of forced interaction on individual members, group discussion and decision, social structure, and feedback mechanisms.

The Effect of Group Size

Practitioners who work with groups want to learn what optimum group size is for the likelihood of behavior change. A number of studies have been made, and they indicate that increasing the group size has certain inherent effects on its members. For example, the psychologist Paul Hare has found that group members have less opportunity to speak in groups with twelve than in those with five members and are less satisfied in the larger meeting because of this limitation on their participation.[2]

Further, the member has more persons with whom to relate as group size increases. Since he has less time at his disposal to devote to each other individual, he relates to them in qualitatively different ways. For example, the sociologists Robert Bales and Edgar Borgatta report that as group size increases from two to seven, the individual increasingly relieves his frustration at not being able to participate as much as he would like to by behaving in ways that release more tension, maintain his social relationships, show solidarity, and make a more forceful use of the limited participation time at his disposal by giving more information and suggestions and fewer opinions, indications of agreement, and requests for the opinions of others.[3]

Increasing group size also has certain effects on the performance of its leaders. The psychologist John K. Hemphill has found that in large groups (more than 31 persons) the demands on leaders increase, but at the same time, there is a growing tolerance of a leader-directed group among the members.[4]

In general, the preceding evidence indicates that—for both members and leaders—as the group gets larger, there is an increase in the problem involved in maintaining effective interaction. And, indeed, a number of studies have shown that smaller groups are more efficient and productive than larger ones. For example, the English psychologist R. Marriott compared 251 task groups in an industrial setting and found that the individual output of work decreased as group size increased.[5] This study defines productivity in terms of the individual, but there are situations in which individual productivity is not as important as that of the total group. The psychologist Jack R. Gibb has shown that in such cases, using groups varying in size from one to ninety-six, idea productivity is positively related to group size.[6] Thus, while the productivity per individual may go down as group size increases, the productivity of the group, in terms of the number of ideas per unit time, goes up. Another study by the psychologist E. B. South highlights the contrast between individual and group productivity.[7] South finds that groups with three members are able to arrive at decisions more quickly than those with six; that is, their output per man is faster. Groups of six, however, are superior in their ability to reject a false hypothesis. It should be remembered, however, that while larger groups may increase idea productivity, they decrease the satisfaction of individual members, because of the reduced participation time each person has.

Finally, by increasing group size, the discrepancy in number of contributions between the smallest and largest participator increases. The psychologist Bernard Bass and his colleagues have shown that 83 per cent of the differences in leadership ratings can be accounted for by group size, when the subjects are in groups that have no appointed leader.[8] These findings demonstrate that group size is the central determinant in the degree of variation in leadership attributed to each group member.

These studies all suggest that an increase in group size affects the quantitative and qualitative manner in which the members participate and produces a decrease in output per man along with an increase in total group productivity. A smaller group facilitates quick decisions. A larger one increases the scope of the leader's influence, extending it to more members in any given time. However, such a group requires greater leadership skill to counteract the greater variation in member participation rates and the general decrease in the amount of participation by each group member. A larger unit reduces the opportunity members have to talk to one another and consequently to influence each other. Moreover, members of a large group are less likely to come to a quick decision, which may or may not matter, depending on the nature of the goal. It cannot be said that a large group is better or worse than a small one, but it is possible to point out the relative effects of each and on this basis to decide the optimum size for attaining the purposes of a particular unit.

In addition to effects associated with increasing size, there are those associated with groups of a particular number of individuals. Bales and Borgatta, in the study referred to above, have found that among problem-solving groups those composed of two members form a unique case. The two-man group, as compared to all others, shows a high rate of tension and of requests for orientation and opinion, and displays low rates of disagreement, antagonism, or giving of opinions. This is because in two-man groups there is no possibility of forming a majority. Either both members agree, or there can be no action. Consequently, both individuals are polite to each other. They ask each other for opinions and orientation and avoid disagreement and antagonism or offering opinions that might lead to disagreement. However, the strain of maintaining cordial relations is indicated by the high rate of showing tension overtly.

In groups of three, the situation is quite different, since a majority is possible. The sociologist Theodore Mills has studied the power relation in such groups and has found that if the two stronger persons can agree and support each other, a stable structure develops. If, however, they cannot agree, no such structure is formed.[9]

Beyond the effects associated with groups of two and three, characteristic patterns have been found by Bales and Borgatta to be associated with odd- (3,5,7) as compared to even-numbered (4,6) groups. Even-numbered groups were characterized by more disagreement, more antagonism, and fewer requests for suggestions. This pattern is virtually the opposite of that found in the smallest even-numbered unit, two members. This apparently is due to the fact that, in contrast to the two-person groups, in those composed of four and six, all members do not have to agree for a decision to be reached. On the other hand, if members are evenly divided on a question, they cannot come to a decision. This accounts for the increase in disagreement and antagonism and a decreasing interest in suggestions. With an odd number of members, however, division of the group into opposing halves cannot occur. Even when disagreement exists, a majority decision can always be reached. These findings, which apply only to initially leaderless problem-solving groups of between three and seven members, indicate that an odd number of participants are more efficient, both in terms of emotional strain and the easy attainment of majority decision. In general, a group size of five is recommended.

The Composition of the Group

One of the more intriguing topics in small-group research is the relationship between the characteristics of the individuals and the efficiency and productivity of the group enterprise. There is frequent need in many areas to form small groups for a variety of purposes, including the facilitation of behavior change, but little objective knowledge exists as to whether different types of persons actually will function more or less effectively in a group.

The issue is complex, involving the nature of the task and the setting in which the group functions as well as the background and experience of its members. Because of this complexity, investigations have been difficult to execute successfully. The psychologist Richard Heslin recently reviewed twenty-six such studies.[10] He grouped personality characteristics into six classes: ability, adjustment, extraversion, dominance, authoritarianism, and a miscellaneous category. The analysis showed that both the ability and adjustment of group members significantly contribute to their capacity to function together effectively. While this conclusion is not surprising, it aids in distinguishing characteristics that are significant for effective group performance from those that are irrelevant. This is particularly so when the small group is to be a vehicle for significant social or environmental rather than personal

85

change, since success in the larger endeavor will be in part determined by the ability of the group to perform its task.

Group Power Structure

The control of power is a central issue in most small groups. It is possible to place most arrangements for the distribution of power into one of three categories: the laissez-faire system, in which all members have equal power and the leader acts as an observer who takes no part in the activities; the democratic system, in which the leader acts as a coordinator, taking an active and guiding role but encouraging all to participate and share in the leadership; and the autocratic system, in which the leader discourages interaction among the members of the group and makes all decisions himself.

A number of scientists have studied the effects of these three kinds of power structure. The psychologists Malcolm G. Preston and Roy K. Heintz compared laissez-faire with democratic groups.[11]

They found that in democratic groups the leaders have more influence, there is more group agreement on relevant issues, and this agreement is more permanent. Both leaders and members reported that participation in the democratic group is the more enjoyable experience.

In a series of studies democratic and authoritarian groups have been compared. Kurt Lewin and the social psychologist Ronald Lippitt in earlier studies have found that democratic groups show less tension, more cooperation, objectivity, constructiveness, cohesion, and stability of structure than authoritarian ones.[12] Lippitt also found that authoritarian group members do more individual jobs, compete for status, and show hostility more. Democratic group members have clearer group goals, more cohesion, less tension, and produce more creative work.

In general, authoritarian groups produce leader dependency, intermember irritation and aggression, low levels of cohesion, lack of group goals, dissatisfaction, and low quality but high quantity of output. Laissez-faire groups show little leader dependency, great intermember irritation and aggression, many suggestions for action, but dissatisfaction with progress and achievement and a medium amount of productivity. Democratic groups produce low leader dependency, low intermember irritation and aggression, a high number of suggestions for group action, great satisfaction with group, and medium quantitative and high qualitative productivity.

On the basis of these findings it seems quite clear that the democratic group has received an experimental mandate. However, the situation is not as simple as it appears. For example, psychologist Lauren Wispe has found that when students are preparing for an examination, they prefer an authoritarian approach from the instructor rather than a democratic one.[13] Further, the psychologist Leonard Berkowitz, in a study of seventy-two business, industrial, and government conferences, found an inverse ratio between democratic groups with shared leadership and group cohesion.[14] There are situations in which democratic structure is not desired. For example, the conflict produced by ignoring the role expectations of members of a business conference may make the meeting uncomfortable, in spite of its democratic character. The findings suggest, therefore, that in forming a democratic group one must consider the previous experience and expectations of its members. If they expect and have accepted authoritarian leadership, the problems involved in social change may be greater than the advantages brought by democracy.

The value of democratic group structure has further been questioned by the American psychologist Harald McCurdy.[15] His studies indicate that there is no difference between authoritarian and democratic groups in problem-solving ability. In addition, it was found that authoritarian individuals function less efficiently in a democratic group than in an authoritarian one, indicating that the personality of individuals partially determines the reaction they have to a particular structure.

Thus, the democratic type of group seems to be superior to the laissez-faire type in terms of satisfaction and productivity. The weight of evidence also favors democratic over authoritarian organization, but a number of studies have qualified and even questioned this superiority. In any case, the personality of the participants, their previous experience, and their expectations affect the ease with which they are able to adjust to the democratic pattern.

This implies that there is little reason for the practitioner to act as a laissez-faire observer. It appears most desirable that he should act as a democratic leader, but it is necessary for him to consider the expectations and personalities of group members in order to judge whether a slight degree of autocratic leadership may enable them to function more effectively.

87

Group-Member Reward Systems

Another important aspect of group functioning concerns the use of rewards to achieve cooperation or competition. The social psychologist Morton Deutsch has studied this problem extensively.[16] He compared a series of discussion groups; in some, individuals were rewarded for successful competition against the other members of their group (competitive group), and in others, the rewards were for the performance of the group as a whole competing against others (cooperative group). It was found that the members of the cooperative groups were less resistant to change, more interdependent and friendly, communicated more effectively, were generally more productive, and had more influence on each other than those in competitive groups. Deutsch's study clearly suggests that cooperation is superior to competition in terms of effective group functioning. However, in evaluating the results of the study, it is important to realize that he was comparing the effects of intragroup competition with the effects of intergroup competition.

Natural Detrimental Processes in Group Development

A number of naturally occurring processes are detrimental to small-group functioning from the point of view of the practitioner. The first of these is unequal distribution of participation among group members. The psychologists Frederick Stephan and Elliot Mishler have demonstrated that a few individuals do most of the talking, an undesirable condition from the viewpoint of behavior change, since the members are influenced by a group experience to the degree that they participate in it.[17] One of the leader's functions may, therefore, be to help equalize participation rates by encouraging those who speak little and quieting those who speak too much.

A tendency toward unequal distribution of group rewards is somewhat less accessible. It has been described by the psychiatrist Jacob Moreno as a "sociodynamic law."[18] This law states that the social statuses of group members are unequal; that is, some persons are chosen by group members as friends and associates more frequently than others. Since the extent to which his experience as a group member influences an individual is, in part, a function of whether he is accepted, it would appear that the leader should accept and encourage those who are ignored or rejected by the others and so help counteract the natural tendency toward differential social status.

88

A third such process inherent in the operation of small groups is their natural tendency to form norms and standards that express the will of the majority. This is certainly necessary if the group is to function, but such decisions can exert an overwhelming influence on the actions of group members. Individual behavior change has to take place in spite of the tendency of groups to develop norms leading toward conformity of action. Again, if varied individual alternatives are desirable, it would seem necessary that the leader set an example of tolerance and interest in a number of alternative solutions to the same problem.

A final undesirable aspect of group development, closely related to the previous one, is the differentiation of roles and status. From the viewpoint of behavior change of the individual, the development of a role structure is unfortunate, since it interferes with his free expression by creating an unequal distribution of group resources. To ensure equal access to group facilities, the leader may attempt to counteract the effects of status differences by casting all members in the same role—for example, the patient—thus minimizing the social differences among them.

In each of the processes described, conscious effort by the leader is required to counteract the natural processes of the group that, if allowed to develop, would interfere with the attainment of the intended behavior change of individual members.

The Effects of Forced Interaction

It has been assumed that the degree to which an individual participates in a group determines the effect of that experience upon him. A number of experimental studies indicate that this is so. For example, the psychologist H. J. Leavitt has investigated the effect of different communications networks on group members.[19] These networks consist of artificial restrictions upon how the group members can communicate. He found that the members were most satisfied with a circular network, an arrangement in which each individual can talk to the two persons adjacent to him and in which all have an equal opportunity to participate. In a wheel arrangement, however, the individuals located around the edge of the wheel were dissatisfied, because they were allowed to communicate only with the person at the hub. He, however, was very satisfied, since he was the center of interaction. Studies of decision-making conferences in industry have similarly shown that satisfaction is related to the opportunity to participate, even if it is not actually utilized. Thus, the freedom, or lack of freedom to participate influences the emotional satisfaction of group members. What is the effect, however, of forcing group members to participate more than they normally would wish?

A partial answer to this question is provided by a series of studies of the effects produced on the individual by *role playing*, a procedure requiring him to create spontaneously a role that has been assigned to him. These studies consider whether heightened participation produced through involvement in role playing produces changes in personal attitudes or characteristics.

One of these investigations, performed by the psychologists Irving Janis and Bert King, has shown that role players change their opinions on issues relevant to their portrayal more than observers.[20] In general, it has been shown by other investigators that the degree of attitude and behavior change are proportional to the degree of participation in the role-playing situation.

These findings underline the importance of encouraging infrequent participators to enter the group discussion so that they may be subjected to its influence. At the same time, it is suggested that forcing of participation is a feasible procedure for producing individual attitude and personality change.

The Effects of Group Discussion

It is assumed by most practitioners using groups to produce behavior change that the discussion process itself produces personality change among the members. The power of group norms, which are transmitted through discussions, is sufficient to produce change in personal preferences and even in sensory perception. The social psychologist Solomon Asch has shown, for example, that a person will see two unequal lines as the same length if other group members do so.[21] There is also evidence that heterogeneity of opinion, such as is likely to exist in a group, facilitates adequate problem-solving processes more than, say, a lecture in which only one view is presented. For example, the Russian psychologists V. M. Bechterew and M. de Lange found that individuals perceive a series of events more accurately after they have heard others describe their version of the same events.[22]

While rational grounds exist for supposing group discussions to be an effective agent in producing behavior change, the evidence to support this fact is surprisingly scarce. Some indirect reinforcement is, however, available. The psychologist W. A. Timmons has found that individuals who study the facts about a given social issue and then have a group discussion about it are more in agreement with the view of experts than persons who merely study the facts.[23]

A series of studies have considered the effectiveness of group discussion that culminates in a group decision. The psychologists Lester Coch and John French have shown that changes in industrial methods were more successfully introduced when the workers took part in decision-making discussions concerning these changes.[24] Similarly, the psychologists Jacob Levine and John Butler have found that discussion followed by group decision reduced the bias in ratings of workers made by plant supervisors more than lecturing to them did.[25] Kurt Lewin has made extensive studies of group discussion followed by group decision and reports that this procedure produces greater and more lasting changes in a variety of behavior than either lecture or conversation between two individuals.[26] These studies seem to leave little doubt about the effectiveness of such a procedure on behavioral change. However, it is not clear from this evidence whether the alterations reported are due to group discussion, group decision, or an interaction between the two.

Some evidence on this point is supplied by the psychologist Alex Baveles.[27] He studied workers who had group discussions followed by group decisions and compared them with other groups who discussed the same topics but came to no decisions. Members of the first group increased their piecework productivity 50 per cent during the experiment and stabilized at that level. Men in the second group did not change their piecework productivity during the experiment. This seems to indicate that all of the change was due either to an interaction between discussion and decision or to the group decision alone.

More recently, the psychologist Edith Bennett has further analyzed the process involved in group decision.[28] She reports that the effectiveness of group decision depends on how it is made and on the degree of unanimity of the participants, but it does not depend on whether the commitment is made in public or in private. Even more important is the fact that the effectiveness of the decision is unrelated to whether the members participated in a discussion or listened to a lecture.

Thus, little objective evidence exists to support the utilization of group discussion alone as a behavior-change procedure.

Sociometric Reassignment

Sociometric reassignment is a procedure that allows group members to select those persons with whom they would like to work or to socialize. The psychologist Helen Jennings has evaluated this approach in a study of the effect of assigning newly arrived reformatory girls to groups of their own choice.[29] Some girls were assigned to groups representing their first choice. Others were assigned to groups representing their third or fourth choice, and still others were assigned at random. The results showed a direct relation between being assigned according to one's sociometric choice and the social integration of the subject in the group. After a thirty-two-week period, girls who had been assigned to groups of their first choice were better integrated than those assigned in accordance with their third and fourth preference, who were, in turn, better integrated than the control group.

A further study of this procedure has been made by the psychologist R. H. Van Zelst.[30] Working in an industrial setting with carpenters and bricklayers, he divided these workers into an experimental and a control group of each occupation. The workers in the experimental group were selected on the basis of mutual sociometric choice. The composition of the control group was determined by random selection. The effect of the sociometric reassignment was determined by various indexes including turnover rate, labor cost, and material cost. The experimental group was found significantly superior to the control group on all criteria. This evidence suggests that sociometric assignment procedures produce greater cohesiveness and productivity among groups than would otherwise occur by a process of random assignment.

The Influence of Objective Feedback

Feedback as a means of producing improvement in individual and group performance has been of special interest to communications theorists, who have studied it as an aspect of the communications network. They have found that feedback increases the accuracy of information transmitted as well as the transmitter's confidence that his message has been understood.

Feedback has other, more notable, effects. For example, the psychologist E. Paul Torrence has studied the impact of a highly structured objective feedback on the performance of U.S. Air Force crews in a problem solving situation.[31] Torrence found that the objective feedback of test data produces significantly more improvement in problem-solving ability than when the crews feed back their reactions about mutual performance to each other in a group discussion. This finding suggests that the feedback must be objective in order to be effective. These results have been replicated by a series of studies carried out by the Rand Corporation—a private research organization in Santa Monica, California, primarily engaged in research for the Air Force—in connection with the training of teams designed to operate radar facilities.[32]

Objective feedback apparently is an effective method by which to improve individual and group performance. It would seem, therefore, important to apply this finding to attempts to change behavior in small groups by providing members with the opportunity for such feedback. This might be done by administering an appropriate standard psychological test to each person, who could then compare his response with the norms for the test and with those of other group members. The test could be repeated toward the end of the meetings and the comparative results could be the feedback information of any changes that might have occurred. Such a procedure would also provide useful research material for evaluating the effectiveness of the group, and in this way the measurement of change could actually become part of the behavior-change process.

Principles of Behavior Change in the Small Group

In 1951, the psychologist Dorwin Cartwright summarized his interpretation of small-group research as it bears on the problem of inducing behavior change in terms of eight general principles.[33] While some of these are qualified by later work, no one has made a more recent attempt to approach the material in this way. They can, therefore, best be viewed as indicative of the kinds of principles one might expect to arrive at, rather than the most recent research in this area.

These principles can be summarized in the following terms. In order for the group to act as the medium of change, its participants must have a strong sense of group membership, that is, they must value the sessions as a social experience. Further, when a process to induce change is introduced, its success will be in proportion to the relation it has to the members' reasons for belonging to the particular unit. Thus, a public-speaking group will be willing to listen to an analysis of the members' public behavior, though they might ordinarily ignore or reject such comments.

Within the group itself, the greater the individual's prestige, the more influence he can exert and the greater the changes he can produce in others. Whether or not the attempted changes will be successful is, in part, determined by the position the changed persons have relative to other group members. If, by virtue of their altered behavior, they become deviants in the eyes of other participants, the resistance to such a change will be increased. Thus, effective revision of behavior can most easily be induced by creating a shared perception of the need for different behavior, so that its desirability becomes a group norm. While this shared perception provides the necessary preconditioning, it is not sufficient to carry through and successfully conclude whatever alterations and improvements may be required. To maximize the likelihood of successful change, it is important that plans for it and its consequences be understood by all relevant persons. This kind of objective feedback provides the best guarantee against unintended deviation from the original group goals.

The foregoing principles are coherent and organic to the small group. However, they do not begin to cover all of its components pertaining to behavior change mentioned earlier in the chapter. They are but a first attempt to clarify and generalize from accumulated findings that are vast in magnitude and complex in character.

Group Dynamics

One of the major influences in the development of small-group research has been the *group dynamics* movement. Scientists involved in it have made two major contributions. First, they have emphasized the need for obtaining an objective understanding of the functioning of small groups. Second, they have attempted to utilize this understanding to facilitate individual and group change. What is particularly important about this development is that it exemplifies one of the very few attempts to use scientific knowledge to create procedures designed to enhance the function of normal persons rather than of those who are physically or emotionally crippled. It represents a systematic effort to carry individual and group activities beyond their customary limits through the application of established principles of small-group organization.

The major fruit of research into group dynamics, in addition to the solid scientific studies that have been performed, was the evolution of the laboratory method of human relations training, and more specifically the utilization of the *T*, or training, *group* as a vehicle for the production of insight and behavior change.

The T-group consists of normal persons who meet for a number of sessions under the guidance and leadership of a professionally trained scientist who, during the meetings, will educate them in the processes that characterize small-group functioning. The T-group is unusual from several points of view. First, it has no assigned task. If the members had one, they would be too busy fulfilling it to observe their own actions and those of others. The members can do what they want to do or do nothing at all. Second, the members are encouraged to analyze their reactions to themselves and to each other. Third, the trainer refuses to provide positive group leadership by telling the members what to do. Rather, he tends to interpret to them the reason that things are happening as they are. It is generally assumed by most trainers that enhanced understanding of small-group processes will not only increase the diagnostic skills of the group members, but may also lead to new forms of behavior as members become aware of how others are reacting to them.

At this point, it is necessary to clarify the relationship between the training procedure as a behavior-change technique and the group dynamics research that has been performed parallel with it. Both the research and the training share a mutual dedication to the scientific model of a search for greater objective understanding of social processes. But it would be inappropriate to say that the T-group training method represents the logical outcome of the research of group-dynamics adherents. What has tended to happen is that the scientists who perform the research and those who conduct the human-relations training concentrated only on their own areas of interest, though there are individuals who both train and conduct research. When these scientists are observed or interviewed, however, it soon becomes evident that they lead two distinct professional lives. When they act as human-relations trainers, they put their research out of their minds. When they perform research, they withdraw into an abstract realm of theory, formulas, and variables. In other words, they are no more able than anyone else to bridge the gap between research and practice.

This is not meant to suggest that T-group leaders have not devoted a good deal of thought to what they are doing, both as an aid to clarifying their action and also to aid them in transmitting their experience to others interested in becoming trainers in their own right. Recently, a number of leading practitioners in the group-dynamics movement brought together their theories in the book *T-Group, Theory and Laboratory Method*.[34] Much sophisticated thought has gone into the description of the way in which groups operate and the definition of the group-leader's role. However, the diversity of viewpoints among the contributors is considerable. Clearly, in spite of the unique intent of combining research and training, the methods of group dynamics are no more scientific or exact than the variety of other methods currently used for training purposes.

However, a more objective basis for assessing this general conclusion is provided in the volume by the psychologist Dorothy Stock, who has performed the valuable service of reviewing the research studies of training groups.

A number of topics are touched upon in her review, but only one is directly relevant to the present discussion—namely, the effectiveness of training groups in creating behavior change. The resolution of this issue involves the utilization of evaluative research, the deficiencies of which have already been extensively discussed. A variety of positive effects have been reported, but these studies were characterized by various kinds of methodological error. Thus their conclusions can best be taken as tentative.

In any case, the assessment of the method's effectiveness is unrelated to the question of whether it was formulated on the basis of conclusions drawn from scientific studies of the small group. It seems reasonable to conclude that the group-dynamics movement has separated the training and research function, in spite of a temperamental and historical commitment to their integration.

This analysis of small-group research has indicated that scientific information that bears on the use of the small group as a change medium is currently available. In addition, the experience of the scientists studying group dynamics suggests that the direct application of these findings in the design of new behavior-change techniques may be more difficult than originally envisioned. Thus, through experimental investigation and case history, studies of the small group suggest both the hope and limitations of the experimental analysis of the social aspects of behavior-change processes.

CHAPTER EIGHT

Attitude Change Produced by Interpersonal Influence

O NE of the conclusions suggested by small-group research is that group members engage in a variety of efforts to influence each other's attitudes on a number of relevant issues in order to attain both individual and group goals. This conclusion parallels one of the most noteworthy recent developments in social psychology, namely the rapid accumulation of studies of attitude change.

In general, these studies are designed to determine whether a particular form of influence does produce a discernible attitude change in a specified individual or set of individuals. A variety of attitudes has been used as change criteria, but the general assumption has been that, for purposes of measuring change, one attitude was as good as another.

Research of this kind has been performed for more than three decades on such topics as the reduction of prejudice, the analysis of propaganda, and the like. But it is only within the last fifteen years that the field has become organized around the topic of attitude change and research developed programmatically.

Of all topics relating to ways to alter human behavior, attitude change has been the most carefully studied. Investigations of attitudes have always been in the mainstream of social psychology. Because of the large number of research projects, methodology has been developed successfully. Further, attitude behavior is a suitable subject for experimental investigation and does not involve the diverse problems that tend to occur in clinical research.

Perhaps the only major criticism that can be made of this body of research as a whole is that attitudes are not, after all, the most profound aspects of an individual, nor is a change in attitude necessarily followed by a change in behavior. The alteration of attitudes is, therefore, often a relatively trivial affair. This need not be so, but many laboratory studies have made it so, preferring to investigate peripheral attitudes, such as reactions to the likelihood of finding a cure for the common cold or beliefs about proposed monetary reforms, because it was felt that the use of such criteria would enhance the likelihood of success in inducing change.

It is convenient to date the acceleration of progress in this field from the programmatic work of the psychologist Carl Hovland, which began as early as 1949 during his early work at Yale University.[1] Only in retrospect is it evident that these efforts were the first of a long line of fruitful investigations that would, as they grew, gather a number of separate subspecialties into the important field of attitude-change studies.

A major distinction that should be made in organizing the results of the attitude-change investigations that have been conducted is whether direct personal influence is used or whether the attempt to change attitude is made through the mass media. In the present chapter, the first type of study will be discussed. In Chapter Nine, the impact of the mass media on attitude change will be analyzed.

In many of the investigations to be described the major interest has been in relating patterns of communication to the degree of attitude change. The central issue has often been the determination of which kinds of communication produce the most attitude change. Such studies involve *communications analysis,* a study, not only of the nature of attitudes and their development, but also of the communication process and the ways in which it can be varied systematically. Thus this body of research brings together two important lines of development in the social sciences.

Abelson's Study of Attitude Changes
Produced by Communications Processes

In 1959, the psychologist Herbert Abelson reviewed the literature of attitude-change studies in order to evaluate the extent to which, taken as a group, they suggested well-defined principles that might have practical and theoretical implications of a broader nature. In his analysis, he focused on 139 pertinent experimental studies whose common elements he sought to extract. The results were reported in a small, paperback book, *Persuasion*.[2] Abelson's conclusions are interesting because they provide a direct guide to the more practical aspects of the accumulated knowledge in the area, and they also aid in any assessment of the level of utility and sophistication of this knowledge. Moreover, they indirectly indicate the kinds of conclusion one can expect from this general approach to the study of behavior change.

The reported conclusions are as follows:

The communicator talking to a friendly audience, when he is interested in only temporary change or when he alone will be heard, should give only one side of the argument. If, on the other hand, he desires long-term change, or the audience does not agree with him, or if they are likely to hear different views of the issue from other persons, then it is better for him to present the audience with both sides of the issue.

When both sides are presented, one after the other, the final presentation tends to have the greater impact. However, in any given communication, it is not clear whether the important material should be placed near the beginning or the end of the talk. Greater opinion change is likely to occur if conclusions are explicitly stated than if the audience member is allowed to draw his own conclusions.

The use of different kinds of appeal has varying effects. The relative impact of emotional as opposed to intellectual approaches depends on both the nature of the audience and the material, but, in general, where threats are employed, a moderate or mild threat is more effective than a strong one.

It is well known that an individual's behavior and attitudes are strongly influenced by the groups to which he belongs and whose membership he values. However, more recent research has clarified the nature of this influence and the way it can be manipulated to produce change. Its central form, as wielded by small groups, is the reward of conformity and the punishment of deviance. Further, individuals are influenced by communications that conflict with group norms in direct proportion to the extent that they value their group membership. If the group is to exert its greatest influence, it is necessary that all attitudes be made public, so that each member is clearly aware of how the others feel. Also, the group must be aware of how each individual feels, so that it can have a real opportunity to change him.

Another important issue in attitude-change research involves the persistence of the change once it has been produced. Not unnaturally, the effects of a persuasive communication tend to wear off, though periodic repetition delays this effect to some extent. What is of greater interest, however, is the *sleeper effect,* a term that describes the situation in which the amount of change produced increases over time. This effect has been experimentally demonstrated, but its mechanisms are not clearly understood.

All attitude-change attempts presuppose the availability of appropriate subjects to influence. Unfortunately, the persons whom one would most like to influence are least likely to expose themselves to communications that conflict with the convictions they already hold. Within this limitation, the level of intelligence of the audience and the underlying motivations of its members influence the relative effectiveness of different kinds of appeal. Recently, the personality characteristic of *persuasibility,* the extent to which one can easily be persuaded, has been emphasized. It has been clearly demonstrated that such a trait does exist and that it is somewhat independent of the particular issues and attitudes involved.

The final set of findings relates to the persuader himself and how his personality characteristics affect the reception of his message. The credentials of the source have a definite influence on the reception of the communication, though this effect becomes diluted some time after the influence has been attempted. People tend to forget just where they received the message, but they remember its content.

The motives the audience attributes, correctly or incorrectly, to the communicator influence its reception of his message. Since such attributions are difficult to assess and often hard to change, their impact may be important in determining the outcome. The converse is also true. The opinion the audience holds of the communicator is influenced by the attitudes he presents. It is partly for this reason that it is helpful for him to mention at least some opinions with which he knows his audience will agree, though in the end, the more extreme the change the communicator asks for, the larger the change he is likely to produce.

Additional Implications of Attitude-Change Studies

Such are the main conclusions of Abelson's review of pertinent research materials; a number of conclusions beyond the particular relationships that are described are suggested. First of all, this form of research clearly is deeply committed to one underlying research model of social influence; in it, a relatively static, one-way process of attitude change is envisioned. The emphasis is, by implication, on attempts to influence attitudes of a relatively normal character and mild degree, including debating and lecturing, rather than on the more intimate and fundamental two-way approaches, such as psychotherapy. This is an important aspect of the model, since this kind of research was originated by persons who were interested in communications and attitudes as such. They hoped, by studying their mutual interaction as mediated by the personal characteristics of the communicator and the audience, to clarify not only the basis of attitude change, but also the underlying nature of communications and attitudes as modifiers of human behavior. Thus, one may conclude that what was lost in depth was gained in generality.

A second major observation that can be made is that, for the most part, these findings are not very startling. In terms of their practical fruit, the harvest seems pedestrian. On the other hand, any summary of over-all conclusions is bound to be misleading. In almost every study they were qualified either by partially contradictory findings or amplified by additional analyses that they suggested.

For example, though it is generally found that, as already stated, the motives attributed to the communicator affect the amount of change he is able to produce, the results have not always been so straightforward. In one study, the audience was presented with a standard talk favoring the devaluation of currency. The speaker was introduced to the group as a prominent importer who had, by inference, something to gain from the devaluation. Another group heard the same speech, but this time the speaker was presented as an economics instructor who was presumably impartial. As expected, the students rated the first presentation as biased and the other as fair and impartial, in spite of the fact that the speeches were identical. However, unexpectedly, there was no difference between the amount of change produced in the two groups, despite the difference attributed to the motives of the speakers. In order to explain this, one would have to examine the experiment very carefully, determining whether the nature of the topic was suitable for a study of attitude change, whether the reliability of the instruments was adequate, and so on.

Sometimes the design of the study is sufficiently complex to enable fairly sophisticated conclusions to be drawn. In one case individuals with three kinds of personality characteristics—authoritarianism, self-confidence, and complexity—were compared for general persuasibility. Because of the simultaneous investigation of all three personality characteristics, it was possible, not only to state the relationship of each to persuasibility, but also to determine whether particular patterns of characteristics were uniquely related to persuasibility. In this study, it was found, for example, that persons who had little self-confidence but who were able to tolerate disorder and confusion were highly persuasible, both by authority figures and by colleagues. Presumably, their orientation toward complexity made them more open to the opinions of others, while their lack of self-confidence led them to undervalue their own opinions. This type of finding is certainly of much greater interest than the general conclusion reported by Abelson that persuasibility is a characteristic related to underlying personality patterns. For this reason, it is not useful to judge the direct importance of research from the simple conclusions that have been reported.

Further, these studies collectively help to illustrate the possibilities inherent in a systematically pursued, long-term program of research. This impact is particularly evident when one examines the sites at which such research was conducted. In the early 1950's, only Yale University was active in this area, under the direct stimulus of Hovland. He designed and obtained financing for the early efforts. In the course of this work, a number of young scientists were trained by him. As they matured and moved elsewhere, they carried with them his insight and particular vision of communications-oriented research and continued to pursue this line of investigation in their own studies, training other graduate students and publishing themselves. In this simple manner, the whole subject has become central to modern social psychology, even though not long ago there was just a trickle of interest in it. The secret of this success must be attributed in part to the continuity of effort. However, it is equally important that an appropriate methodology was employed from the first to deal with the problem of behavior change. Each major component and variable was carefully analyzed and subjected to variation under experimental control. In this manner, one study could build on another with confidence and precision, and the cumulative result became ever more impressive, until the whole area was tacitly accepted by other social psychologists.

Finally, the limitations of the findings in terms of behavior change of a more fundamental and enduring character do not in any way reflect on the strategy that produced them. Hovland and his disciples have never really been interested in major personality changes that are produced by intense and unusual experiences. Their concern has always been with the less basic but more usual influences that are exerted in society through readily accessible communications channels. Their work must be appreciated in those terms. What they actually have provided is an interesting example of how the more difficult and lasting aspects of behavior change might be approached in a manner that is suitable in terms of existing scientific methodology and appropriate in terms of our current understanding.

Theoretical Models of Influence Processes

A further aspect of these investigations of attitude change produced by communications processes relates to the theoretical models that have been employed to interpret their conclusions. Theoretical models are precise expressions of the relationships among specific variables that are derived from a general theoretical position. Such models can be developed and tested only when research is carefully formulated and the variables are selected with an eye to their relation to already existing systems of analysis. When these conditions are met and appropriate models are created, the character of research may be greatly improved, since each investigation not only produces specific findings of interest in their own right but also tests the validity of the model, which contains implications that go far beyond the conclusion of the study.

To illustrate this point, three models that are now widely employed in the design and explanation of research findings in attitude-change research will be described. The seminal line of development of these models can be traced to the psychologist Fritz Heider, whose basic work, "Social Perception and Phenomenal Causality," published in 1944, though admired, was generally ignored for almost a decade.[3]

The first model of behavior change can be called a *congruity* approach. Only its simplest aspects will be presented here. Its basic proposition is that when two objects, persons, or events are related in an individual's mind, their effect on each other depends on their relative quantitative strength and qualitative character. If they differ in strength, his attitude toward both is modified. If their strength is equal, no attitude change will occur. If an American president who is highly valued by a given individual criticizes a Russian official who is negatively evaluated by him, no change of attitude will occur if one is liked as much as the other is disliked. However, when new mental associations are formed or old associations are disrupted, the balance of forces is no longer in equilibrium. In this situation, attitude change is likely to occur. The congruity model not only states the general conditions and directions of the change but attempts to predict the actual amount that will be produced if the balanced state is disrupted. It is clearly less difficult to predict direction than extent, but the two problems are interwoven.

The general principle employed in deciding the most likely position for the creation of a new equilibrium is that change is inversely proportional to the initial extremity of the two positions. This relatively simple principle is easily tested by experimental study and has been supported.

For example, if a Russian who is evaluated as a strong negative (—2) criticizes a mildly liked American politician (+1), it is probable that the greater change will occur in the evaluation of the American. The direction of the change must oppose the nature of the attack if equilibrium is to be restored. According to the model, it is also necessary to conclude that the Russians are not quite as bad as one thought. This latter change would not be due to the attack itself but to its lack of proportion. It is unnatural, for a very bad person should not attack a mildly good one. Either the good person is much better and more important than he seems, and, therefore, deserving of the attack from an enemy of equal stature; or, conversely, the bad person is not so bad or so important as he seems, and, therefore, he is attacking his proper counterpart. Since the first alternative is in keeping with the assumption that extreme positions are harder to shift, it is natural to predict that the attitude toward the person about whom feelings are weaker will undergo the greater change, even though some compensatory movement must also occur in feelings toward the extremely negative position.

The only limitation to this general model is the plausibility of the communication. If one is told, for example, that an individual whom one scores +4 has attacked someone valued at +3, it may not seem plausible, and, therefore, no attempt will be made to arrive at a resolution.

The second theoretical approach, and the one that is most widely employed in current experimentation, is the theory of *cognitive dissonance*. Its basic concept is that if an individual holds two opinions that are logically contradictory, a dissonant situation is created for him. Since such dissonance is inherently uncomfortable, the individual will attempt to reduce it by undergoing an appropriate attitude change.

This principle is extremely simple, but it has been applied in a number of different situations with valuable and sometimes unlikely results. For example, in a study of compliance due to social pressure, it was hypothesized that a minimal use of influence would be more effective in changing attitudes than a stronger one.

This hypothesis was based on a chain of logic. Forced compliance will in itself produce dissonance, since the person is being pushed in a direction he does not want to go. If this force is very strong, the dissonance will be less than if the influence is just sufficient to obtain compliance; conflict is stronger when two opposing forces of equal magnitude are matched. When one is much greater than the other, the contest is eliminated and the resultant dissonance reduced. It therefore follows that since the more dissonance existing the greater the resultant attitude change, minimal social pressure should produce greater change than a more heavy-handed approach. This, in fact, has been established by the use of experimental procedures.[4] Such a considered use of social pressure has implication for the production of attitude change among the opposition in the political, economic, and even the interpersonal spheres.

The major difficulty in the application of cognitive dissonance to attitude-change processes is in clarifying and controlling the dissonance-producing aspects of the situation. This can be quite difficult, since the experimenter cannot always be sure how subjects interpret certain features of the experiment. What he intends as a dissonance-producing event may be dismissed by the subjects as merely amusing, or, conversely, an action of whose significance the investigator is unaware may create strong dissonance in the subjects. Thus, if the subject dislikes the experimenter, dissonance may be created in response to having to follow any instructions he might give. This may, in turn, interact with any of the more formal aspects of the study, producing unexpected conclusions.

The final model of attitude change employs *balance* as a central concept. Although it is quite similar to the congruity model, they differ significantly on several issues. In one sense, the balance model is less precise than its counterpart. It does not assign a numerical value to each element but utilizes only equal, minus, and plus signs to indicate the general quality of reaction. However, in other respects the theory is more refined. It implicitly recognizes, for example, that the presence of imbalance is not enough to create attitude change. This imbalance must be perceived consciously by the individual before change is likely to occur. A further implication is that one solution to the stress produced by the perception of imbalance is to avoid or repress the perception rather than to change any attitudes.

Another interesting way to attain balance is by redefining or differentiating among one of the elements in the conflict situation. This mechanism has been demonstrated through the experimental use of hypnosis.[5] A subject who was strongly concerned with maintaining her independence of action was told that on waking up she would favor a city-management plan. She had originally been against it, because she felt it would reduce her own autonomy. After the hypnotic session, her opinion shifted as had been suggested. When questioned about why she had changed her view, she indicated that somehow her perception of the plan had been altered. She now saw it as work people would do together and independently rather than being something imposed on them from without. Thus, by revising the nature of her analysis of the plan, she was able to rationalize and accept her own change of opinion, which she considered to be genuine and not the product of a hypnotic suggestion.

This experimental use of hypnosis is very illuminating. It indicates a means of manipulating the elements of attitude formation as well as of inducing attitude change under conditions in which the subject is unaware of what has happened. Thus it allows a careful analysis to be made of the way in which a person is able to accommodate himself to the change that has been experimentally forced upon him.

In conclusion, the study of attitude change produced in interpersonal situations remains today an area of extreme interest. New syntheses, theoretical reformulations, and substantive accumulations, if not revisions, are all to be anticipated. Any review is soon out of date, and a complete assessment of trends is difficult because of the extent and growing complexity of the material. Nevertheless, the basic approach is simple, almost traditional. Only the area of application is new.

CHAPTER NINE

The Mass Media as Vehicles for Attitude Change

THE same investigators who provided the original impetus for the development of research into attitude change through interpersonal communication have had an equal interest in the effects of the mass media on attitude. They have made their initial model broad enough to encompass both forms of intervention, though experimental work has focused more on interpersonal influence rather than the mass media as arbiter of change. Both areas therefore can be subsumed within a more general category of attitude change. In practice, however, it is helpful to distinguish between them, since the conclusions that have been drawn in each field are somewhat different, and the techniques of study are, of necessity, characteristic of the material employed to produce change. Those who emphasize one type of study have different professional affiliations from their colleagues who are primarily interested in another type. Market research analysts, advertising psychologists, and communications analysts are clearly identified with the study of mass media, while social psychologists, educational psychologists, and others are associated with the field of interpersonal influence. On the whole, those who have been most active in the experimental study of attitude change under laboratory conditions have had little contact with mass-media research and little commitment to it, though there are noteworthy exceptions.

The mass media appeal to those who wish to influence attitudes because they reach the largest possible audience with the least possible expenditure of manhours. In many large-scale attempts at influence, communication through the mass media is the only feasible method, and in most situations it forms the natural one, even if the change attempt is also supported by the use of interpersonal influence. Thus the politician uses posters and television and radio appearances, but he also shakes hands, organizes political units to go from house to house seeking to convince neighbors, and the like.

While the mass media are relatively cheap in terms of the human labor required to reach a given number of individuals, they are expensive in terms of over-all cost. Thus it is natural that a good deal of interest has been centered on the question of their effectiveness in comparison to each other and in relation to more direct approaches. Reports of research on the impact of the various media read something like the reports of evaluative studies of behavior-change processes. They are designed to show that a given medium does, in fact, produce an effect under certain conditions and is, therefore, useful and valuable. Each of the major media has been evaluated with varying degrees of precision. The motivations for these studies are mixed. Sometimes the research is supported directly by an organization, such as a newspaper or a TV station. At other times, it is the indirect product of more broadly conceived investigations sponsored by the government or by private foundations. The issue in each of these investigations is whether the particular medium can be demonstrated to have any impact on the audience toward whom the message is directed. If such an effect is demonstrable, the study then attempts to clarify its limitations and character.

Effects of the Mass Media

One would be tempted to predict that probably all media have some demonstrable effects, but that they vary considerably, depending on a number of uncontrolled circumstances. This prediction, which is no more than an extrapolation from the conclusions about evaluative research in general, is, unfortunately, quite accurate. Numerous studies have been conducted of the impact on attitudes of books, pamphlets, magazines, newspapers, comic books, motion pictures, radio, and television. All media do produce some attitude change under appropriate circumstances. For example, a relatively well-conceived series of studies of propaganda films has indicated that such material could influence soldiers' attitudes about war. In another study, it was demonstrated that students were influenced in their opinions of a congressional investigating committee by the newspaper accounts they read.

Investigators may have in mind more sophisticated ends than this research denotes. They may be interested in whether certain features of the mass media—violence on television, for example—encourage social disorganization. Such a question involves a more subtle analysis than a simple evaluation. Others may be interested in the relative impact of different kinds of media on one particular behavior, such as voting. Both of these issues are clearly of great practical importance as well as of general scientific concern.

Another type of investigation compares various media with each other in terms of such characteristics as the complexity of stimuli they can present, the duration of the exposure, and their relative effectiveness in presenting certain types of messages. For example, printed materials may have lengthy exposure, since they are permanent, whereas television and radio programs are generally available only for a single presentation. Television can appeal to several senses, radio only to one. It is of interest to determine whether these obvious differences among the media have discernible effects on the impact of communication transmitted by them. The comparison is further enlightened if the impact of mass-media methods of communication are compared, not only with each other, but also with those created by interpersonal approaches, such as have already been discussed in the preceding chapter.

While the experimental comparisons that have been made are not comprehensive, some sample conclusions can be offered. For example, when the impacts of radio and printed materials are compared, it is found that people who listen to the radio also read more than those who do not listen to it. However, when an individual is asked which exerts the greater influence on him when he reaches a decision—whom he will vote for, for example—radio is usually selected as the more important influence, presumably because of its greater personal impact. Similarly, studies have demonstrated that television has greater impact on attitudes than radio.

A number of investigators have studied the impact of television on voting. This analysis was motivated by the assumption that television was the most potent of the mass media and could be presumed to have the greatest effect. This research has clearly shown that when television's influence is compared with that of radio and newspapers, it is the most important. However, information is not equivalent to attitude. And, when attitude is considered, the conclusions are less positive. Television does not appear to have any particular impact on the act of voting, though it has been demonstrated that television-set owners increase their exposure to opposing viewpoints and consequently improve their general opinion of the opposition, even though they do not actually change their vote. However, the clearest and most general distinction that can be drawn is between the influence of direct personal contact and that which is exerted by the mass media. Here, the evidence seems quite clear. Personal influence is much more effective in producing attitude and behavior change. Unfortunately, it is also much more expensive per influence attempt, so that its higher potency has to be evaluated against its higher cost.

The importance of personal intervention in creating change serves to emphasize once again the centrality of the group setting as the most powerful and, in a sense, the most natural arena for the induction of change.

Personal Influence as Opposed to the Mass Media

A number of studies have attempted to explain the superiority of personal influence in decision-making, such as the choice of political representatives, what movies to go to, and household appliance and food purchases. The results have indicated that the superiority of face-to-face persuasion lies most of all in its greater flexibility. The approach can be modified in terms of the subject's response. Further, this technique is more likely to reach those who are most desirable subjects. One of the major difficulties faced by mass-media attempts to alter behavior is that those who need to be influenced generally refuse to expose themselves. When the influencer appears in person, he can make direct efforts to reach the appropriate audience, even if it does not, at first, present itself.

Much of this comparative research is undertaken for practical ends. Advertisers wish to know how much change different media will produce for a given financial investment. Educators must decide whether films should supplant lectures or whether closed-circuit television should take the place of field trips in the achievement of specific educational objectives. These questions are of some moment to those faced with such decisions but do not have great general scientific importance, because the circumstances surrounding the study are largely uncontrolled. Specifically, the impact of a medium depends, not only on its own nature, but also on the audience to whom it is directed; the nature of the message being transmitted; its presumed source; related social, political, and economic conditions; the initial attitude of the subjects toward the issue; and so on.

Because of this inherent complexity, communications scientists tend to study the way influence is achieved in mass media in terms of the particular character of the message and the nature of its appeal rather than to investigate the medium by which the message reaches its intended source.

The Effects of Advertising

A somewhat different approach is taken to much of the same material by the psychologist studying problems of advertising. His job is to advise advertising agencies on the best way to design and communicate particular kinds of advertisement in order to ensure the greatest rewards for their clients.

The advertiser wishes to capture the attention of the consumer, hold that attention once it has been attracted, and make an appropriate impression that will result in overt action in relation to the product or services that are being advertised. Presumably, this impression will later influence buying habits, though agencies tend to feel that if they can demonstrate, through appropriate use of market-research interviewers, that a lasting impression has been made, they have performed all that could reasonably be required of them. What the individual actually buys is another issue.

Once the objectives are defined so clearly, the relevant topics fall rather neatly into place. First, it is necessary to analyze the basic and relatively constant needs of the consumer, studies usually performed by the *personality psychologist*. These needs constitute a frame of reference. Satisfying them is inherently desirable to most persons and, therefore, it is advantageous to relate any message to them in terms of gaining and holding interest. Thus, the advertisement with the pretty girl and the successful-looking man appeal to the sexual and security needs that are so emphasized in our society.

The advertiser wishes to relate the product to a need in an original and appropriate manner. This principle is simple to state but permits infinite variety. One can emphasize positive or negative needs (love or hate, security or fear). A sentimental focus designed to arouse positive emotions can be used or a more rational, "scientific" approach—"independent surveys have shown" that the product is superior. In view of the very realistic choices involved, it is surprising that a great deal of published material is not available to clarify the relative impact of the various alternatives. Some research indicates, for example, that both positive and negative appeals may be useful. But if a large number of studies to determine the merit of certain components of advertising exists, it lies buried in the files of agencies. Such research represents a valuable commercial asset and, therefore, is not published. Clearly, the standards of science in the market place are different from those applied to research conducted in the ivory tower.

Psychologists involved in advertising are concerned with the relative advantages of different sense modalities in attracting audiences, particularly the relative advantages of eye over ear. However, they draw their conclusions from evidence obtained in other fields. Much attention has been devoted to the physical makeup, or layout, of the advertisement when it is visual in magazines or both oral and visual on television. Since the design of any ad involves many variables, there is much to be said. Unfortunately, the impact of the advertisement bears little relation to the layout.

Some relevant factors in the design of magazine or newspaper ads include their location, size, and format. Each variable has numerous alternatives. Location involves a selection of a particular page and a particular section of that page. Such choices must take into account the nature of surrounding material, the relative attractiveness of placements in terms of attracting the eye, the advantages of being in the beginning, middle, or end of the publication, and so on. An ad's size is not independent of its location; while the size of any particular piece of advertising, regardless of its placement, may be a very important factor in gaining attention, the relationship between the two factors is not always a simple one. The results of research into this area are either trivial or equivocal.

While the actual design of the ad is a coordinated artistic enterprise, it can be subjected to exact analysis. One can distinguish the efficiency with which the space is used, the pattern of eye movements it induces, the contribution of pictures as against the printed word. The whole question of typography permits an endless degree of analysis of arrangements of style and size of type and the influence of all this on various kinds of pictorial material. And, of course, the impact of color cannot be ignored.

All of these distinctions are of some interest to the advertiser but are only effective in changing human behavior at a rather trivial level. No one ever changed his mind on an important issue because he liked the kind of type employed by the opposing side. It is only because advertisers traditionally deal with choices that in a real sense do not matter, such as which soap flakes to buy, that an accumulation of relatively unimportant details such as these may have a demonstrable effect.

Naturally, the advertising psychologist is extremely interested in the impact of the advertisement on the consumer. Many efforts have been made to study this influence. For the most part, the methods employed are traditional, though occasionally somewhat unusual approaches are employed. For example, the eye camera has been used to follow a subject's eye movements in order to study the way in which newspapers or magazines are read. Again, a survey can be designed to determine whether persons are engaged in two different kinds of activity, such as reading while listening to the radio, and what effect this has on his reception of a message on either medium. Generally, however, the methods are similar to those already described. It is reasonable to conclude that the advertising psychologist does not seem to be the possessor of any vital secrets of behavior change.

The Laboratory as Opposed to the Field Setting

One basis of comparison between the interpersonal and mass media approaches to the creation of behavior change has yet to be discussed. This comparison is indirect, but its results are instructive. For the most part, the mass media are studied through surveys involving interviews with many people. Most investigations of the effects of interpersonal influence are performed in a laboratory or under circumstances that approximate this condition. This methodological divergence has arisen largely because in each case the easiest and most natural deployment of research strategies has been utilized. Nevertheless, the effects of the relationship between the method of investigation and the mode of influence have proved as interesting as they were unintended. They were a source of concern to Carl Hovland, who did so much to stimulate interest in the whole area of attitude change.[1] His analysis of the situation did much to clarify the conflicts that were emerging and their source and ultimate mode of resolution.

The most striking divergence between studies conducted in the community and studies of interpersonal persuasion was in terms of the amount of change in the subjects. Naturally, the effectiveness of any process of attitude influence must relate in part to the use to which it is put, the message conveyed, and its source and target. Nevertheless, with all these factors given due weight, it is quite clear that the results of the two kinds of research are quite different. On the whole, surveys have indicated that perhaps 5 per cent changed their attitudes on whatever issues were investigated. However, when laboratory investigations are reviewed, the amount of change reported ranges between one-third to one-half of all subjects. In view of the generality of these findings, the difference in effect can scarcely be ignored.

Another important divergence involves the effect of the attitudinal distance separating the communicator from the audience on the amount of over-all opinion change he induces. Laboratory studies provide definite substantiation for the belief that the greater this divergence is, the larger the attitude change created. However, in survey studies, the relationship is reversed; the greater the discrepancy, the less the change.

Another contradiction relates to the impact of the order in which the information designed to change attitudes is presented. In general, the results of laboratory research have suggested that presenting the message first is not an important determinant of its effectiveness. However, survey studies of consumer choice have clearly indicated that such primacy is important.

It is unusual to find a situation in which the same problems have been approached from two such different methodological vantage points. This very atypicality led Hovland and others to suspect that the basic contradictions obtained in this research were not so much a reflection of the material as of the procedures. In other words, the findings were being manufactured partially by the methods used to attain them, a possibility that always haunts the scientific investigator.

The first issue to be analyzed from this viewpoint was the question of why experimental studies indicated extensive attitude change in the face-to-face approach, whereas survey research did not indicate a like amount of change when mass media were employed. A number of pertinent explanations seemed possible. In laboratory studies, all subjects are forced by the experimenter to expose themselves to the communication. Under natural conditions, however, the individual can choose whether or not to read a newspaper, tune in a particular television station, or buy a certain book. People do not generally expose themselves to points of view with which they disagree. Therefore, as has been stated, under natural conditions they will not expose themselves to communications advocating opposing views and such mass-media attempts at persuasion cannot possibly influence them.

Moreover, the nature of the communications is very different in the two kinds of study. Experiments may deal with only one brief communication. Surveys usually attempt to assess the impact of a long-term effort, such as that involved in a political campaign. This choice is strategic and practical, but it naturally produces somewhat different conclusions. A related issue is the time period involved. The experimenter of necessity employs a limited time during which he measures the change. Under these conditions if any altered behavior or attitude occurs, it is likely to be detected. Survey research, on the other hand, usually covers months and even years of time through retrospective analysis. The longer the time span of the study, the less likely would one be to find changes. Such effects would be diluted by intervening events.

Further, under experimental conditions, communicators are usually more credible than under normal circumstances. Experiments always have the authority of scientific method and usually the indirect aura of the sponsoring institutions behind them. Thus the subject is inclined to accept any communication offered as reliable. However, communication received under natural conditions from the mass media is not so well taken. One is often not sure of the origin of such material or of the intent of the messages. A good deal of distrust or uncertainty exists. Related to this point is the stabilizing influence of the individual's friends and associates. Under natural conditions, an individual has an opportunity to talk over any new communication with others. This tends to reinforce his previous attitude at the expense of the communication. Under experimental conditions, however, such checking is controlled or eliminated, so that the message itself can have greater effect.

Another very important difference between the two types of research involves the kind of change being attempted. In experimental studies, the attempted changes are often trivial. They are selected in order to increase the likelihood of finding some altered behavior in a relatively short time. Survey research bearing on issues of attitude

115

change, however, is generally more reality oriented and focuses on opinions about socially significant issues, which are also intrinsically more difficult to alter. This conclusion excludes large-scale studies of the effectiveness of advertising directed toward relatively minor attitude shifts.

Most laboratory studies are performed in universities with college students as subjects. Surveys, by their very nature, are far more representative of the adult population at large. These differences of sampling could well lead one to expect different kinds of conclusions.

All of the preceding distinctions hold in any comparison of findings obtained from survey and laboratory studies. However, other qualifications must also be introduced to explain the additional contradictory conclusions. The explanation of the effect of attitude discrepancy involves the further refinement of issues that have already been raised. In this instance, the important difference in the two types of study seems to be the degree of involvement the individual feels with the issues under investigation. In most laboratory studies, the degree of involvement is relatively small, and it is, therefore, easy to produce an attitude shift. However, when the individual is deeply concerned about the issue, as is the case in most survey research, he reacts more unfavorably to disagreement. When he hears communications with which he is in conflict, he tends to reject them. Only opinions slightly different from his own will be tolerated, and only such opinions can possibly influence him.

Finally, one has to account for different findings in relation to a *primacy effect* in communications, that is, the degree to which one is influenced by the message one hears first. A review of this issue in survey research suggests that in many cases the communicant does not really hear two sides of the argument. He listens to the first presentation and then leaves psychologically or physically. Under such conditions, there can hardly be anything but a primacy effect. Of course, in an experiment, it is harder for the subject to leave. He has to sit there and listen to all arguments.

Other influences are also involved. Primacy effects are greatest when it is not known that the issue is controversial, the communicator is believed to be impartial, or where different communicators present the same point of view. Under natural circumstances, these conditions can arise only when communications are carefully controlled, as in an advertisement. However, in the laboratory, where all conditions and viewpoints are systematically presented, primacy effects would be minimized. Thus, the contradictions are once again related to the accidental or concomitant conditions associated with the research rather than to any inherent contradiction of the facts themselves.

These illustrations serve to highlight the basic point that to properly interpret the results of attitude-change studies, one needs to be fully aware of the impact of the research design. Otherwise one may take for fact a conclusion that is produced more by the method of study than the nature of the material.

In conclusion, it is necessary to note the existence of several gaps in this discussion. Studies of the effectiveness of the mass media as aids to learning new material have not been dealt with, for learning intellectual information or new motor tasks is not the same as changing previously established attitudes or behavior patterns.

Similarly, there are many studies involving the relative effectiveness of different communications designed solely for entertainment, such as movies, radio programs, or TV series. While results of such studies have great practical value for the people involved in such enterprises, no attempt in entertainment communications is made to change the audience. Therefore, these findings are also irrelevant.

In some ways, the study of attempts to use the mass media to influence behavior is encouraging. It suggests that the individual can become immunized to the effects of large-scale assaults on his behavior patterns when he lives with them daily and when the messages themselves tend to conflict. On the other hand, under certain conditions, the mass media can exert an effect that—in conjunction with other circumstances, such as a political campaign—creates a definite result. Further, in those societies in which mass-media communication networks are carefully controlled, the effect is probably greater; this is not due to any increased effectiveness, but rather to the lack of competing viewpoints. Thus, in an open society, any attempt to use these media to affect behavior provides its own antidote. Such communication becomes dangerous only when specialized power groups are able to control it for their own ends.

CHAPTER TEN

Improving Intergroup Relations

ONE aspect of attitude change that currently engages widespread attention is the study of how attitudes can be altered to reduce the tensions between racial, religious, and national groups living in the same or adjacent territories. The issues involved in these accommodations are generally studied as aspects of intergroup relations. The negative aspect of these relationships is prejudice.

The existence of racial, religious, and national prejudice is one of the most clearly established findings in social psychology. As long ago as 1933, the psychologists Daniel Katz and Kenneth Braly found a consistent pattern of stereotypes attributed by Princeton students to certain national groups.[1] An almost identical pattern was found in the following decade by other investigators using a number of student subjects of various racial backgrounds in this country and also in Great Britain. Finally, in 1951, the psychologist Gustave Gilbert duplicated the original study on a new generation of Princeton students with almost identical results.[2] Very few findings in social psychology have been as widely replicated on different samples over such a long period of time.

Social psychologists have also been interested in devising and testing methods of reducing prejudice, because of the urgent social problems that its existence creates. For many years, such research was actively conducted. However, in recent years, this field has been ignored for the most part. This oversight is strange in view of the increasing prominence of the national issues produced by intergroup tensions and the important part that the early research findings played in supporting and supplying scientific justification for such steps as the Supreme Court decision on school desegregation.

Two explanations can be offered for the paucity of recent research in this area. First, many social scientists felt that the answers had already been found and became interested in other problems. Second, the study of ways to change intergroup attitudes was absorbed into the broader area of attitude change. Presumably, if one could affect one attitude one could affect another, and, in this sense, prejudice was only a small sample of a larger population.

At present, we are faced with a new crop of intergroup problems that are indirectly related to the impact of the first wave of scientific answers that helped to support school desegregation and other more recent social legislation. In order to view these problems in proper perspective, it is necessary to review the studies performed in the thirties, forties, and early fifties to gain an understanding of what they established and where they logically led.

The Earlier Evidence

Most researchers who studied intergroup relations were quick to realize that they either had to be content with investigating a relatively small aspect of the larger problem or divide the over-all area into a set of mutually exclusive categories. More specifically, they had to distinguish among the cognitive (intellectual), affective (emotional), and behavioral (action) components of prejudice. An individual might increase his knowledge about other groups, but fail to alter either his feelings or actions. Or, he might change his actions, due to legal sanctions, but not alter either his understanding or beliefs.

With these distinctions, it was no longer sufficient to determine whether prejudice was reduced. One had to specify the type of prejudice to be influenced and also to study the relationships among changes of different types. This approach was recognized in theory but often ignored in practice. When the components were studied separately, the results were often surprising. The author, for example, performed such a study.[3] His conclusions were that these three components were unrelated for a sample of white subjects, but highly related for a Negro sample.

However, the situation is even more complicated. Recently, the psychologists Stuart Cook and Claire Selltiz have described how the techniques by which prejudice is measured influence the kind of results obtained.[4] In general, they found that prejudice and other similar attitudes have been measured using self reports, the observations of overt behavior, projective tests, standard attitude tests, and physiological reactions to set situations. Since all of these approaches can be used in any investigation, it can be said that prejudice can be measured on three levels and by five different kinds of instrument. Both the instrument and the component studied partially determine the experiment's result. The problem of defining the proper criterion for the measurement of prejudice is a complex one. Since so many alternative measures are available, it is not unnatural that the results obtained from studies of prejudice reduction do not tend to fall into an orderly pattern.

When the focus of the research is upon attitude change, an added complication is introduced: namely, the nature of the technique used to produce the change. Thus, any attempt to improve intergroup relations must define the method of change inducement to be applied, the component of prejudice to be reduced, and the way in which this component will be measured. Unfortunately, most studies in this area have given primary attention to the first of these requirements, assuming that prejudice was an undifferentiated trait that could be measured in any way that seemed convenient at the time.

Most of the research that is to be described can be classified as evaluative. Therefore, the criticisms directed toward such an approach in the earlier chapters can be applied here. However, the nature of these techniques is somewhat more specific, so that results are less ambiguous. It is convenient to organize these techniques under three headings, though the approaches are by no means totally different from one other.

The Effects of Education

It is usually assumed that prejudice is the result of ignorance. Consequently, it is believed that the more educated the person, the less likely he is to be prejudiced. Some general support for this position can be obtained from survey research. Of course, alternate interpretations are possible, since the degree of education a person has relates to other significant variables, such as his financial position and social class.

Studies have been made of students as they pass through college to determine whether they are less prejudiced toward minority groups as seniors than they were as freshmen. In this instance, the results vary. In a college in Michigan, the seniors were less prejudiced than they had been as freshmen. In a North Carolina college, they were more prejudiced. Students attending other schools showed no particular change. Evidently education does not automatically produce a constructive change of attitude or behavior. Other factors are involved, such as community attitudes and parental beliefs. Education may, under certain circumstances, only supply rationalizations for previously held beliefs rather than acting to correct unjust conditions.

For this reason, specialized educational courses have been developed specifically for the purpose of decreasing the prejudice of the students enrolled. Most studies of such courses are of dubious quality, since the individual conducting the class was usually also the experimenter. Further, little provision was made for distinguishing which aspects of the course were responsible for its impact.

Some of these studies indicate that if more information about the minority groups in question is provided, prejudice toward them tends to be reduced. This relationship appears to depend, however, on a number of contributing factors, including the assumptions that the information presented is less prejudiced in content than that already possessed by the students; that the instructor indicates he is less prejudiced than most of the students; and that the instructor has a satisfactory relationship with the students, so that they can accept his viewpoint and the material he presents. Thus, the reduction of prejudice depends on interpersonal as well as cognitive aspects of the teaching situation.

Most of these investigators took a rather simple approach to the problem. An example of a more subtle one is provided by the work of Rabbi H. E. Kagan, who taught a course designed to improve the attitude of Christians toward Jews.[5] Three separate approaches were used. In the first, the contribution of Jews to the development of Western morality and Christianity was stressed. This had no effect on student anti-Semitism. The second approach utilized biblical material as a springboard to a discussion of anti-Semitism in the modern world. The third technique was similar to the second but also utilized individual discussions between the rabbi and each student. Both the second and third methods significantly reduced the original level of student prejudice. The value of this experimental design was that it helps to clarify which aspects of the educational experience produced the attitude change and helps us to better understand the processes involved.

Propaganda: the Utilization of Mass Media

One usually thinks of propaganda in a negative context, but in an objective sense it only involves the use of mass media to influence opinion. Whether this influence is beneficial or detrimental depends on the viewpoint of the observer. Numerous approaches have been used, including movies, oral persuasion on TV and radio, and written material. Since the intensity and nature of propaganda is largely uncontrolled, it is hard to equate the results obtained from different studies. However, there is little doubt, for example, that movies can improve intergroup relations.

One of the earliest of such studies was performed by the psychologist L. L. Thurstone.[6] Not only did he find that three out of four movies that he presented to the subjects of his experiment produced changes in their attitude, but when subjects were retested five months later, 62 per cent of the change produced was still in effect. When subjects were additionally tested nineteen months later, 60 per cent of the original shift in attitude was maintained, indicating that the majority of the change was stable over time.

More important than the particular type of propaganda employed seems to be the type of person to whom it is directed. In general, it appears that college students alter their attitudes substantially, whereas adults show little change under more or less the same conditions. This seems due both to the relative maturity of the adults' attitudes and to the authority that an attempt to influence college students is likely to carry, since it indirectly represents the opinion of school faculty and administrators, who have agreed to allow the material to be presented.

Intergroup Contact

The support for the Supreme Court decision on desegregation was drawn in part from studies of the effects of intergroup contact and the tendency of such contact to reduce prejudice. In this one instance, scientific investigation has helped to support sweeping social changes.

However, these studies were generally of an *ex-post facto design;* that is, they measured the impact of intergroup contact after it had occurred without having benefit of precontact measures.

Such an investigation may be practical, but its conclusions are open to some doubt, since the previous opinions of participants can only be measured retrospectively. This type of evidence cannot be equated with the direct measurement of individuals before the intergroup experience. With the exception of this one caution, the evidence relating to intergroup contact is impressive. During World War II, for example, enlisted white soldiers who had served in companies with Negro platoons displayed much less resistance to accepting such an assignment in the future than white soldiers who had not had such experience.

In a well-known study of housing developments, the psychologists Morton Deutsch and Mary Collins found that 53 per cent of the white housewives living in interracial projects favored such a policy for all city projects, while only 5 per cent of white women living in nonintegrated projects favored such a policy.[7] Deutsch and Collins broke down their study of prejudice into affective and cognitive components. Their analysis suggested that changes of feeling were usually related to changes of belief; the reverse relationship, however, did not necessarily hold. This finding suggests a hierarchical pattern of change; that is, when feelings change, they alter the beliefs below them. However, beliefs cannot affect feelings, since influence only proceeds down the scale. The nature of such a model, however, is partially obscured by research findings that altered behavior has no direct relationship to changes of either attitudes or feelings. Either behavior is the lowest member of the hierarchy, or it is only indirectly related to the other two components.

A number of similar studies support the thesis that opportunity for contact reduces intergroup prejudice, but this finding is not consistent under all conditions. In communities in which national groups are replacing each other in a given residential area, considerable friction may occur despite the opportunity for contacts, suggesting that, in such situations, economic and social resentments may be stronger than the influence of direct contact.

The effectiveness of intergroup contact in work situations has not been clearly demonstrated. Similarly, in a recreational boy's camp, the opportunity for intergroup contact produced mixed effects. Some boys became more prejudiced and some, less. There are relatively few studies of the effects of intergroup contacts in schools, and the results of existing investigations have been equivocal.

Clearly, more than one factor must be operating in order to produce such different results. The psychologist Gordon Allport has analyzed this material extensively.[8] He concludes the intergroup contact is an effective aid to the improvement of intergroup relations only when certain other necessary conditions are fulfilled. These include equal status among the members of the interacting groups, the support of social sanctions for the interaction, and the pursuit of common goals in a setting leading to the perception of common interests and problems. The integrated housing development tends to satisfy these conditions. Work situations and other settings that have produced equivocal results do not. Thus, intergroup contact depends for its ultimate effect on environmental and social conditions.

There are alternative approaches to the reduction of intergroup prejudices, including individual psychotherapy of prejudiced individuals, specific action programs, and group retraining using role-playing procedures. However, the evidence concerning the effectiveness of these approaches is sparse, even though they seem to offer some degree of promise.

Prejudice, of course, is only one of a variety of problems that these procedures have been used to alleviate. It is a pertinent focus because of its timely interest and the existence of relevant research, but in a sense such focus tends to create the illusion that it is a unique problem. This is not the case. Studies of human behavior require greater emphasis on the means of change and less on the object, since it is the general efficacy of the means that is in question. Presumably, effective ways to alter attitudes of prejudice would change others equally effectively.

The Implications of Social Action

In contrast to most of the research described in this book, the studies of intergroup relations have had a direct and immediate impact on a large segment of society. Recent history has served to illustrate some of the naïveté that surrounded earlier ideas on the subject and perhaps the degree to which nonscientific motives entered indirectly into research in spite of investigators' caution.

While in recent years relatively little has been done by psychologists to study directly the reduction of intergroup tensions, much has been accomplished in law and politics. The results of this effort have been and will continue to be around us for some time to come. It is clear by now that the problem of prejudice does not dissolve before any abrupt revision of circumstances. This practical experience has led some social scientists to reevaluate the many factors involved and to clarify the full complexity of the situation that exists when alteration of prejudiced behavior is accomplished through social and legal means, rather than through voluntary group action. In particular, for example, interest has centered on the academic performance of Negroes in integrated schools, since it has been assumed that one of the great benefits of integration would be an increased opportunity for them to attain a higher educational level. The evidence on this issue is complex. It serves to document the uncertain effects that are the inevitable handmaiden of any sweeping social change.

A number of studies of this issue have recently been analyzed by the social psychologist Irwin Katz.[9] He concludes that the performance of Negroes in newly integrated school systems depends on many factors. When there has previously been a marked discrepancy between the standards of the white and Negro school systems and consequent low expectations and feelings of inferiority were generated in the minority group, Negroes do not perform well. Further, where social threat is present and the fear of punishment for failure is strong, minority group performance will tend to be poor.

On the other hand, when the majority genuinely accepts the minority, other, negative influences tend to be reduced or mitigated.

These conclusions are simple enough in themselves, but they have considerable weight because they are drawn from a sizeable body of data. They also suggest certain practical steps that may assist successful attempts at integration. First, it might be desirable to raise the levels of Negro schools to those of white schools before integrating the two systems, if this can be done in a practical manner. Second, it may be useful to work with the parents of the minority group to help them prepare their children for the new experience and inculcate in them the interest in achievement that may characterize the majority. Third, teachers need some retraining to deal effectively with the complex emotional reactions occurring in a biracial school. Fourth, the widely adopted practice of grouping children in terms of their achievement or ability should be partially or completely abandoned, because it places most members of the minority group in a lower position than the majority due to their hitherto poor education; adequate provision for flexibility is necessary if they are not to be frozen there. Finally, integration should begin in the lower grades, since younger children are less likely to be threatened by failure at that level or to have formed strong intergroup attitudes.

The most interesting aspect of these suggestions is that they serve to illustrate the naïveté of the social scientists who recommended desegregation as a direct approach to the reduction of racial prejudice. As in all attempts at major social engineering, the conditions require careful specification and proper preparation. Otherwise, the results are mixed and the consequences difficult to anticipate.

CHAPTER ELEVEN

Creativity

THE previous material indirectly suggests that there is little evidence of any serious scientific concern with the development of the potential inherent in normal humanity. This is a very curious and serious omission in view of the need for general improvement in human behavior to help mankind cope with the destructive forces that have been unleashed in recent times.

However, this need for more constructive human activity in the face of possible annihilation is only the most acute example of a situation that has been chronic throughout recorded history. Men have seldom acted rationally, kindly, or even effectively, but have been crippled by hate, frustration, improper education, societal constrictions, and a variety of personal, social, and historical influences that do not further either the individual or the collective good. Yet this destructive behavior is perpetuated through ignorance, vested interests, and inertia.

There has been no end to the number of systems, methods, and procedures proposed by philosophers, theologians, mystics, and artists to resolve the situation. But science, the powerful hope of our age, seems to be mute. At least, such is the implication of the material discussed so far. However, this conclusion is not entirely justified. Recently, a small but growing group of behavioral scientists has become interested in, and received support for, studies of *creativity*. Creativity is an extension of normal functions. It is not something of which one must be cured or a change of attitude or behavior to be manipulated externally. It represents an ability to restructure a limited aspect of psychological, social, or physical reality, the ability to perform in a flexible and unprecedented manner. Whatever definition of creativity is adopted, its study stands as a lonely beacon indicating that the possibilities for altering behavior toward a development beyond normal levels of performance are not totally ignored by modern psychology and other related disciplines.

Recent interest in creativity has been stirred by a concern for the future of the United States. It has become increasingly evident that we must utilize our existing intellectual and creative resources more fully if we are to survive in the modern world. Creativity helps to provide the fresh vision that is required to solve the many modern social and scientific dilemmas. Thus, what was once a minor topic in the study of intellectual functioning has become a thriving, though still relatively modest, area of research.

Established Facts about Creativity

In any new research area, it is difficult for the scientists involved to come to firm conclusions about their investigations. A number of facts about creativity seem, however, reasonably certain at this time. For the most part they are rather pedestrian, but this should not belie the careful investigation that has substantiated them.

For example, creative persons typically show a preference for complexity, asymmetry, and novelty rather than the simple, regular, or routine. This preference occurs not only in relation to problem solving, but throughout the personal experience of the creative individual. He follows his own impulses and is able to accept paradoxes and contradictions with humor. In a sense, all these traits are inherent in the very definition of creativity.

In terms of its limits, creativity is usually at its height early in most productive careers, typically in the 30's, though of course notable exceptions occur. Also, in most arts and sciences the great majority of creative contributions are made by relatively few persons. There seems to have been through history a creative aristocracy of excellence which has exerted an influence out of all proportion to its numbers.

These conclusions are, of course, relatively obvious. One more subtle conclusion has been reached. Most studies of creativity have indicated that intelligence and creativity are only slightly related to one another. In virtually all such investigations a number of highly intelligent people are found in the noncreative group. Since most of our educational methods are based on the development of intellectual ability, it is reasonable to conclude that our schools do not seriously attempt to educate or enhance students' creative ability, though some educational researchers are interested in these problems. Emphasis on the assimilation of facts and on learning traditional views of the universe is an appropriate basis for intellectual development but may be deleterious to creativity which depends upon fresh approaches to problems and a free expression of ideas.

Yet it is not so much the findings of recent studies as the over-all scope of the approach characterizing them that is of greatest interest. Most research into creativity can be considered as investigating one of four categories: the creative process, the product produced by the process, the measurement of creativity as an ability, and the personality of the creator. These topics are not mutually exclusive, but in most cases a study deals primarily with only one of them.

Research into the Creative Process

The earliest research attempted to study the nature of the process by analyzing what people do while they are engaged in creative actions. As long ago as 1926, the psychologist Graham Wallas described creative thought in terms of a four-stage process: preparation and study of preliminary materials, incubation, illumination via a creative insight, and final verification by the use of objective criteria.[1]

Later theorists have not argued with the basic approach but have demonstrated that Wallas was presenting an ideal model. In fact, these stages may overlap, occur in a different order, be partially repeated, and depart in various ways from the simplified picture originally suggested. Further, it has been emphasized that description is not explanation. The basic problem of how creative insight is obtained is described, but it is not explained. At best, this model has documented the developmental nature of the creative process and helped to abstract some of its important phases.

A much more recent interest has been the evaluation of creativity in terms of what it produces. Products, of course, can be rated in a number of ways—their gross amount, originality, what evidence they are of the subject's problem-solving ability, the subject's ability to produce, that is, to complete jobs that are undertaken, and so on. In order to utilize products, such as the number and quality of works of art or of scientific papers, as measures of creativity, some judgment must be made. Unfortunately, it has been demonstrated in many other areas of psychological research that the role and personal bias of the judge tends to influence his judgments.

The psychologist Donald Taylor and his colleagues obtained the dismaying total of fifty-six different aspects of creativity to measure from such diverse raters as the subject himself, a peer, the examiner, the work supervisor, the number of creative products, official records, and membership in professional organizations.[2] From these measures he was able, by the use of *factor analysis,* a statistical technique designed to reduce complex measurements to their simplest common denominators, to convert the total number to twenty-seven demonstrably different ways to measure the products of creative effort. This kind of study raises serious questions as to whether it is meaningful to speak of creativity as a single ability, since it clearly has many independent aspects.

The third major research area has focused on a way to measure the existence of creative ability in a subject as distinct from rating the finished products. The assumption underlying these studies is that creativity is a capacity that varies from person to person and can be assessed and measured in the same general manner as intelligence or mechanical aptitude. Three approaches have been used to obtain standard measures of creative ability. The first, an inductive one, involves an attempt to specify and assess each aspect of creativity by an independent test. It has been most convincingly advanced by the psychologist J. P. Guilford, who has developed a model of intellect that includes an assessment of creative abilities.[3] Guilford has developed tests, the Guilford Creative Battery, presumably related to some more general concept of creativity, for such characteristics as fluency of thinking, flexibility of thinking, originality, redefinition, and elaboration. The tests can be administered singly or in various combinations. The advantage of this approach is its precision.

Precision, however, does not necessarily produce conceptual clarity or insure completeness of coverage. Thus, several researchers have found that independent ratings of creativity have little relationship to the characteristics measured by Guilford's tests. These results serve as a caution against simply taking test scores of some components as a direct measure of creativity at this time. Either an extension of the number of components is required, or a different, less complex measurement procedure may be appropriate.

Another kind of attempt to assess creativity involves the use of nonverbal test materials consisting of some kind of illustration, about which the subject is asked to comment. One such test uses pairs of figures drawn in black ink. The examinee is requested to indicate which of each pair of items he prefers. His preferences are scored in terms of norms supplied by a group of artists. It has been found that such a test correlates quite highly with independent ratings of creativity, in spite of the fact that it was originally designed to measure artistic taste. In one study, for example, this test correlated more highly with other judgments of the creativity of research workers than eleven other scales, including tests of values, vocational preference, and the Guilford Creativity Battery. Thus, the nonverbal tests seem extremely promising as a simple means of obtaining an estimate of creative ability.

The major effort of research into creativity has been the study of the personality characteristics of individuals identified as creative. This research has been conducted both in order to clarify the function of creativity in the personality of the creator and also to aid in its identification by attaining an increased understanding of the kinds of people in whom it is likely to occur.

Several scientists have attempted to understand something of the dynamics of creativity through the use of projective tests and other dynamic approaches, such as clinical interviews. Unfortunately, the instruments required for this kind of analysis are those that are most difficult to interpret. Findings have suggested that creative individuals tend not to repress anxiety-provoking experiences and have less certainty about their sexual identity than less creative persons. They are also more inner-directed and relatively unconcerned about the opinions of others.

However, discussions of material drawn from projective instruments have tended to revert to quasi-theoretical descriptions of ideal types, which may or may not have any resemblance to actual data obtained in direct research. Certainly, the attempt to uncover the underlying motivation of creativity has not been notably successful, since equivalent motivational patterns are found in others who are not creative and, in any case, motivations do not explain the creative process but merely identify some of the preexisting conditions that may be necessary for its fuller expression.

Most behavioral scientists utilize some measure or set of measures of creativity and relate them to a variety of personality components, which they also measure and compare to norms obtained from a given sample. A good deal of this kind of research has accumulated. The results, generally, confirm the popular stereotype of the creative individual, with the one exception that they suggest that creativity is not necessarily associated with eccentricity, as is often believed.

Taken as a whole, the systematic nature of the development of research on creativity is impressive, and the quality of the studies itself is, at least in some cases, exemplary. But a remarkable aspect of the subject has been omitted. Everything is dealt with but the development of the creative capacity itself. It has been assumed that creativity is a given aspect of the personality, and that its normal development can be recorded. This assumption may or may not be justified in terms of scientific strategy, but it is certainly dangerous if left unquestioned.

In one sense, it is not surprising that behavioral scientists should consider creativity an innate ability and study how to measure it and the personality characteristics to which it relates. This view falls within the established tradition. But it would be tragic if serious attention were not given to the question of whether and under what conditions creativity, whatever its sources, can be enhanced.

Not unexpectedly, educational researchers have been interested in this problem, since progressive education stresses the development of independence of scholarship and creativity of approach.

Unfortunately, while modern educators and psychologists have been eloquent in their praise of creativity and have stressed the importance of fostering its development, they have been extremely vague about how this was to be done, beyond the presentation of case histories or suggestions for the use of largely untested methods. One exception is the recent emphasis on *brain-storming* both in education and industry. The basis of brain-storming is that the members of a group considering a given problem offer any solution they happen to think of, regardless of its apparent practicality or rationality. While this approach has many enthusiastic followers, the results of studies evaluating its efficacy are mixed. Some have supported brain-storming as a method of enhancing productive thinking; others have suggested that it depressed the problem-solving ability of the group. The issue will be settled in time. Aside from this one technique, there is almost total ignorance in educational circles about how creativity is to be enhanced.

Synectics

However one outstanding example of a full-scale attack on the development of creative ability is provided by the method of *synectics*, which has been described in detail by one of its originators, William Gordon, in *Synectics: the Development of Creative Capacity*.[4]

In the early phases of synectics, particular emphasis was placed upon developmental analysis of the creative process of successful problem solving; it can be summarized as follows: First comes a feeling of detachment from the situation and the problem; then a reidentification with it from the viewpoint, not of the person, but rather of the problem itself, as if the person himself were a part of it instead of being on the outside thinking about it. Next comes the attempt to avoid a premature solution, however tempting it might be; following this deferment of resolution comes a speculative period in which the participant allows his thoughts to roam freely along lines suggested by the problem. Finally, he comes to feel, as in the first stage, that the problem is independent of him; shortly thereafter the solution is attained.

These stages were derived from studies of individuals and groups involved in creative activities, including those seeking new forms of artistic expression, industrial invention, and scientific understanding. While the existence of these stages of creative activity was psychologically interesting, it was soon observed, as with many psychological findings, that theoretical knowledge of the necessary stages was not really helpful in bringing about the process. It did not make anyone more creative. People could not become more involved or more detached merely by willing it. The process had to be more natural and organic.

From the early days of its existence in the late 1940's, synectics has utilized groups of individuals meeting together to pool their creative abilities. In one sense, these synectic groups resembled the T-groups employed by group-dynamics practitioners; some of the discussion mechanisms are similar, and the participants in both types of group are normal persons functioning successfully. However, the goals are quite different, and the nature of the interaction between group members in the two experiences is of quite another order. Members of a T-group join it to study how groups work and how they themselves act in such situations. It is axiomatic that such participants in groups are not particularly interested in producing any particular product, but rather in understanding the process.

In contrast, the members of the synectics group are interested in process only to the extent that it affects what they produce. They have a definite goal: the attainment and testing of creative breakthroughs. The group session is task oriented.

As a direct result of the analysis and experimentation engaged in by individuals in synectics groups, a systematic approach to the development of creative ability was slowly and painfully evolved beyond the initial statement of abstract stages of creative problem solving.

The analysis suggested that the basic obstacle to enhanced creativity in the synectics group was insufficient individual expression. The range of expression had to be increased so as to allow greater freedom for unlikely and unsuspected solutions to emerge. This freedom could be obtained only by lifting some of the repressions that ordinarily serve the function of maintaining an ordered and consistent personality. Thus creativity would be enhanced in a way similar to the psychoanalytic process. The prime requisite was to gain access to unconscious and semiconscious material. The goals of the two techniques, of course, are quite different.

Two basic processes were soon identified. The first involved the incorporation of new materials into old conceptions in order to make them more familiar and accessible to analysis. This stage is characteristic of all problem-solving situations. It is first necessary to understand the nature of the problem and to have technical knowledge of the materials related to its possible solution. This stage is necessary to, but not sufficient for, a creative solution; therefore, a second general mode of operation must be used. The familiar must be made strange, or unfamiliar. The members of synectics groups employ four analogical mechanisms to facilitate this latter process.

The first of these mechanisms involves taking the role of some part of the problem. For example, a physicist concerned with atomic particles might ask, "How would I feel if I were an atom dancing around?" He thus enters, through his imagination, into intimate physical contact with the problem in a way that would never occur under conditions of ordinary life.

The second mechanism involves the use of direct analogy—

attempting to think of some aspect of another field that bears some relation to the problem—much as Alexander Graham Bell utilized the membrane of the ear, which vibrates as sound waves hit it, thus transmitting the sound to the nervous system and the brain—as the model for the metal diaphragm of the telephone, which transmits sound in a similar way.

The third mechanism is symbolic analogy. It utilizes an aesthetically satisfying poetic approach, even though it may be technically inaccurate. In this category might be placed the concept of a biological auto jack that would operate only when fed. The idea is impractical as it stands, but it is an interesting notion that might be practical with suitable modifications.

The fourth mechanism is that of fantasy analogy, in which no attempt at being reasonable is maintained. This approach is nearest to free association. For example, when a synectics group was trying to design a method for closing the edges of a space suit, one member had the fantasy that the suit would close when the astronaut wished it to. Later this fantasy was transformed into one in which insects climbed up the suit trailing steel wires behind them, and those wires closed the suit. This possibility was finally transformed into a realistic probability by the use of overlapping interlocking springs that performed similarly to the insects of the group's fantasy.

In contrast to the more typical descriptive approaches of most psychologists to the creative process, these analogical mechanisms have the advantages of being guides to action rather than categories of analysis. While they form the core of the synectics approach to the release of creative ability, they are only a skeleton upon which a complex group interaction must be built. To date, synectics has been applied mainly to industrial and scientific problem-solving situations. Practical experience has indicated that an extensive training program, lasting about a year, is necessary to create a successful group that can function independently over a period of time and produce useful concepts and models that serve the ends of the sponsoring organization. As these experiences have accumulated, a variety of practical principles have been formulated, including guides to the selection of likely candidates for synectics groups and the design of proper settings for them.

Generally, it is desirable in an industrial setting to select men who represent all the major aspects of the company's operation. Candidates should be chosen for their high energy levels, since the synectic group experience can be extremely wearing; for this reason, the age range of participants is generally between twenty-five to forty. Some relation to both administration and selling is useful in translating the ideas generated to practical products. Men who have changed from one specialty to another, held several different jobs, and never quite realized their potential in any of them may perform excellently in the synectics group. Finally, the ability to function by using the four analogy mechanisms is important.

Experience has suggested that a simple environment is best for the group meetings. The only machinery that should be new is the typing and recording equipment. For the rest, it is better that it appears second-hand to avoid the envy of other employees, reduce the over-all cost, eliminate status differences among members, and set the stage for unconventional thinking, which might be hindered by symbols of status and technology.

Perhaps the best way to gain some sense of what the synectic approach actually involves is through a brief transcript of a group in action:

A: The client wants a new can opener, a better one. . . .

B: What does better mean?

A: What would an ideal can opener have?

C: Ideally cans shouldn't have to be opened. . . . They should open themselves.

D: Okay, okay. But we're working for a can opener client, not a can company. If you don't like this assignment go sell a new product job to American Can.

E: I hate the way a can opener gets so filthy. . . . Ever looked at the knife part after opening a can of sardines? It smells for days.

A: All right, . . . our job must be perfectly clean. What else?

C: Well, if we must stick with the mundane limitations . . . I don't like to think that I have to eat a little steel every time I open up a can.

B: What the hell are you talking about?

C: Listen. When the cutter goes around it removes material. Just be happy that you don't get a big sharp sliver of metal in your tomato soup.

A: Whether present can openers do what you say or not our job better be free of it. What else?

D: It would be great if you could put the top of the can back on . . . you know, for cat food and stuff like that.

A: I'll buy that, but I don't think that it's a matter of life and death.

D: How about having the unit automatic? Just put in the can and the top is off.

A: That wouldn't be a basic invention. It would just be putting the thing on wheels.

B: We aren't going to get anywhere if we limit our thinking to improvements. My understanding is that the client wants a radically new can opener . . . not a slightly better one.

A: I think you're right. Let's back way off from the problem. . . . What does "open" mean?

B: To me, "open" means that something was closed . . . now it's open.

C: What about a crater? It's always open, isn't it?

D: Sure . . . but that's not what "open" means to me.

E: Both of you are using "open" to describe a state. I think of it as describing an action . . . I "open" the book. The book was closed, now I open it.

A: I wonder if we can universalize it. If we use the word as a verb, does it always imply a previously closed state? . . . I guess it does at that.

E: In nature . . .

A: What?

E: In nature there are things that are completely closed, then open up . . . a clam for instance.

B: But with a clam the process is reversible. We don't need that for our problem. We don't need to close the can up again.

B: I thought it would be great if we could.

D: All right. But the clam isn't actually sealed. The shell fits nicely together but it's not soldered like a can. The only analogy from nature would have to be a case where something is wounded and heals immediately.

E: If a starfish loses one of his legs he grows another one in his place.

B: True. But that's not an opening, is it?

E: I guess not. . . . How about a pea pod? That really opens up along a line . . . it's got a built-in weakness and splits along a weak line.

A: Has a can a built-in weakness? A weakness we can take advantage of?

C: Maybe it's weak where the top is put on. Around the seams.

D: Hell no! It's stronger there than anywhere else. It's double thickness there on the seam.

B: Maybe it's only apparently stronger there. If you cut along the outside edge at least you wouldn't get the cutter all dirty. . . . And no filings could drop into the food either.

E: (*At the blackboard.*) Let's see. The seam in a can looks like this . . . double where the two layers of metal are rolled over. If we just cut into the first layer and peeled it back. . . .

B: You know that's not bad. If you did that then you'd have a top that could be put back on. It would be larger than the diameter of the can itself.

A: Not only that, but the top couldn't fall back into the can. Wouldn't need magnets the way they have them on the models I've seen. Just pick the top off the can.[5]

This extract has illustrated the use of direct and symbolic analogy in the enhancement of creative activity as well as the general character of synectic group activity.

However intriguing the synectics approach may be, it is important to realize that it has not been scientifically validated. Such evidence could be attained easily, and it is surprising that this has not been done. But regardless of its ultimate validity, what synectics does illustrate is the possibility of approaching the extension of a normal human function beyond its usual level in the context of normal human activities. As such, it represents an important model that is both contemporary and pertinent to long-range human concerns. It suggests something of the atmosphere and interests that are necessary if we are to progress beyond our present scientific stalemate in relation to human potential in this and the other areas that have been reviewed.

CHAPTER TWELVE

The Extension of
Human Development

With the exception of research into creativity, the studies with which we have been dealing have interpreted "changing human behavior" to mean either the correction of deviant or the manipulation of normal behavior. Doubtless both of these areas are important and functional, but they do not exhaust the possible meanings of the term "behavior change."

Clearly, it would be desirable to restore all mentally ill persons to the community so that they could function in an approximately normal manner, just as it would be desirable to find a cure for cancer. But society can continue functioning without either of these discoveries being made and will probably be very little more creative when they are.

Studies that add to our ability to manipulate each other will certainly have great economic and political value, but their net effect may only be to threaten freedom of action. It is necessary to pursue this kind of research, but the results at best will keep us strong and at worst make us even more vulnerable than we are to special-interest groups who might use such knowledge to control us.

In contrast to these areas of research, studies of how to aid the normal person to function beyond his present levels would be beneficial to the person himself, others around him, and, ultimately, to the whole social order of which he is a part. It is curious that scientists should have left such a vital area of investigation to those who do not pursue it objectively. This tendency constitutes an important and possibly disastrous oversight. The only reasonable basis for it would be the belief that the normal person functioning with reasonable success in society represents the full development of human potential. If this were true, then there would, of course, be little reason to attempt to extend the limits or nature of his current performance. However, behavioral scientists themselves have provided clear evidence that such is not the case.

Studies of Deprivation of Needs

One of the traditional ways psychologists study basic needs, such as those for food, water, and sleep, is through the systematic deprivation of these necessities from animal and human subjects. Scientists have not been primarily interested in the potential limits of human endurance, but rather in the strength and influence of the motivations involved. However, such studies have clearly indicated that, with the exception of such vital functions as breathing and heartbeat, normal human patterns can be violated with relatively little difficulty unless an alteration is carried to extremes.

For example, during World War II experiments were conducted, using conscientious objectors who volunteered, to test the effects of an extremely limited diet for a three months' period.[1] During this time, the men's weight dropped about 25 per cent from their starting weight, but even under these conditions of semistarvation no deterioration in intelligence was noted.

Studies in which subjects were deprived of sleep suggest that the human ability to tolerate long periods of wakefulness is much greater than has been assumed. In one investigation, for example, a subject was kept awake for nine days.[2] The fact that his behavior became disorganized toward the end of the experiment is scarcely surprising. What is noteworthy is that he was able to stay awake for that length of time at all, when the average person feels out of sorts if he misses an hour or two of his normal sleep for one night.

Cultural Differences of Behavior

Anthropologists have made us only too aware of the adaptability of the sex drive to social requirements by their studies of comparative cultures. In various societies the structure of marriage ranges from monogamy to polygamy and polyandry. Standards of premarital and marital sexual behavior vary widely in terms of social tolerance and specificity of actions. Thus, human behavior is flexible even in regard to functions crucial for the survival of the individual or of the species, and in special instances vital behavior, such as sexual activity, may be suspended altogether—as in the members of certain religious orders—without apparent harm to the person.

With functions such as cognitions, perceptions, and emotions, the differences produced by cultural influence among persons raised in different societies become more pervasive and subtle. The conceptual systems of cultures are to some extent nontranslatable, so that the same events have different meanings to members of varying cultures. Perhaps the most dramatic illustration of this fact is provided by *projective instruments* such as the Rorschach ink-blot test. These tests use only nonverbal stimuli, such as blocks or pictures, and are, therefore, easily administered in different settings. They indicate that, despite individual human variation, cultural influences are so pervasive that a Rorschach protocol can be identified with a given culture, regardless of the personality pattern of the particular individual who has taken the test.

One's social heritage is so important that all aspects of human behavior can be shown to depend upon it. Anthropologists devote a great deal of effort to documenting this relationship. They have shown that different cultures produce different types of personality, arts, ethical beliefs, and philosophies. What they fail to appreciate, because of their own professional predispositions, is the implication of this array of evidence. What is impressive is not so much the impact of society on human development, but rather the implications for human potentiality that these conclusions suggest.

All persons are conceived in the same manner and grow during the first nine months of their existence according to a remarkably regular pattern. Most research indicates that the genetic endowments of members of different societies is remarkably similar, though such studies are technically difficult to perform. If this is true, then the numberless individuals going through the routine operations of the day— these relatively dull creatures with mass-oriented amusements and mechanized employment—could have been entirely different people, engaged in other activities, holding diametrically opposed beliefs with equal conviction and perhaps greater proficiency. Overt actions are largely the result of being born into a given society.

Intellectually, this is quite an acceptable notion, but on a more fundamental level of awareness it is hard to accept, since we have lived with ourselves so long and have come to accept the patterns that constitute our existence as somehow inevitable. Nevertheless, one of the clearest scientific conclusions in the social sciences is that the potential flexibility of human behavior is truly incredible.

At the same time, however, social scientists also find that it is in a society's interest to make routine whatever patterns it helps to develop. In that way a relatively high degree of predictability of the social behavior of those who compose the society is possible, thus enhancing the efficient functioning of the social order. Within a culture, the conformity of its members is impressive, but when we compare cultures, we are struck by their diversity. Adults are not ordinarily able to make the great transition from one culture to another, because of the hold their own society has upon them. Nevertheless, research in the social sciences, particularly anthropology, clearly suggests that such cultural transformations might be possible if they are begun early enough in the individual's life. The process by which one learns to take on the attributes of a new culture cannot be very different from those involved in psychotherapy or human-relations training, whose ends differ only in the extent of the change intended and in the degree of cultural acceptability of this change.

However, even if fundamental alterations in adult cultural identification could be created or induced, they would, in the end, merely resemble the stereotyped characteristics of another culture group. The demonstration would be impressive, but the ends would not seem to justify the effort.

These observations suggest an important distinction between natural variation produced by differing cultural influences and the enhancement of function, regardless of cultural conditions. The latter possibility requires a positive demonstration of new levels of human performance that are directly produced in a given culture, rather than an indirect conclusion derived from culturally determined individual differences. Even studies of physiological limitations are indirect in this sense. They only document the extent to which one places artificial constraints on one's own performance in that sphere, rather than offering methods for extending the levels of that performance. However, even at face value, these studies suggest that individuals rarely push themselves to their own limits—a fact of which we are all aware from personal experience and from the accounts of those who have been forced by circumstance to extreme efforts.

The Realization of Human Potential

It is not unusual to leave the whole question of the range of human potentiality in the hands of science-fiction writers, who have no difficulty in imagining all kinds of extensions of normal levels of behavior and experience. While many of their speculations are wild, others such as the space ship have come true. However, psychologically, a curiously stilted view of human nature seems to inform their imaginative projections of human experience. However fantastic the situation and however great the abilities of the individual, he nevertheless is usually recognizable as an ordinary person with unusual powers in an unparalleled situation. These writers basically cannot imagine people any different than they are, except in terms of an increase of relatively familiar attributes, such as strength or intellect.

Yet the possibility of a fundamental transformation of human personality must also be considered, since it provides the most natural extension of the present discussion. There are certainly precedents in all the great religions for just such an occurrence. The lives of Jesus, Buddha, Mohammed—if they are considered to have been men when they were born—and, even more clearly, many of the saints, whose life histories are less encrusted with myth, document just such a fundamental alteration of human behavior and activity.

The reports of these lives must be examined to determine whether, after these individuals were enlightened, reborn, or whatever the appropriate religious term may be, they in fact functioned in a different manner due to some fundamental change within them. Naturally, the religious would believe such to be the case. Divinity, or a superhuman status, is usually ascribed to the founders, saints and heroes of religions. Unfortunately, these figures are found only in history. It is difficult to identify them while they are alive from the host of lesser men who imitate and compete with them. But we cannot afford the luxury of ignoring these examples, even though scientific predilections might lead us in another direction.

It is not a question of the efficacy of religious belief that is important, but rather the implications for human potentiality suggested by the changes that have been documented in persons who have believed. It is claimed that such alterations in behavior range from moral reformation to a change in world concept and basic personality structure. And the evidence is rich enough to merit careful review in the search for reliable data concerning the paths and procedures that may lead beyond the state of experience we generally describe by the somewhat misleading term "normal" to one that is more general, rich, and objective.

Thus, a variety of evidence—studies of the effects of drugs and hypnotism, anthropological investigation of cultures, investigation into the causes of creativity, biographical data of religious leaders, and experiments in physiological limits—suggests very clearly that for brief periods of time, under suitable pressures and motivations, humans are capable of freeing themselves from existing limitations and attaining higher levels of performance. The precise means of attainment does not have to be demonstrated in order to establish the possibility of the event. Graphic evidence exists that the normal man uses only a small portion of his abilities and performs in a relatively inefficient manner.

This unhappy statement might represent the conclusion of this volume, but it can also be a new point of departure for a somewhat different kind of analysis.

It would be naïve to suppose that men have ignored their own inherent potential and made no attempts to utilize or extend it, even though science has been mute on this issue. Methods have been developed, more fully and over a longer period of time in certain Far Eastern countries than in the West, but well-established traditions exist in both cultures. In the next two chapters some of the principles upon which these procedures are based will be examined briefly to determine whether they seem to provide any aid in the formulation of a scientific approach to the problem.

CHAPTER THIRTEEN

Eastern Religions
and Philosophies

Most Western people view Eastern religions and philosophies with pity, reserve, distaste, or suspicion. Those who do not, accept these often strange beliefs uncritically and with inappropriate enthusiasm.

These reactions have justification, but all of them are irrelevant to the present subject. The only question that interests us here is whether, buried in the strata of religious heritage, there are methods that enable men to reach higher levels of development than would ordinarily be available to them. If such levels are attainable in an orderly and understandable manner, the act of reaching them should be scientifically verifiable. If such verification is not possible, the speculations and beliefs will be disregarded, regardless of whether they may happen to attract or repel us.

This approach is easy to state but hard to adhere to, since the one viewpoint that has not characterized Eastern philosophy and religion is the scientific one—philosophy, theology, personal experience, mysticism, even politics, but not the objective canons of the scientific method.

The Types of Eastern Religion

It is best to admit at the start that one can speak of Eastern religions and philosophies only in very global terms. In actuality, the Far

Eastern countries have given birth to a startling number of religious and philosophical schools that have differed on a variety of criteria but shared a common concern with the general issue of extending the limits of human potential. In some of these systems this theme is obvious. In Japanese Zen Buddhism, for example, the objective is to attain a direct experience of enlightenment. In other religions, the central direction is buried under centuries of religious dogma and philosophical decay. One must excavate to find the living core.

To the specialist, any attempt to discuss the contribution of Eastern thought and practice to the area of changing human behavior would seem naïve and ludicrous. The subject matter is vast, technical, and obscured by language and cultural barriers. Nevertheless, the task is not impossible, because others have faced the problem before and attempted over-all syntheses or looked for recurrent themes in systems as different as Yoga, Taoism, Sufism, and Zen.

Indian *Yoga* consists of a set of systems of exercises designed to aid the aspirant in identifying with, or "yoking" himself to, the divine. Four major systems of Yoga are commonly identified: Bhakti (love), Hatha (bodily control), Raja (control of thought), and Jnana (philosophic insight). The lesser known approach of Shakti, or Kundalini, Yoga utilizes direct work with spiritual energy. These methods are designed for persons of different types and collectively represent a set of procedures and principles of great generality and flexibility.

Chinese *Taoism* emphasizes simplicity, intuition, and the attainment of profound understanding through the development of an ability to perceive "Tao," the primal cause, in the midst of everyday phenomena.

Japanese *Zen Buddhism* has many of the same characteristics as Taoism. It differs chiefly in the greater intensity of its approach and the development of a series of training procedures designed to facilitate the attainment of insight and enlightenment.

Finally, Persian *Sufism* is a lyric form of mysticism in which the aspirant views God as an idealized beloved, much in the spirit of Bhakti Yoga.

The recurrent theme in Eastern thought is human perfectibility. This central concept integrates philosophy, religion, and psychology as alternate and concurrent paths by which men seek to promote their inner growth and to attain new levels of experience and perfection.

146

The view that these activities are distinct and pursued for different ends is only a recent Western development.

Human Development as a Standard of Attainment

Teachers of Eastern religions have always held human development as their standard of attainment. Ideas, beliefs, and the understanding of human nature are not taken as ends in themselves, but only sought to the extent that growth can be achieved through such knowledge. Deviations from this central theme have generally led to the decay of religious life and the foundation of new religious movements designed to correct this condition.

This general approach is seen very clearly in the life and teachings of the great Indian Saint Gautama Buddha, who founded Buddhism in the 6th century before Christ. He did not argue about beliefs in gods; in fact, he did not stress the need for such belief, nor was he engaged in an objective analysis of human values and behavior. His message was very simple. The human condition is one surrounded by fear, disease, and death; the wise man, realizing his situation, looks for a way to resolve it. Toward this end, Buddha gave his message, but always in the context of showing the path to a new kind of existence on which he had traveled himself.

From our viewpoint, the particular context of the message is less important than the assumption that the experience of liberation from the human condition, which it describes, could be attained following a known path. Whether one believes in the religion or not, the path itself has its own intrinsic validity. It either guides one to greater objectivity and understanding or it does not. These are matters that can be tested if the nature of the path is clear enough to be viewed as an experimental procedure.

The nature of human potential is itself a thorny problem. It is not entirely obvious how men might evolve if such a possibility actually exists. Most of the alternatives that occur to us consist of merely improving on what we already have, such as creating in people more intelligence, greater emotional balance, improved physical health, and the like. But would this really be enough, and are its implications fully clear? Many Eastern systems describe quite different possibilities.

Perhaps the most striking and important characteristic of the evolved man in Eastern religions is that he has ceased to exist as a personality. He has, as it were, extended the potentialities of his individual nature to become more universal and more objective, almost superhuman. Of all changes that one can easily imagine, this is the most fundamental. It does not affect the perception of events but the perceiver. In one sense, there is a god-like quality about this characteristic. From a slightly different point of view, this development approaches the goal of the scientist who attempts by all the means at his disposal to prevent subjective and personal influence from biasing his work.

As a corollary to the above state, the individual is able to manifest a variety of powers that were very rare or nonexistent in his previous state; that is, he is able to perform miracles. Regardless of how one interprets these claims, whether as realistic events or subjective experiences, they are made so universally that they cannot be ignored.

Attainment of a superhuman state is not the matter of a minor personal commitment. It requires, as T. S. Eliot has said in his *Four Quartets*, "nothing less than everything." It is one of the paradoxes of this condition that in order to become universal in scope the individual has to surrender his own existence to what is called God, Atman, or simply the void. Thus, the part of a man that would have felt pride in such an attainment has to die before the change is actually wrought.

This rather summary description can scarcely do justice to the complexity of the literature dealing with these matters, but it is sufficient to indicate that these systems, whether Yoga, Sufism, Buddhism, or Taoism, are not engaged in the mere improvement of human virtue as it is usually defined. Believers in them attempt to produce a fundamental reorientation in their natures. The religions are, therefore, viewed by their adherents as paths to the further evolution of human experience, to a condition that is as different from man as man is from the animals.

It must be emphasized that these goals do not characterize all Eastern religious systems. That would be an enormous simplification, but they do represent certain recurrent tendencies that can be traced through most of them. These goals are interesting intellectually and worthy of further analysis in their own right, but they do not by themselves change anybody in any way. They only represent a beacon toward which efforts might be directed, if we knew what to do.

The central issue is whether these systems also provide methods that enable an individual or a group of individuals to achieve the goals

148

that have been described. This question cannot be answered directly since scientists have never seriously explored this problem.

Some Techniques of Eastern Religions

Certain preliminary generalizations can, however, be made before examining any particular system of Eastern religion. First, to achieve any substantial development, a tremendous amount of work is necessary. There is apparently no shortcut to paradise. The story of the great twelfth-century Tibetan saint, Milarepa, is typical. He was told by his teacher to build a house. After many months he was finished. His teacher then told him to take it down. When that was done, he was told to build it up again. This cycle was repeated several times. In this way, his teacher tested the firmness of his resolution and brought his work to a pitch of intensity that enabled him to attain the growth that he desired.

Second, work by oneself without the guidance of a person who has in fact himself extended his faculties is not productive. A teacher is necessary. It is not only the ignorance of the aspirant that will prevent his success when working alone, though certain kinds of knowledge are viewed as essential. Of even greater importance is the need for guidance from an impartial but benevolent source who can detect just those areas and issues that the individual would avoid.

Third, the nature of the work, whatever its specific content, is difficult and painful in the sense that it goes against the natural tendencies of the person. The individual grows by opposing himself. The teacher functions in part to create the right kind of obstacles or to show how the ones that already exist can be attacked.

Fourth, at some point complete surrender of individual effort is required. He must recognize his own helplessness and ask for guidance from his teacher or from some great spiritual source.

Fifth, the process of work is gradual, though the rate of development at different times may vary greatly. As successive stages are passed, new methods may be required; what is useful during one stage may be harmful at another.

These five principles are sharply reminiscent of many of the psychological processes with which we have dealt. Certainly, modern insight psychotherapies stress the need for difficult work under the guidance of a healer who helps the person to face those situations and aspects of his self that he seeks to avoid. It is not surprising that the same principles seem to hold in very general form, since the process of growth must have certain common denominators, regardless of the point from which one starts.

Certain psychotherapists have been struck by this resemblance. Recently, the psychologist Edward Maupin has discussed the relation of Zen Buddhism to western psychotherapy.[1] That such a discussion is even possible suggests a loosening of taboos against the study of religion and mysticism among professional psychologists, which is in itself a hopeful sign. Naturally, in such a presentation, it is necessary to go to some pains to relate familiar psychotherapeutic approaches to the relatively unknown character of Zen Buddhism. Of particular interest to us is the discussion of the general process of Zen training and also the specific techniques employed to attain an experience of enlightenment. Zen can be seen as representing the most highly purified of ancient Eastern traditions and is, therefore, a convenient point of departure.

Zen training occupies many years, perhaps decades. In a sense, it is perpetual. The techniques that are employed will be described shortly. However, regardless of the particular procedures to which the Zen aspirant is subjected by the master with whom he studies, three stages of development can be distinguished. In the first phase, the individual practices some form of concentration, gradually attaining a sense of relaxation and self-immersion. However, when this is attained, thoughts and feelings begin to arise that disturb the tranquility of the state. It is probable that most of the recorded Zen exercises are designed to facilitate the development of this first phase of self-immersion.

After a suitable time has elapsed, if the individual can accept these disturbances calmly, his concentration becomes effortless and he is possessed by a feeling of quiet power. In this stage the individual is in great danger. The very freedom that he has gained makes him the potential prey of various illusions, including a desire to withdraw from social contact, ecstatic feelings, or attack by what Zen students call demons, which are more reasonably thought of as personalized forces opposing the kind of growth produced by the Zen exercises. These conflicts, temptations, and doubts grow to a point of great intensity in which the subject finally and completely recognizes his inability to solve them. At this point, if he abandons all hope, he may attain the experience of enlightenment called *Satori,* which enables him to integrate and resolves all his former doubts and experiences within one unified and universal conception of himself and the world in which he lives. This is not a permanent enlightenment; the experience must be repeated, but the general level of his existence is slowly raised. In the future, less effort is required to get to the same level. This is the Zen pathway, and schematically it is typical of many other Eastern systems, though it does not utilize the full array of exercises and elaborate analysis of developmental stages described elsewhere. In fact, religious and mystical writings of all countries contain many accounts that seem very close to the Zen sequence, regardless of the tradition involved or the country of residence of the individual. What is remarkable about Zen Buddhism is not so much the outcome, but the use of a systematic training procedure to attain it.

Zen masters have invented various original means to facilitate this general process, the best known of which is the *Koan*. A Koan is a logical impossibility that the student is asked to solve, such as "what is the sound of one hand clapping?" There is no reasonable answer to the Koan. The only possible solution requires a new form of consciousness that resolves the logical contradiction in some greater perceptual unity. By concentrating on these Koans to the exclusion of all other matters, the student may bring himself to a pitch of intensity in which his own limited self and personality are blotted out long enough to permit Satori. There is a tendency to equate the use of Koans with Zen; this, however, is incorrect. Zen existed before Koans were employed. It is more clearly viewed as relaxation coupled with vigilant detachment. A similar attempt to reach this state can be traced throughout Buddhism, in certain forms of Yoga, and in Taoism.

The main aspects of Zen training, as they have been described, have certain similarities to Western therapies that emphasize relaxation training and even more directly resemble insight therapies emphasizing spontaneity and free association of inner experiences. These similarities are certainly interesting, since they represent independent developments and thus provide indirect confirmation of each other. But while psychotherapy and Eastern religious processes share the common aim of human growth, the point along the continuum at which they aim is quite different. This, in turn, affects the nature of the effort they require of the participant.

The minister Alan Watts has devoted many years to the analysis and interpretation of Eastern systems from a Western viewpoint. He has recently summarized his thinking in the book *Psychotherapy: East and West*.[2] His conclusion, based on an extensive examination of original sources, is that most Eastern systems of personal development are designed to undo the ill effects society has upon the individual. He argues that the human ego, far from being at war with society, is actually created by it. Society fosters socialization processes that encourage in us the notion that we are distinct individuals. Once this concept is firmly embedded, society can exist as the structure within which individuals perform their ascribed tasks. However, it depends on the availability of individuals who are convinced of their own separate existence, just as a play depends on the availability of actors who are willing to act the assigned parts. Thus society creates the illusion of diversity so that the characters it requires for its existence will be available. It is the task of religions and other systems of development to undo this work, so that the individual becomes free of such illusions and is able to experience the inherent objectivity and universality with which, in a sense, he was born.

The discipline of Zen and psychoanalysis share the common characteristic of allowing the individual to lose himself, redefine his boundaries, and come to grips with buried and rejected aspects of his experience. This process is greatly facilitated by the existence of a socially sanctioned figure (Zen master, psychoanalyst) who is surrounded by situational, physical, and social marks of authority and wisdom. All of these sanctions, however, are employed, not to force the individual into accustomed patterns, but to force him from these patterns to new experiences and relationships. Thus, the therapeutic and spiritual teaching relationship turns society against itself to help the individual regain some more general and fundamental sense of himself and his basic potential.

All of the preceding is suggestive and integrative, but it is not scientific. It can at best be viewed as establishing underlying points of similarity. The crucial question from our viewpoint is not how the processes and systems are to be classified and related to our own, but whether they work.

Here science stands mute as a timid sphinx. Behavioral scientists have not seen fit to determine whether the physical postures, controlled breathing, and mental exercises that are described by Eastern systems do, in fact, produce dependable and important results beneficial to the individual who practices them.

There are a few exceptions to this general situation. Several doctoral theses have been devoted to physiological studies of the effects of Hatha Yoga, a system of exercises designed to help the student gain complete control over all body functions. Anthropologists have given some attention to the description of Eastern religious practices, but their interest is comparative rather than in an experimental verification of their effectiveness. Thus, the scientific studies that do exist are either irrelevant to the subject of changing behavior or trivial. A vast realm of human experience has been bypassed and ignored, though it purports to deal with the enhancement of human function and the fundamental alteration of human behavior.

In each of the Eastern religious systems that have come down to us, there are endless numbers of practical exercises embedded in mystical and theological writings. The efficacy of each of these can be tested by scientific methods. In view of the desirability of the fruits these techniques are intended to produce—varying from the improvement of health to the creation of wisdom—it is incredible that such experiments have been so studiously avoided.

It is difficult for one who is not familiar with these systems to believe in the richness of practical methods that they contain. The difficult bodily postures of Hatha Yoga are widely known. They are, however, analogous to training procedures that characterize other forms of Yoga, each of which is actually a collection of exercises of progressive difficulty for different types of persons seeking to develop themselves. The best way to describe them is through example.

One of the most fundamental exercises of Buddhism, "the setting up of mindfulness," provides a direct insight into the character of the effort that is typically involved.

> Let a brother, going into the forest, or to the roots of a tree, or to an empty chamber, sit down cross-legged, holding the body erect, and set his mindfulness alert.
> Mindful let him inhale, mindful let him exhale. Whether he inhales a long breath, let him be conscious thereof; or whether he exhales a long breath, let him be conscious thereof . . . Let him practice with the thought: "Conscious of my whole body will I inhale." Let him practice with the thought: "Conscious of my whole body will I exhale."

Let him practice with the thought: "I will inhale tranquilizing my bodily organism"; let him practice with the thought: "I will exhale tranquilizing my bodily organism."

. . . And moreover a brother, when he is walking, is aware of it thus: "I walk"; or when he is standing, or sitting, or lying down, he is aware of it . . . whether he departs or returns, whether he looks at or looks away from, whether he has drawn in or stretched out his limbs, whether he has donned underrobe, overrobe, or bowl, whether he is eating, drinking, chewing, reposing, or whether he is obeying the calls of nature—is aware of what he is about. In going, standing, sitting, sleeping, watching, talking, or keeping silence, he knows what he is doing.[3]

There are no intrinsic difficulties in measuring the effects of this exercise on the extension of self-awareness, on the character, personality, physical state, and social adjustment of the individual who practices it. It is accessible to scientific investigation.

Another exercise derived from Yoga has a slight, though suggestive, resemblance to certain psychoanalytic techniques. It is called a meditation on the past. The individual attempts before going to sleep at night to review in reverse as objectively and vividly as possible the events that occurred during the day. He continues this process through the dreams of the previous night until he completes the twenty-four-hour cycle and has returned in his memory to the time when he last performed the same exercise. He makes every effort to look at his actions and motives in the detached manner of an impartial observer. This exercise is intended to improve the character of those who practice it by helping them evaluate their own actions. It also is supposed to have the much more interesting effect of beginning to intrude into the day's activity. At these times, it is as if every day's experience becomes the memory of a larger mind in whom the world and the individual are all interwoven in some greater whole. The exercise presumably has direct effects on the individual in terms of reducing his anxiety and increasing his empathic understanding. These effects could certainly be detected by current testing methods.

Eastern systems of enlightenment contain a vast collection of such practical procedures that are designed to improve, elevate, and evolve men to higher levels of performance and being. These methods have the stamp of historical validation, that is, they have been used over long periods of time with subjectively reported success. This, of course, proves nothing about their objective effects or whether they produce the changes that are attributed to them. Nevertheless, any reasonable scientific strategy would suggest that these processes are worthy of investigation, since they represent the crystallized heritage of the efforts of countless men, known and unknown, who have left them to us as a precious, though objectively untested, legacy.

CHAPTER FOURTEEN

Western Religions
and Philosophies

As in all religions, the literature of Western mysticism is obscured by the theological framework within which it has been developed. Thus, the evangelical and messianic tradition of Christianity may account for its unique position among the world's religions, but it does little to encourage a more objective and scientific evaluation of the methods by which Christian mystics have proposed to attain higher states.

Nevertheless, a more careful reading of the religious writings of the West—Christian, Hebraic, and Moslem—reveals a concern and interest with the development of man's potential similar to that of the Eastern religions.

The four Gospels, for example, can be viewed as a poetic historical record of the possibility of the further development and evolution of humanity. We do not customarily think of them in those terms, because the religious experience that is described has become so overlaid with historical accretions that this emphasis is obscured. If one can put aside the associations with this material to which one has been culturally conditioned, it becomes more evident that Christ had a central purpose, which was not very different from that of Gautama Buddha: showing men a path out of the wilderness of the world. The idea of Christian salvation is easily viewed as a theological equivalent of the fulfillment of man's inner potential. We are led by the urgency with which the message is presented to overlook its psychological implications. If one views the Gospels in a psychological rather than a religious context, they can be interpreted as a vast drama portraying the conflicts, temptations, and possibilities inherent in the human situation. Christ's teachings and life point the way to those who wish to evolve. The unique characteristic of the Gospels is their unremitting emphasis on the need for change and the countless indications through parables and example how this change is to be produced. A more fully developed exposition of this viewpoint is given in *The New Man* by the English physician Maurice Nicoll.[1]

The Old Testament and the Koran are less clearly focused on this one theme, but both are deeply involved in the issue of how men should act in order to be true to their own higher nature and to God, their creator. The prophets are quite explicit about this problem. The various parables of the Old Testament, including the Garden of Eden, the Tower of Babel, and the Flood are still relevant today as summaries of the human conditions and diagnoses of the difficulties that must be resolved.

It is, unfortunately, difficult to separate the psychological elements from the historical when dealing with religions that are close to our own tradition. Further, religions have a way of contradicting their founder. Buddha, who specifically said that he should not be worshiped, is now worshiped by millions. Christ, who came to lead a few to heaven ("many are called but few are chosen"), is worshiped hopefully by hordes around the world. The peaceful message is utilized to justify war. Such ironic reversals of intent characterize all human intellection and are in no way uniquely associated with religious institutions.

The central point is that each of these religions was intended to transform the individual. Men were to be guided by procedures that were sometimes written down and sometimes transmitted verbally by teachers who undertook to train others in what was called the religious life.

Most of the Western religious leaders were also mystics. It is in the writings and lives of these great mystics that one finds the clearest indication of the procedures that were utilized to help the aspirant attain greater universality and objectivity.

The greatest stumbling block to a serious evaluation of the methods employed by Western mystics is that the ends to which they were directed do not seem as acceptable as those found in many Eastern paths. Since this point is not obvious some explanation is necessary.

In the higher forms of many Eastern religions, God either is viewed as impersonal, very much like some universal higher form of energy that physicists might study, or he is not even mentioned, as in the early forms of Buddhism. In Western traditions, God is more personal. One can only worship him as a great father and work toward becoming a saint, or the child of a personalized god. There is no doubt that such an approach exerts a tremendous appeal, but it is bound not to satisfy those who prefer a more scientific orientation, who do not find that a belief in a personal god, with assorted prophets and a son, is meaningful to them. In such a situation one tends to discard the theological trappings of the tradition along with the tradition itself. This could, however, be a serious error. The Christian saints and mystics were striving toward self-improvement, and in the course of their lifelong efforts developed and passed on methods for achieving this goal. These methods, like those of Eastern religions, may be potent irrespective of the climate in which they evolved. We shall, therefore, bypass the question of the existence of God, heaven, hell, and all of the beliefs with which religions are encrusted and examine the methods of human enhancement connected with them.

Unfortunately, as in writings on psychotherapy, there is a much greater attempt to describe philosophy and belief than there is to describe actual procedures in the writings of many saints and mystics. There are, however, some notable exceptions. Before discussing them, it is helpful to establish links among Western mysticism, Eastern religions, and modern techniques of psychotherapy.

The Similarity between Eastern and Western Religious Tradition

First, there is again a common belief that a great amount of effort is necessary to attain any real growth or change in the human condition. St. Augustine states: "If thou shouldst say, 'It is enough, I have reached perfection,' all is lost. For it is the function of perfection to make one know one's imperfection." [2] Or, even more explicitly, the words of Meister Eckhart, the great German medieval philosopher and mystic: "I tell you that no one can experience this birth . . . without a mighty effort." [3]

Second, the need for a teacher and guide, while recognized, is treated less directly in Western religions than in other traditions. The existence and the structure of the church is intended to aid the individual. More particularly the minister, rabbi, or priest is officially the guide and intermediary, though particular sects may eliminate this function and emphasize the direct relation of man to God. In the East, this tradition is very clear. The teacher is the path, the representative of the aspirant's hope of attainment, to be treated with awe and respect, held in greater reverence than one's parents. A similar tradition is found in the West only within religious orders in which the rule of obedience to superiors approaches the absolute and in certain sects such as the Chasidic Jews. While this arrangement is meant to humble the spirit, it also is built on the assumption that those in charge are wiser.

The third common theme is the emphasis on the need for work that is difficult, because it goes against the natural tendency of the individual. This has been described by the seventeenth-century French prelate François Fénelon in a manner that is strongly reminiscent of the previous description of Zen procedures.

> The first step, then, is for the soul to put away outward things and look within so as to know its own real interest; so far all is right and natural; this much is only a wise self-love which seeks to avoid the intoxication of the world.
>
> In the next step, the soul must add the contemplation of God, whom it fears, to that of self. This is a faint approach to the real wisdom, but the soul is still greatly self-absorbed; it is not satisfied with fearing God; it wants to be certain that it does fear him and fears lest it fear him not, going round in a perpetual circle of self-consciousness. All this restless dwelling on self is very far from the peace and freedom of real love; but that is yet in the distance; the soul must needs go through a season of trial, and were it suddenly plunged into a state of rest, it would not know how to use it.
>
> The third step is that, ceasing from a restless self-contemplation, the soul begins to dwell upon God instead, and by degrees forgets itself in Him. It becomes full of Him and ceases to feed upon self. Such a soul is not blinded to its own faults or indifferent to its own errors; it is more conscious of them than ever, and increased light shows them in plainer form, but this self-knowledge comes from God, and therefore it is not restless or uneasy.[4]

Finally, the need for complete surrender of self is very prominent in Western religious writings. When St. Ignatius Loyola, the sixteenth-century Christian mystic, was asked what he would do if the Pope suppressed the order that he had founded, Loyola replied that he would need a quarter of an hour for prayer and after that he would think no more about it. Saint John of the Cross, who lived in the sixteenth century, put the matter simply: "The fitting disposition for union with God is not that the soul should understand, feel, taste or imagine anything on the subject of the nature of God or any other thing whatever, but should remain in the pureness and love which is perfect resignation and complete detachment from all things save God alone." [5]

Thus, while language and theology may differ, Eastern and Western traditions share certain basic concepts of the enhancement of human experience and how to attain it. This underlying agreement is not surprising, since common goals are being pursued, but it is important to make it explicit so that the generality of the religious experience is fully appreciated. This emphasis is a particularly needed antidote in an age in which the scientific model of man is a rat and a computer.

The similarity between Eastern and Western traditions does not end with general principles but can be carried into the area of the training procedures employed. While they were generally developed in greater detail and at an earlier time in the East, they certainly have their Western counterparts.

St. Ignatius Loyola developed a well-known handbook of exercises for aspirants and members of the religious order he founded. They are, in a sense, designed to turn the practitioner into a holy man. These exercises were particularly widespread in monasteries during the early years of the Counter Reformation, but in various forms they have existed throughout religious history as an integral part of worship. Prayer, fasting, performing good deeds, and many of the other traditional marks of the religious life are actually training devices and best understood in that light. Similarly, traditional church services, whatever their social implications, are intended as powerful aids in the maintenance of proper attitudes, beliefs, and aspirations in regard to the growing improvement and purification of human experience.

These training devices are too familiar to be seen in their intended perspective. Those that are somewhat removed from us are easier to appraise. For example, one of the oldest and most widely recommended exercises of early Christianity involves the utilization of a sacred word as a shield against evil or threatening influences. In the remarkable volume *The Cloud of Unknowing* the following comment on this exercise is made:

The word shall be thy shield and thy spear, whether thou ridest on peace or on war. With this word thou shalt beat on this cloud and this darkness about thee. With this word thou shalt smite down all manner of thought under the cloud of forgetting. In so much that, if any thought press upon thee to ask what thou wouldst have, answer with no more words than with this one word. And if he offer of his great learning to expound to thee that word, say to him that thou wilt have it all whole, and not broken nor undone. And if thou wilt hold fast to this purpose, be sure that that thought will no while bide.[6]

Behind the poetic and biblical quality of the writing hides a simple but powerful idea. The best defense against difficulties is to cling to a stronger symbol. However, it is not the meaning or the implication of the exercise that is important, but whether it has any demonstrable effects. Does such an action increase the assurance of the individual who practices it? Does it enable him to behave more calmly in crisis and view situations more dispassionately? Modern scientific methods are designed to answer this question, even though the experimental psychologist and the religious leader might be horrified at the idea.

Modern Views of Mysticism

One of the major stumbling blocks to a psychologically oriented science of religion has been the widespread belief among many scientists who were themselves nonbelievers that religion was dysfunctional and that mysticism was either an escape from the realities of life or a dangerous area of experience, replete with illusions and unnatural unconscious regression. It belonged, they believed, most properly to the historians, since religion and mysticism were developed in a prescientific era.

Even the Church has not always looked kindly on the experience of potential saints and their reported miracles, taking the longer more pedestrian view of all bureaucrats, who must be concerned as much with the implication of events for their organization, as with their intrinsic validity.

The issue that must be faced is the utility of saintliness. In one sense, any unusual development is dysfunctional, since the social system within which the individual lives is geared to the maintenance of a homeostatic condition. Any individual or group change may require a readjustment of the entire community. In this sense, a genius and an insane person both place stress on those around them, though the social implications of their activities are quite different. A prophet or a saint is not necessarily easy to live with or to have as a neighbor. He may upset the social organization of which he is a part and even found a new one. It is only in historical perspective that we can gain some sense of the validity of his actions.

However, it is very difficult to prove or disprove the value of religious systems by historical records, since contradictory versions of any particular event can always be found. Further, the beliefs that are accepted unquestioningly in one time and place are viewed with suspicion and ridicule in another. No one has ever been convinced of the relative merits of religions solely by logical argument, since this area of experience is extremely personal. What then remains but the right of the individual to define his own beliefs? The answer would seem to be that at a certain level these experiences and the methods that have been designed to facilitate them can be evaluated by the procedures and standards of controlled scientific assessment. In such an evaluation, judgment is traditionally suspended. It is for scientific study to determine whether the claims of religion to enhance human behavior are valid or misguided. If this approach were pursued, it would soon become clear that it is not so much the scientists who are resistant to it, since they suffer only from a limited perspective in their definition of scientific material, but the religious practitioners, who utilize these methods without ever subjecting them to impersonal appraisal. Whatever the source of difficulties, it should be possible to separate the practical from the theoretical, the living exercise from the mythic content, and to establish the nature of the effects involved. Such investigation would not undermine existing institutions any more than has already occurred, but it could place them in quite a different light.

To facilitate this process, it is helpful to reanalyze the nature of the condition mystic states are designed to foster. Mystic states can be characterized in very general terms as having four attributes. These include the creation of a new kind of understanding, an inability to describe the full nature of the mystic experience to other persons, a lack of permanency, and the induction of surrender or passivity in the recipient. It is true that these experiences have been sought as ends in themselves because of their intensity and unprecedented quality. A careful reading of the history of most religions with hardy survival power will, however, suggest that mystical experiences were not viewed as the end but rather the products of spiritual evolution. Where they became the ends, the experience itself tended to decline and decay. When viewed as steps toward greater understanding, compassion, and power they were accepted thankfully but without attachment to them.

Much of the negative modern reaction to mysticism, Eastern or Western, comes from an inappropriate search for experience as an end in itself, rather than for growth and understanding. Experience without growth becomes ever more personal and subjective; on the other hand, personal development bears fruit for many, since understanding can be described and transmitted, and the concomitants of human enhancement and growth are shared by all who are in contact with it, whether it takes the form of artistic fulfillment, scientific investigation, or the expansion and objectification of inner experience.

From this cursory review of Eastern and Western mysticism emerge recurrent themes among the practical methods used to expand consciousness and extend the limits of human behavior, even though the surrounding theories and beliefs may vary widely from each other. Thus, the practices of Western religious saints and mystics can be taken as further historical validation of the procedures advocated in the earlier Eastern traditions.

Finally, it must be emphasized that only an extremely limited review of the potential evidence has been possible. Even this, however, is sufficient to suggest the richness of the available material if one can view it with an impartial and uncommitted eye. Certainly the high ends toward which these methods are directed suggest the necessity for bringing them within the more traditional framework of scientific investigation, so that their vital core can, if it exists, be extracted.

Conclusion

F ROM the various sources that we have analyzed emerges a confused picture in which certain common trends can be found. It is confused in the sense that it has been obtained unsystematically, for a variety of different ends, with varying degrees of precision, and in different conceptual areas.

Among the common trends are first, that current scientific capabilities are sufficiently developed to provide the necessary base for research into ways to alter and enhance behavior. While improvements in methodology can be anticipated, one cannot attribute insufficient progress to a lack of proper instrumentation. Second, there is no dearth of theory in relation to a number of topics relating to such change, such as psychotherapy, group dynamics, and learning theory. Third, there is no lack of intriguing and important aspects of behavior-change research awaiting further investigation or original exploration.

If these conclusions are even partially correct, it is evident that something is quite wrong in the segment of the behavioral and social sciences to which they are directed. With a few notable exceptions, such as the study of the influence of communication procedures on attitude change, research devoted to changing human behavior has simply not achieved the importance or the scope to which it is entitled, because of the centrality of the topic and the practical implications of the findings.

This misapplication of priorities has many causes, ranging from scientific amorality to the system of differential rewards employed for different kinds of scientific investigations. Nevertheless, relevant work has been done within limited subareas of the general field. From this work, come glimmers of common findings.

For example, the conclusions about behavior change derived from small-group research into the effects of personal interaction have been duplicated in studies of attitude change and group therapy. Studies of a nondirective approach to change have been conducted in fields as diverse as group psychotherapy, individual psychotherapy, individual and group counseling, education, and small-group organization. The effects of faith can be traced in studies of psychotherapy, hypnotism, and psychopharmacology. To the extent that such common tendencies can be validated in quite different contexts, a unified scientific approach to the problem of changing behavior is possible.

However, another, quite different conclusion must also be drawn. Namely, the scientific community seems to have avoided any direct attempt to study the problem of behavior change and development except in its mechanistic and negative aspects. This book actually understates the problem, since it has called upon positive evidence that seems to have relevance, whether or not it was collected in a scientific environment.

When one concludes that a basic oversight has occurred, it is necessary to determine how this situation can be corrected. The first stage is the recognition of the problem. The second is to review alternative solutions. If it were possible for a substantial number of behavioral scientists to recognize the need, the problem would be solved quite easily. Monies would be assigned for research in this area and it would grow along with the other topics and subtopics that currently occupy psychologists and sociologists. But it would be naïve to suppose that this is what will happen, since the present situation is the outcome of forces that have determined the shape of current scientific investments.

Most advances are created by a few dedicated individuals who persuade others to join them in the mutual exploration of new territory. Leif Ericson did not lead an invasion. Magellan did not guide an armada. A few ships with courageous men of mixed motives were necessary, plus some dedicated dreamers who could not be convinced of the impracticality of their visions. However, the present situation is more complex, since there is no physical destination to reach. Rather, what is required is the systematization and reformulation of a field marked by chaotic minor adventures.

The simplest means of achieving this end is to visualize some enduring enterprise dedicated to the exploration of scientific studies of behavior change and development in the sense that these terms have been used here. Such an entity could, over an appreciable period of time, exert enough influence to polarize slowly other segments of the scientific community in this direction. For the sake of identification, I have labeled this institution the Human Development Corporation (HDC). HDC would perform several essential functions.

First, it would collect, analyze and file all scientific studies related to the problem of changing human behavior. This in itself is a large undertaking requiring extensive library facilities, the evolution of an appropriate coding system, and provision for continuous review of new materials. To perform this task, HDC would become a repository of scientifically established findings in this area. This by itself would tend to give a certain weight and dignity to the whole endeavor and provide a substantive frame of reference from which new investigations could be developed in a logical and natural manner. The very existence of such a library would lend a great impetus to the acceleration of behavior-change research and would help to relate areas that are presently treated as conceptually independent, such as psychotherapy and group dynamics. However, it must be emphasized that it is not enough to merely collect relevant research materials. They must be abstracted and coded in some general form so that they can be compared with a variety of different criteria and from various viewpoints. Ultimately, the major aspects of each study should find their way onto an IBM card or tape to facilitate comparison and analysis by means of an electronic computer.

Second, members of the corporation would themselves perform research that would be highly selective in nature. It would not consist of relatively minor extensions of work already undertaken elsewhere, since such extensions would occur in the normal course of scientific study. Rather, HDC scientists would search for new avenues of exploration. They would then perform model pilot projects in these areas, not so much to answer specific questions, but to help to determine the kind of question that is answerable and the sorts of techniques required. These studies would be based on a careful and imaginative review of already existing reports of experimental investigations to determine which avenues might most profitably be explored and the nature of their relative priorities. Thus the second function of HDC depends upon the existence of the first.

A third area of concern for HDC involves consultation. As the corporation matured, it would tend to take a leading position within its own areas of concentration. Inevitably, it would be consulted, not only by other scientists whose interests were similar, but also by governmental, industrial, and social organizations with related practical concerns. A vital function of HDC in this field would be to provide interested parties with the latest, most comprehensive information available on relevant subjects, and, in turn, to learn which areas needed further attention from the viewpoint of practical issues, such as administrative policy and human performance.

Finally, HDC would mount pilot projects designed to test scientifically recently acquired knowledge. It would, in other words, provide limited services both to individuals and to groups. This function would have to be carefully defined and closely supervised to prevent the corporation from turning into another psychosocial consulting firm. HDC would not provide service tailored to the client's unique need, as is usually the case, but rather on the basis of what methods are under current development. The service would not be altered appreciably to fit the client.

For example, if new methods had been evolved for increasing worker production incentives, they might be taught to business executives who would be interested in the economic consequences of such procedures. However, the methods would not be extensively modified by the corporation to fit each particular problem that these executives might face. They would merely be made available to those who felt that they could utilize the techniques. Thus HDC would not be in the business of industrial consultation any more than it would be directly involved in psychotherapy. But it would make available the newest procedures to those persons whose interests and affiliations made them logical consumers. This service would, in turn, provide HDC with a natural testing ground for studying the effectiveness of new methods of behavior change in a field setting.

There is nothing fundamentally unrealistic about HDC, at least on the conceptual level. It would perform a vital set of functions. All that is necessary is for it to come into existence. Someone must pay the bills and someone must promote the vision.

Traditionally, long-range scientific enterprises are located in universities or in large corporate structures, such as the Bell Telephone Company or IBM. Neither of these solutions seems entirely suitable in the present case, though the former alternative is more natural than the latter. The complexity of HDC's activities is not naturally suited to an academic background in which a given institute performs a given function. On the other hand, one would not like to think of industrial influences controlling the kinds of study to be conducted. Perhaps the most feasible alternative would be to operate the corporation as an independent entity in its own right. Precedents exist for such operations. The Rand Corporation in California and its associate, the Systems Development Corporation, engage in fundamental research in the physical and behavioral sciences as well as in developing new training procedures. The Educational Testing Service in Princeton, New Jersey, and the Psychological Corporation in New York City provide instances of independent psychological organizations operating commercially and scientifically.

However, it is not necessary for HDC to be economically independent. It might with equal appropriateness be the research and training arm of an organization already engaged in behavior-change work on the service level, such as a hospital or social agency. What is vital is that HDC have autonomy in the development of its own goals and projects. With such an administrative arrangement, connections could be established with universities, government, industrial, and clinical groups without handing over control to any of these sources. The financing of the corporation is a vital practical step in its implementation, but this problem need not involve us here, since we are concerned with what should be done, not its actual organization.

Let us picture a time, perhaps a decade after its establishment, when HDC has become an established and respected member of the scientific community, performing actively on the four levels that have been described. How might it appear on a typical day? First, it is located in a large, modern building, such as is identified with any corporation. Each of its functions are symbolized by the building's architecture. The library contains both traditional facilities and standard summaries of all materials on microfilm and tape in a form that can be easily located as needed by interested investigators. In this wing, one might see a librarian at work locating the microfilm of a particular thesis done fifteen years before at the University of Minnesota on training procedures used to improve the maze-running ability of rats.

A visiting scientist is requesting all available information on nondirective approaches from the central file system. After a short wait he is supplied with a list of 325 references. Summaries of these materials are on direct call to him by a simple numerical classificatory scheme. If he needs a fuller account, he can consult the original sources in the library.

In this wing, inquiries are received from scientists in other countries who are unable personally to utilize the facilities. For a limited fee, magnetic tapes, a set of IBM cards, and microfilms containing codified and original information on the topic requested are forwarded by mail, direct telephone conversation between computers, or by other procedures that may have been developed.

Basic information on all studies is stored in external storage banks for an electronic computer to which scientists from other portions of the building have direct access. Thus, a steady process of inquiry and information processing is constantly, though silently, proceeding. This computer forms the substantive heart of the entire organization, since it is the repository of known facts on the subject. Its value is cumulative and its functions multiple. Research on particular topics is vastly accelerated by having quick access to pertinent materials. Reports can be regularly and relatively painlessly issued from the library arm of the corporation, summarizing recent developments in various key areas. The computer itself can be programmed to study the materials stored within it in order to report general conclusions and suggest new areas for investigation.

The research wing of HDC contains varied equipment and flexible spatial arrangements. Experiments are being conducted on topics such as the creation of hypnotic states through subliminal stimuli, the implementation of creative activity through the use of synectics-like groups of young children over long periods of time within experimental school settings, and an analysis of the normal social and psychological forces that inhibit the individual from developing his inherent potential.

Three long-range efforts are currently under way: the comparative psychotherapy program, the behavior-change components program, and the ancient recovery and testing program, devoted to evaluating ancient mystical exercises.

The comparative psychotherapy analysis involves the simultaneous application of various procedures utilized in different cultures for the amelioration and cure of psychosocial difficulties. An international sample of individuals are randomly assigned to the various treatments. Practitioners of known repute from various parts of the world including Yogis, shamans, and psychiatrists, are each applying their own kinds of procedure to patients under scientifically controlled circumstances. By this program scientists hope to solve the basic issue of the relative effectiveness of different kinds of behavior-change approaches.

A related endeavor is the behavior-change components program. This activity involves the systematic and progressive assessment of the relative effects of various components of all behavior-change procedures, such as faith, reinforcement, and interaction, in all possible variations and combinations. Ultimately, this program will derive a series of scientifically evolved procedures for producing behavior change in which each component is combined with others in proportions that have been demonstrated to have highest efficiency.

The ancient recovery and testing program involves a searching analysis of the training procedures used by various religious and mystical systems as recorded in their literatures and reported by contemporary practitioners. Its first phase concerns the recovery of these procedures from the confusion of historical and cultural alterations and distortions. The second phase involves the scientific assessment of the effects these training methods have on subjects and their eventual reformulation and utilization in the enhancement and extension of human experience.

In a separate, though connected, wing consulting services are provided. Clients receive direct information about topics of interest through connections with the central computer. They have the opportunity to talk with scientists about work in progress and to observe this work through a system of television cameras that enables them to monitor ongoing experiments without interfering with their progress. One such experiment involves an investigation of a new type of synthetic drug. A subject is lying on a cot waiting for the effects to begin. It has been reported that this drug causes the individual to take on aspects of the identity of persons with whom he comes into contact. A

number of different individuals are waiting outside the door of the subjects' room to test this claim.

On another monitor, showing a second study, a group of subjects
are being instructed in the proper pronunciation of an Eastern
mantrum, or sacred chant, designed to fill the individual with a sense
of relaxation and quiet energy. Various physiological measurements are
being taken, and the effects are being observed by scientists who have
studied the subjects in other situations.

On a third monitor, the latest techniques of implantation of micro-
electrodes in special areas of the brain are being studied. A monkey is
recovering from brain surgery. The effect that stimulation of these electrodes has on his ability to learn new complex behavior is going to be
investigated, using the electricity as a direct system of reinforcement
and reward.

Finally, on a fourth monitor, the observer can watch the latest of
a long line of tests for effectiveness of components of changing emotional reactions to anxiety provoking situations. The present test involves the assessment of the combined factors of objective feedback,
nondirective leadership, a chain-communication network, minimization
of the factor of faith, and the use of intermittent negative reinforcement.

Nearby are seminar and conference rooms for consultation with
corporation personnel. Common problems can be discussed, and the
visitor can share the latest ideas and inferred implications of the work
he has observed with the scientists engaged in it.

Finally, the service wing, though spatially isolated from the others,
looks much like the laboratory center, with flexible arrangements for
individual and group activities. This wing has provisions not only for
the services themselves, but also for the training of practitioners who
will apply them. For example, classes are being given in which established psychotherapists learn to perform and teach certain types of
Yoga breathing useful in calming the individual or, conversely, in stimulating his emotional and thought processes. The use of visualization
exercises adopted from St. Ignatius Loyola's manual are taught as an
aid in objectifying the individual's behavior and enabling him to understand and analyze the source of his own difficulties by becoming
able to see himself as others do.

In another area, housewives are being trained to teach new methods of child rearing that combine firmness with maximization of crea-

tive potential. In a third area, military personnel are learning new methods for resisting influence attempts from hostile sources. Psychological procedures are being demonstrated under simulated field conditions. Finally, a group of ministers, rabbis, and priests are listening with mixed feelings to a demonstration of methods drawn from many of the world's great religions that have been found to enhance the religious experience.

Current clinical work, as distinct from training activities, involves certain findings and principles uncovered in the research programs previously mentioned. In one room, neurotic individuals are being treated by automated psychotherapy. Recent developments have enabled the computer to interpret human speech directly and to react appropriately in the therapeutic role, using a variety of prerecorded messages. Recovery rates of these subjects are being compared to those of human therapists.

In another room, a selected group of subjects are being taught to take the roles of other people without producing any visible sign that this is occurring. Previous tests have shown that when this is done the individual is able to understand the other person better, and interpersonal difficulties can often be resolved in a totally unexpected and satisfactory manner, since the inherent two-person conflict cannot occur if the other person in one sense ceases to exist.

Elsewhere in this wing, a group of executives are being educated in the use of exercises derived from Hatha and Raja Yoga and certain Zen practices so as to be able to think more clearly in emergencies and maintain greater emotional control. As all of these group experiences progress, they are studied and analyzed to clarify ways in which they might be modified to ensure their successful and widespread adoption. The more limited form in which they were originally evaluated under laboratory conditions must be extended to the more varied conditions of the naturalistic situation. This is at least the image that has been projected.

At present, HDC is science fiction. But this is only because of neglect, repression of relevant information, and tradition. It could be created today for a relatively small amount of money. It could integrate and stimulate the study of human potential and produce a harvest that is difficult to anticipate fully at this time. Doubtless, other strategies are possible. A number of minor centers might be started around the country. An industrial complex might encourage such work.

What is certain is that, left to its own devices, the investigation of the development and enhancement of human behavior will continue to run its restricted course as it has for the last century. World conditions today are, however, too saturated with danger for us to allow ourselves the luxury of such a casual approach. While something has been done, the important steps are yet to be taken. We must overcome both prejudice and tradition if science is to provide mankind with any lasting blessings instead of the uncontrolled advances it generates today. The time has come for man to turn his most powerful analytic weapons on the subject that is closest to his own happiness and ultimate survival: the fulfillment of his own potential.

Appendixes
References
Glossary
Suggestions for Further Reading
Index

Technical and Social Difficulties in the Conduct of Evaluative Research

Evaluative research and its effect on scientific understanding of behavior change has been discussed in the preceding chapters from time to time. In the Appendixes, the subject will be reviewed in greater depth. Underlying the physical realities of evaluative studies is a clear scientific model. It is so simple that it can be stated in one sentence: In order to perform an evaluative study it is necessary to compare the amount of change experienced by members of two equivalent groups, only one of which is exposed to the behavior-change process.

To design such a form of investigation it is necessary to define the method of behavior change to be applied, select appropriate measures of the change, and apply the process to one of two similar subject groups. Nothing could be simpler than this, or so it would appear. However, in practice the application of this straightforward abstract model leads one into a maze of technical obscurities and problems created by social pressures, which collectively interact to make evaluative studies one of the more difficult ventures in the social sciences. This Appendix is designed to document this statement and can be taken as a sad example of such scientific experiences, an illustration of the vast gap that may separate the logical model underlying the experimental investigation and the realistic issues that must be faced to translate this model into research experience.

The relevant material is presented in two parts: first, the technical requirements that complicate this form of research endeavor, second, the types of hindrances that arise from the social environment within which the research is usually conducted. Both the design elements and practical necessities must be resolved in order to perform evaluative research successfully. It is this joint requirement that traps those who are attracted to evaluative research as the direct approach to the study of processes designed to alter and improve the quality of human performance.

TECHNICAL ISSUES

Measuring the Effect of the Treatment

All evaluative studies are designed to measure the nature and extent of the change induced by the given treatment. However, it is the reliability, appropriateness, and independence of the instruments used to measure the change that help to determine the extent to which it can be detected. The results of any study are, therefore, partially determined by the instruments selected. This selection needs to be carefully considered in terms of (a) the claims made for the process under evaluation, (b) the instruments currently in use, and (c) the amount of time actually available for testing.

Unfortunately, all instruments, regardless of their degree of methodological sophistication, are open to various forms of *bias*, which must be either controlled or taken into account when one interprets the data that they provide. Even the best evaluative technique remains open to misuse and some instruments, such as rating scales to be filled out by practitioners regarding the progress of their subjects, almost demand biased response. The practitioner, for example, may want to demonstrate his competence and, therefore, indicate change where none has occurred; or he may have faith in his method and believe that change must have occurred, even if, in fact, it has not.

Similar problems arise with regard to the subjects' self-ratings of progress, which may be influenced by desire to please or to be socially acceptable. Even such objective and standardized instruments as personality questionnaires are subject to response biases of various kinds, such as a tendency to give only moderate or only extreme responses, a tendency to agree with all statements, or an attempt to provide answers that are acceptable rather than true.

Another problem relating to the measurement of change concerns the interaction between measurement and method. Certain test instruments in combination with certain change processes may indicate an amount of behavior alteration that is out of proportion to the actual change produced by the method itself. Such an interaction between measurement and method can occur when the experimental subjects, because of the nature of the change procedure to which they are subjected, learn to guess how the experimenter wants them to respond to the test instrument. In other cases, the nature of the evaluative test may simply sensitize the subjects to some aspects of the treatment; in such a case, the instrument actually becomes part of the change process.

The Effect of the Practitioner

In the typical evaluative study reported in the literature, one or perhaps two practitioners are used with one or two groups of subjects, which may vary in size depending on the requirements of the particular study. Under these conditions, it is difficult or impossible to distinguish between the effect on the subject of the method and that of the practitioner applying it. The method itself may produce change; the practitioner, regardless of the method, may produce change by virtue of his own personality; or, a method when administered only by certain practitioners may produce change. Unless the experimental design is formulated in such a manner as to distinguish among effects produced by these possibilities, the results obtained are necessarily ambiguous.

There are a variety of ways in which the practitioner himself may produce change. First, his personality may influence the subjects. This possibility is especially important in view of the findings of the psychologist Fred Fiedler [1] that the personalities of expert therapists of different schools resemble those of well-adjusted persons in the community at large. This suggests that expertness in therapy may be largely due to the therapist's own personal adjustment rather than to any particular method that he uses.

Second, it is necessary to consider the degree of expertness that the practitioner has with the method he uses. Expertness is partially related to the amount of previous experience and partially to ability. Since practitioners are not equal in either ability or experience, it is necessary to control for these characteristics if the results are to be correctly interpreted. The problem in evaluation created by these two factors becomes more serious in direct proportion to the smallness of the sample of practitioners used in a study. Generalization of any evaluative study depends not only on the adequacy of the sample of subjects, but also the adequacy of the sample of practitioners. It is not fair to test a method using either only its expert or its inadequate proponents if generalizations are to be made to situations involving capable, but not outstanding, practitioners.

Third, it is only human for the practitioner to be more interested in and have greater faith in some change processes than others. It is possible that his interest and faith have more effect on the patient than the technique itself. There is evidence to suggest that any systematic approach presented with conviction tends to produce altered behavior in the subjects. Such change is independent of the method and must be separated from it in order to make the experimental findings interpretable.

The Effects of the Subjects

Just as it is necessary to consider the impact of the practitioner on the findings, similar attention must be paid to the effects that the subjects, or influences that are applied to the subjects, may have on the outcome, irrespective of the method. The special attention given to the subjects in the experimental group by professionals and other interested persons may, for example, influence the amount of change they undergo. In many evaluative studies, the subjects in the test group are placed together to receive new and hitherto untried methods; the control subjects, on the other hand, simply are treated routinely. The increase in attention associated with the introduction of a novel type of treatment for the experimental group may by itself produce new behavior in the subjects independent of the method being tested. This may explain why many techniques are found to be successful when first introduced but seem to have little or no effect at a later time when they become routine.

Another important point rarely dealt with in evaluative studies concerns the *placebo effect*. This is the amount of faith the subjects have in the treatment method. A wide variety of sources attest to the fact that faith alone can produce various social and psychological changes. Since any procedure may stimulate faith in some subjects, the effects of faith on the method must be separated from its impact if its potency is to be clearly demonstrated.

The Control of the Experimental Method

One of the essential requirements of any scientific experiment is that it be reproducible, so that independent investigators can verify the results obtained. In evaluative research this requirement is often not fulfilled. The change processes tested are of such complexity and their description so general that it is impossible to form a clear conception of what actually was done. Consequently, the results themselves may be statistically clear but have little meaning, because it is impossible to know to what they are attributed.

A further problem arises from the fact that the experimenters frequently fail to demonstrate objectively that they are actually evaluating the method they believe themselves to be studying. Unless such a demonstration is provided, the research findings may not apply to the technique that ostensively is being tested.

A final problem related to the experimental situation concerns the appropriateness of the instrument for the evaluation of a given method. This issue arises because the demands of evaluative research are frequently in direct opposition to the demands of the practitioner employing a given change technique. The practitioner must be flexible, warm, and insightful; the scientist must be rigid and detached. Unfortunately, the greater the scientific precision in demonstrating the effectiveness of a given method, the greater the likelihood that the experiment bears little resemblance to the method as it is normally employed by practitioners. On the other hand, when a procedure is tested as it is used by practitioners, it is almost impossible to describe the change process in a precise and scientific manner. Consequently, evaluative research at best must represent a compromise between scientific rigor and clinical practicality. In order to ensure that the experimental findings will have practical applicability, the experimenter must determine whether the duration of the subject's work with the practitioner is comparable to that found in practice, whether the motivation for change of the experimental subjects is adequate and comparable to that of subjects who usually undergo the particular change process, and whether the choice of subjects is appropriate to the method. Any of these variables can influence the outcome of the study and obscure a proper interpretation of the findings.

If the experimental conditions should differ markedly from the everyday application of the change process, the interpretation of the findings will be clouded and of little relevance to the practitioner, though the conclusions themselves may be scientifically valid.

The preceding represent some of the technical difficulties that must be overcome in order to conduct an evaluative study properly. While they do not constitute an exhaustive list, they are sufficiently representative to demonstrate that the methodological problems involved in such research are varied and difficult.

SOCIAL CONTAMINATIONS

The second major source of difficulties experienced in conducting evaluative research arises from the social setting within which the method to be tested is placed. These contaminations of the experiment will be organized in terms of seven inevitable problems that arise during the course of evaluation, particularly in those situations where the method being evaluated is also being introduced into the program of the institution in which the test takes place for the first time. This situation is rather typical, since it is usually believed that the time to evaluate the effectiveness of a new procedure is when it is first introduced.

The Control of Communication Channels

The first, and one of the most dramatic, problems encountered by the evaluator as he attempts to translate his beautiful but somewhat unrealistic experimental design into practice concerns the control of communication channels within the institution in which the research is conducted. For the experiment, it is necessary to isolate, insofar as possible, the service or treatment method that is being evaluated from all other treatments or services currently being utilized by the institution. Without such isolation, it is impossible to tell whether change is due to the new treatment or one or more of the old ones. Several strategies are necessary to produce this isolation. First, the subjects are told as little as possible about the change procedure and encouraged not to talk about it. Second, the practitioner is discouraged from describing the method to his colleagues. Third, the records associated with the technique are kept separate from other subject records. All of these operations have the general effect of keeping the nature and effects due to the new procedure fairly well encapsulated, so that they can be studied with a minimum of contamination. It would be easier still if the total study could be geographically relocated, but the practical difficulties in such an approach are usually insuperable.

Further, this isolation tends to keep all other practitioners who are not directly involved in the study naïve with regard to both the nature of the new behavior-change procedure and the identity of the subjects who are involved. This naïveté makes their estimate of progress more valuable, since it cannot be influenced by any assumptions they have about the validity of the procedure, including the general belief that any treatment must have some effect.

Unfortunately, it is almost impossible for anyone to limit communication channels artificially. In most centers where behavior-change techniques are utilized, it is an important aspect of the work to have communication channels open among different professional groups, so that they may share their findings and compare notes. Any attempt to interfere with this or any preexisting communications network is bound to produce a strong reaction and may have repercussions that were not anticipated. The new method may take on the character of a super-secret that may make it important out of all proportion and produce an unrealistic evaluation of its effectiveness. Resentment against the research may be built up among persons who are kept in ignorance of its nature and goals. Or, finally, the restriction of communications may reduce the effectiveness of the change process itself by limiting the opportunity of the practitioner to interact with other staff members.

There is no simple solution for this, or for any of the other confrontations between research requirements and social reality to be described. If secrecy is eliminated, the value of the research may be questionable. If secrecy is maintained, the method that is tested may be applied in atypical circumstances, and the evaluative process impeded by the reactions of other staff members.

The Relationship between Researcher and Practitioner

A second, related situation arises very early in the research operation. It concerns the relationship between the research staff of the evaluative study and the practitioners regularly employed in the institution. For the most part, the job of any practitioner is clearly defined in terms of case load, methods of treatment, amount of time on the job, and so on. The researcher often has a much more fluid position. He may or may not keep a strict time schedule. He does not have a case load in the usual sense. Even more fundamentally, he has no obligation to help anyone, and yet he is functioning within a setting that has this task as its central aim. In one sense, the research scientist has special privileges. In another, his value and importance to the organization in which he is working are uncertain. For these reasons the institution's staff tends to consider the researcher as a necessary evil, who must be tolerated for a time, but whose prime function seems to be to make their difficult life even more complex by giving them more forms to fill out and by introducing research restrictions into certain aspects of the treatment program. These reactions to research are quite normal, but they impede the research process.

The researcher can adopt one of two positions in dealing with this situation. He can invest a good deal of time, emotion, and patience in establishing pleasant personal relationships with various key members of the staff. He would do this on the theory that even if the staff questions the significance of the research, they will be willing to cooperate because they like him personally. This strategy may work if the demands of the research on the practitioners are relatively small, but it is hard for the experimenter to sell the research on a personal basis, since his personality and the study are two distinct things.

The other alternative is for the researcher to remain as much in the background as possible, on the theory that it is hard to resent something that has only a shadowy form. The researcher using this approach avoids as much contact with the staff as is practical in terms of the requirements of the research itself. If he is successful, he is hardly known and the research is accepted as part of the daily routine and soon forgotten. In many ways this is the simplest approach, since it provides the experimental scientist with more time to do his real job and prevents undue emphasis from being placed on the evaluation.

However, whatever he does, the fact remains that the evaluative study is peculiar and unique, and it may be questioned, resented, or misunderstood. For this reason, the researcher must, in the last analysis, have firm support from the institution's administration, so that whatever the experience of day-to-day relationships with the staff, he can, in an emergency, appeal to authority to maintain the operation that has been set in motion. If such authority does not exist or does not support the research actively, the researcher soon may find himself sailing hostile waters in a leaky boat.

184

The Effect of the Control Group

A third problem that arises in the implementation of evaluative research involves the use of a control group that is not undergoing sessions in which the method under study is applied. This problem has been widely discussed and to some extent resolved, but it must be mentioned since it logically falls into the present discussion.

It is not possible to have a worthwhile evaluative study unless a *control group*, equivalent to the experimental group, is used. This means that some persons who should have a chance to undergo the new method do not. This is in direct conflict with the humanitarian ethic requiring that persons who need help should receive it as soon as possible. In this instance, the practitioner and researcher are in direct conflict. However, the problem is not as serious as it might appear, largely because of the prevalence of evaluative studies of various drugs and medical procedures that employ control groups. These studies have become almost traditional, so that practitioners have gotten used to the idea that to study a new technique a control group must be employed. They accept this, whether or not they logically understand its necessity. Therefore, the researcher's problem is not as serious as it might otherwise appear. But there are still many areas in which the control group is either questioned or partially eliminated on humanitarian grounds. Thus, the partial victory of scientific procedure over practitioner's ethics does not mean that the problem can be totally ignored.

The Number of Practitioners Utilized

The fourth difficulty encountered by evaluative research as it is translated into social function concerns the number of practitioners employed in the experimental test of the new method. From the viewpoint of the institution, it is desirable to have as little turnover as possible. Each new staff member must be oriented, and he requires valuable weeks and months of time to learn the intricacies that characterize any complex organization. Unless the staff member remains an appreciable length of time, this investment in orientation is extremely wasteful.

Unfortunately, evaluative research favors and almost necessitates a rapid turnover of those involved in the project, since it is scientifically desirable to use as many different practitioners as is practical. To generalize, an adequate sample is necessary, both of subjects and of practitioners. The number of practitioners that are simultaneously available to work in the project is usually limited, so the most practical alternative approach is to rotate staff members during the course of the study. If the choice is between hiring one practitioner for three years or three men for one year each, the latter would be better.

The Effect of the Study on the Institution

A fifth area of potential difficulty involves the effects of an evaluative study on the institution in which the evaluation takes place. The study most immediately affects the practitioners who are using the method under evaluation. It does, however, tend to spread through the institution, depending on the scope of the study, the findings obtained, and the general adequacy of the practitioners themselves.

It is almost impossible for the practitioners using the new procedure to separate, in their own minds, the effect of the method that they use from their own personal and professional effectiveness. Technically, there are ways to separate the effects of the method and the practitioner on the subject when analyzing research data, but the practitioner is not aware of this. He tends to feel that he is being judged and tested by the research. If no change is noted in the subjects, he may feel that he has failed or been shown to be ineffective. These reactions are natural but extremely unfortunate. The practitioner is driven to protect himself either by making unusual and extraordinary efforts to ensure success or by biasing the results of the study in any way that seems open to him. He may indicate to the clients how he expects them to change, or how he hopes they will change. Whatever he does or does not do, it is hard for him to avoid being threatened by the research.

The practitioner, it must be emphasized, has nothing immediate to gain from the evaluative research. At best, it may provide external validation of the method that he uses. This he already takes for granted. If the evaluation is not positive, however, he is placed in an ambiguous professional position. He must either explain away the research or reconsider the methods he uses. Because of these facts, the evaluation threatens his professional image to some extent, though this may be minimized if the technique is new and untried. This threat is reflected in his reaction to the research process in a variety of undesirable ways.

To a lesser degree, practitioners and administrators not directly involved in the research often suffer from the impact of the study. Once evaluation is started, it is hard to confine its field of operation or the generality of its conclusions. What starts out to be a limited evaluation of a new type of behavior-change technique in a given service spreads to the whole service and even beyond. For example, the control group, which does not participate in the experimental procedure, is still being treated by normal change techniques. Whether or not the control group has changed has direct implications for the effectiveness of the total ongoing program of the institution, since the control group would actually constitute the experimental group in an evaluative study of the effectiveness of the normal program of the institution.

In a different sense, the evaluative research brings to light various weak spots in the coverage of clients and patients among other services. When staff members are required to make detailed evaluations of the progress of particular clients, they become painfully aware of the extent to which they may or may not be successfully inducing change, regardless of what the official records show.

Evaluation can, from this viewpoint, be viewed as a disease. Once instituted it can spread anywhere, with a variety of unexpected effects. Since most institutional structures are designed to maintain the status quo, any evaluation presents a threat, regardless of its initial aim. It is unfortunate that the administration, which supports the original study and may have gone to some lengths in order to obtain finance for it, realizes only when it is too late that it has originated something potentially undesirable, or at least dubious, in terms of its effect on the organization's structure. It is important, therefore, that administrators and staff members be made initially aware of what they are starting. But the researcher cannot tell them about it; he often appears only after the project has been approved. The staff members must learn by experience. The next time, they are more sophisticated in their expectations of and willingness to participate in this form of research.

Because they are threatened the institution's staff and administration may put pressure on the researcher to obtain certain results, usually positive. Most evaluative investigations are instituted to "prove" something in which people already believe. The researcher is generally aware of how the study is supposed to turn out. If the conclusions are not as expected, he may be penalized if he is unfortunate enough to depend on the institution for full-time employment beyond the duration of the project. In this context, research is viewed more as a method of social validation than as an impersonal guide to the truth. If it does not supply the correct answer, it is ignored because its implementation would disturb the homeostatic balance of the institutional structure.

The Effect of the Evaluative Study on the Change Process

A sixth problem that arises when a new service or treatment is evaluated involves the effect of evaluation on the change process. It is common to think that new methods should be evaluated as they are introduced, so as to be sure that they are really effective from the start. Many government agencies require that demonstration projects be evaluated as a condition for providing support. Unfortunately, this apparently logical position contains an inner contradiction. When a new program is first introduced, it does not have the form it develops when it is routinely applied at a later time. It is still being perfected, and the initial amount of attention and interest that it generates is lost at a later time when it is fully accepted. For these reasons an evaluation of an innovation may tell little about its real effectiveness as a routine procedure. Unfortunately, it is the latter situation about which one usually wishes to obtain information.

To further compound the confusion, the process of evaluation itself introduces completely foreign elements into the behavior-change technique. Forms must be filled out, observations must be made, special records completed. All of this data collection influences the method that is being evaluated to some extent. When these research requirements are imposed on the normal problems that occur in the course of any innovation, the effect on the new technique is hard to predict, except to say that the method as it is evaluated may bear little resemblance to the method as it may be routinely applied at a later time. If this is true, it is questionable whether the evaluation at this time serves a useful function. It would appear more useful to evaluate services after they have been routinized.

The Question of Adopting the New Method

In evaluative research, the most immediate, though not necessarily the most important, purpose is to determine whether a new method should be adopted as a routine procedure in the setting where the evaluation takes place. This is one of the central motivations of those who support the research. However, the timing of experimental investigations tends to defeat the end for which the project was originally designed. Research is a lengthy process. Whatever the particular procedures under evaluation, it usually takes about a year at the end of a project to analyze the data and prepare the final report. During this time, since the institutional budget must be finalized well in advance, the administration must decide whether to continue the service that is being evaluated or not; by the time the evaluation becomes available, it is literally too late to have any effect.

The major difficulties encountered in the confrontation between scientific procedure and social reality that have been described all can be traced to a mutual lack of awareness as to what to expect. If such awareness can be attained before the research is initiated, its actual progress should proceed more smoothly. When such an awareness does not exist, the effects are unfortunate both in terms of the research itself, and for the institution in which it is conducted. It is, therefore, not enough for evaluative scientists to study the higher levels of methodological sophistication and for practitioners and administrators to be concerned with the perfection of new procedures. Both groups need to become aware of the limitations, requirements, and opportunities that each brings to the other if the interaction between them is to be changed from an ambiguous skirmish to a fruitful exchange.

The direct approach to the study of behavior change is not necessarily the easiest one. There are a rather overwhelming set of complex problems that need to be overcome to bring such research to a successful conclusion. These snares for the unwary have not in past discouraged investigators from undertaking evaluative research. With varying degress of excellence many such studies have been performed, analyzed, and a majority of them reported in the professional literature. Thus it would be foolish to assume prematurely that such research was to be avoided because of its technical and practical difficulty since, in fact, it has been performed. The more realistic approach would be to turn from the problems underlying this kind of undertaking to the findings that such research has in fact produced. It is in this material that we could reasonably expect to find the basis for determining whether the direct, evaluative approach to behavior-change processes is, in fact, the most fruitful one.

APPENDIX B

The Outcome of
Evaluative Research

The normal channels of professional publication have made readers with specialized interests largely unaware of the true extent of evaluative research, since such studies are published in the type of journal associated with the method being tested. Studies of educational procedures are published in journals of educational research; research in group psychotherapy is published in group psychotherapy journals; and human-relations training studies are published in social psychology periodicals.

Articles published in these periodicals summarizing evaluative studies almost invariably are developed along specialized lines. However adequate and interesting these reviews may be, they fail to provide any comparative sense of the impact of evaluative research. They do not indicate whether such research, taken as a whole, is likely to determine either the general effectiveness of our attempts to change human behavior, or the relative effectiveness of different approaches used in the same field, or the same approaches used for different purposes. These are basic and important questions for any science of behavior change, and it is reasonable to suppose that the evaluation of current behavior-change methods could supply some relevant answers.

This chapter will investigate the nature of the conclusions these studies can reasonably be expected to provide on the basis of a review of the information already supplied. It is difficult to estimate the total number of such studies for several reasons. First, they appear in so many sources that it is hard to extract material from all of them. Second, much of the best such research is done as doctoral dissertations that are not readily obtainable. Finally, much evaluative research is never published because the sponsors or researchers do not want the results made known or because of its inherently poor quality. However, it is safe to say that a careful search of all literatures would accumulate three to five thousand evaluative studies of behavior-change processes.

It is neither practical nor necessary to analyze all of this research. A sample should be sufficient to gain some sense of the general tendency. Further, it is reasonable to assume that the accessibility of research has some relation to its quality and importance.

Several years ago, the author undertook a review of evaluative research conducted in a number of content areas. Since the nature and outcome of this study are directly relevant to the issues under discussion, it will be described briefly.[1]

The first step was the selection of a limited number of content areas for comparison. Two criteria were employed. First, the areas chosen had to contain a reasonable accumulation of evaluative research studies, ranging from 30 to 50, so that some general conclusion about their findings might be possible. Second, the change that the practitioners were trying to produce had to be broad, deep, and of general social significance; in this way, the evaluations would be of attempts to produce important change. With the aid of these criteria, four content areas were selected for intensive investigation: psychotherapy, counseling, human-relations training, and education. In the field of education, only studies of methods that attempted to produce basic personality changes were reviewed; this eliminated the large literature dealing with the effectiveness of educational processes as determinants of intellectual performance.

Even within these areas, it was necessary to be selective, because of the large number and variable quality of the evaluative studies that were available for review. In order to reduce the task to manageable proportions only studies of a relatively high methodological caliber were selected.

A superficial review of the literatures in psychotherapy, counseling, human-relations training, and education indicated that over six hundred studies seemed to meet these criteria. After a more careful examination, approximately two thirds proved deficient in respect to one or another of the selection criteria. It was, therefore, possible to reduce the number of evaluative studies under active consideration to 181. Because of the criteria used to select them, they contained, as a group, findings that had a greater degree of social significance and a lesser degree of experimental error than other research in their area. This sample therefore represented the most likely source for obtaining interesting and important information about the success of evaluative research in contributing to an understanding of the process of inducing behavior change and the methods by which this change can most efficiently be accomplished.

The Analysis of Evaluative-Research Studies

The central problem to be overcome in any analysis of studies obtained from diverse origins is the design and application of a common system of classification that can be applied to all of them. These categories, once they are imposed, form the frame of reference of any comparisons made among studies and thus indirectly influence the findings by limiting the kind of information that can be analyzed.

In the present instance the task of deriving a classification system was simplified by the fact that all studies utilized the same general type of research design, though they varied in complexity. They could, therefore, each be viewed as a sample of evaluative research and described in terms of the general characteristics that all such research must contain.

In order to describe any evaluative investigation, it is necessary to state the nature of the experimental design used, the number of subjects and practitioners included, the nature of the sample, the setting in which the method was tested, the nature of the method itself, the change criteria employed, the findings obtained, and the types of methodological error that may have been present. In the present instance, therefore, it was only necessary to analyze each of these aspects of evaluative research in detail in order to arrive at a coding system that could be used to describe any given study in a relatively complete manner. The end product of this process is given in Table 1 in the form of a coding sheet. One choice in each subsection was coded for each experiment.

TABLE 1

Data Processing Code

NATURE OF METHODOLOGY

Pre post
Post only
Pre post with follow up
Post only with follow up

One method tested and 1 type of control
Multi methods and 1 control
One method and multi controls
Multi methods and multi controls
Multi method only

Subjects matched on less than 4 variables
Subjects matched on 4 to 6 variables
Subjects matched on 7 or more variables
Subjects randomly assigned to experimental conditions
Subjects randomly assigned with equivalence of matching demonstrated
Partial randomization
Matching after the fact
Biased matching (groups not really from same population)
Matched on unspecified variables
Own controls
Basis unspecified

No use of factorial design
Use of factorial design
Induced factorial design by use of analysis of covariance

No replication and no objective confirmation of method
Replication but no objective confirmation of method used
No replication but objective confirmation of method
Replication and confirmation of method used

NUMBER OF SUBJECTS	NUMBER OF CHANGE AGENTS USED
Number not specified	Number unspecified
Less than 10	1
10–20	2
21–30	3
31–40	4
41–60	5
61–100	6
101–150	7
151–200	8 or more
201–	Not relevant

NATURE OF SUBJECTS

Infant	Normal
Child	Emotionally maladjusted
Adolescent	(e.g., mental hospital patient)
Young adult	Antisocial difficulty (e.g., delinquent)
Adult	Underachievers and retarded
Old person	Physically handicapped
Nonhuman (e.g., rat)	Others

SETTING

School	Armed services
Prison or associated conditions such as parole	Private practice
	Others
Out-patient clinic	
Hospital	Individual treatment
Factory	Group treatment
Office	Group and individual treatment
Home	combined

NATURE OF METHODS TESTED

Counseling and guidance
Eclectic psychotherapy
Psychoanalytic psychotherapy or counseling
Nondirective psychotherapy
Unique complex experience (e.g., mental health workshop)

Occupational therapy
Human-relations training

195

Changes in life situation (e.g., desegregation)
Specific methods used in conjunction with physiological therapies
Others

Degree of guidance; varying from laissez faire to authoritarian
Variations in feedback
Amount of participation and exposure to method
Degree of motivation
Nature of group—basis of formation, size, norms, etc.
Comparison of specific techniques (e.g., lectures, discussions, role
    playing, films, television, remedial reading)
Comparison of social approaches (interaction, role) with psycho-
    logical approaches (expression of feeling, interpretation)

CHANGE CRITERIA

Standard personality test
Self-ratings
Ratings by others
Projective test
Intelligence test
Interview
Follow-up questionnaire
Attitude questionnaire
Interaction measures and behaviorial observation
Measures of insight, social sensitivity, and empathy
School records
Test of knowledge and achievement
Aptitude test
Sociometric test
Test of psychomotor efficiency
Reality decisions (e.g., whether to go to college)
Situational test
Nonverbal and performance test
Behavioral records (e.g., discipline marks)
Degree of conformity to group norms
Measures related to learning (e.g., fixation, recall)

AMOUNT OF CHANGE OBTAINED

Considerable change in predicted direction
Slight but significant change in predicted direction
No change
Slight but significant change in unexpected direction
Considerable change in unexpected direction
Results not given

ERRORS OF METHODOLOGY

Possible bias or contamination of measurement

Impossibility of distinguishing between effect of therapy and effect of therapist

No control for effect of therapist's personality

No control for effect of therapist's general level of ability

No control for differential ability of therapist with different methods

No control for previous experience of therapist

No control for degree of interest of therapist

Statistical ambiguities (e.g., regression effects)

Lack of experimental control with consequent impossibility of repeating the experiment

Incorrect control group (not from same population)

No control for effect of providing experimental subjects with attention

No control for subject's degree of belief in the method

No control for interaction between method and test taking

Failure to use appropriate change criteria

Failure to provide an appropriate test of method considered

Failure to use either matching or randomization

No objective confirmation of method

The first step in the preparation of the data for analysis was to code on IBM cards each of the 181 studies that constituted the experimental sample. The information on these cards was then analyzed in order to answer two central questions: first, what are the general characteristics of evaluative research when distinctions of content area are ignored; second, what are the differences in character and outcome of studies that were conducted in different areas. In general, the data analysis was intended to determine whether evaluative studies have as a group accumulated a reliable, valid, and socially significant body of knowledge that can be generalized across content areas or help to distinguish among them.

The General Character of Evaluative Research

The simplest way to attain a general picture of evaluative research when content areas are ignored is to examine the summary statistics of all categories, since these statistics, by definition, describe the general character of the studies under review.

TABLE 2
Aspects of Experimental Design

Pre post	80%
Post only	12
Pre post with follow up	7
Post only with follow up	1
One method tested with one type of control group	74
Multiple methods and one control	13
One method and multiple controls	9
Multiple methods and multiple controls	4
Subjects matched on less than 4 variables	11
Subjects matched on 4 or more variables	22
Subjects randomly assigned to experimental conditions	20
Subjects randomly assigned with equivalence of matching demonstrated	23
Partial randomization	7
Matching after the fact	3
Biased matching (groups not really from the same population)	2
Matched on unspecified variables	2
Subjects acted as their own controls	3
Basis of assignment to groups unspecified	7
No use of a factorial design	93
Use of a factorial design	6
Induced factorial design by the use of analysis of covariance	1
No use of replication	93
Use of replication	7

Table 2 shows the statistics for different aspects of experimental design. An inspection of this table suggests that evaluative research is generally formulated in the simplest possible terms, involving a pre-post test, performed both before and after the course of the experiment of one method and one control group. Factorial design and replication are used in less than 10 per cent of the studies. The method of assignment to experimental conditions is partially or totally unsatisfactory in approximately 25 per cent of the cases. In general, the design of evaluative research appears to be crude and the method of assignment of subject to conditions only partially satisfactory.

TABLE 3
Nature of the Samples

NUMBER OF SUBJECTS

Less than 10 subjects	2%
10 to 20 subjects	8
21 to 30 subjects	16
31 to 40 subjects	11
41 to 60 subjects	13
61 to 100 subjects	18
101 to 150 subjects	9
151 to 200 subjects	3
201 or more subjects	14
Number of subjects unspecified	6

NATURE OF SUBJECTS

Children	8
Adolescents	19
Young adults	30
Adults	40
Old persons	2
Nonhumans (e.g., rats)	1

Normal	49
Emotionally maladjusted (e.g., mental hospital patients)	30
Antisocial difficulties (e.g., delinquents)	11
Underachievers and retarded	9
Physically handicapped	1

NUMBER OF CHANGE AGENTS

Number unspecified	53
1	14
2	11
3	3
4	1
5	0
6	1
7	2
8 or more	9
Number not relevant	6

Table 3 describes the samples of subjects and practitioners that are used in these studies. The number of subjects varies, on the average, between forty and sixty. Their nature is partially determined by the content areas chosen for review. In the majority of studies, the number of practitioners used is not specified. Presumably, in these studies one or two practitioners are used, since a greater number would be likely to receive special mention in the description. In any case, those evaluations that do specify the number of practitioners use an average of one or two.

TABLE 4

Nature and Setting of the Methods Evaluated

NATURE OF THE METHODS

Individual psychotherapy	10%
Individual counseling	11
Group psychotherapy	23
Group counseling	10
Group and individual therapy tested in the same study	9
Components and analogues of therapy	6
Human-relations training	10
Educational procedures	21

SETTING OF THE METHODS

School	61
Prison or associated conditions such as parole	9
Out-patient or mental hygiene clinic	4
Hospital	21
Factory	1
Office	1
Home	1
Armed services	1
Private practice	1

Table 4 describes the nature of the methods tested and the settings in which they were applied. The content areas reviewed determined these components for the most part. It is interesting to note that, among the studies selected in the sample, there were twice as many of group, as of individual, therapy, in spite of the fact that group therapy has become widely used only recently.

Table 5 summarizes the frequency with which various types of measuring instruments were employed as change criteria. Many such criteria were employed in these studies, but no single type of instrument was used in more than 30 per cent of the studies.

Table 5 shows, in addition to the frequency with which a measure was used, the relationship between the change criteria utilized and the findings obtained. The most striking general conclusion suggested by this table is that change was obtained on the various instruments in

TABLE 5
Instruments Used to Measure Change

INSTRUMENTS	INSTRUMENT USED		INSTRUMENT NOT USED
	Change Found	No Change Found	
Standard personality tests	10%	16%	74%
Self-ratings	8	10	82
Ratings by others	12	18	70
Projective tests	15	8	77
Intelligence tests	3	5	92
Interviews	2	3	95
Follow-up questionnaires	4	3	93
Attitude questionnaires	8	17	75
Interaction measures and behavioral observation	5	5	90
Measures of social sensitivity, insight, and empathy	1	4	95
School records	5	7	88
Tests of knowledge	8	11	81
Aptitude tests	1	4	95
Sociometric tests	4	5	91
Tests of psychomotor efficiency	1	0	99
Reality decisions (e.g., whether to go to college)	1	0	99
Situational tests	1	2	97
Nonverbal and performance tests	1	0	99
Behavioral records (e.g., discipline marks)	4	6	90
Degree of conformity to group norms	0	1	99
Measures related to learning (e.g., fixation, recall)	3	1	96

about 45 per cent of the instances in which they were used as change criteria. However, since the number and nature of the instruments varied from study to study, it was necessary to determine whether 45 per cent of the studies also showed evidence of change. This question was investigated by making an independent rating of the amount of change demonstrated and determining whether the amount of change determined in this way agreed with that shown in Table 5. The results of this analysis indicated that the rating of change agreed within two percentage points with the average change shown by the measuring instruments. This substantiated the conclusion that the amount of change found by each of the measuring instruments replicates the general pattern of change obtained by the global change rating and indirectly supported the reliability of the rating itself.

However, several exceptions to this pattern occurred. When projective tests were used as change criteria, change was found in 65 per cent of the cases. This is surprising in view of the generally low reliability of projective tests and the fact that they are supposed to measure aspects of personality that are presumably difficult to alter. In contrast to projective tests, ratings by others and attitude questionnaires showed changes less often than other instruments. This is also surprising, since change is often thought to occur first in surface attitudes and outward behavior. While these findings are intriguing, an over-all *chi-square* comparison of the amount of change found with various instruments failed to indicate any significant differences. The exceptions are, therefore, most reasonably interpreted as chance variation. Chi square is a statistical technique for testing whether different categories of cases occur in a predicted frequency pattern.

The conclusion to be drawn is that all instruments demonstrate the existence of change with approximately the same frequency or, conversely, that change is demonstrated in evaluative research in approximately 45 per cent of the cases regardless of the instruments used.

Table 6 deals with the same data from a different viewpoint by showing the number of different types of instruments used in different studies. This table indicates that fewer than 40 per cent of the studies used more than two types of change criteria. In view of the variety of instruments available, the uncertainty of the types of change to be expected, and the effort involved in even the simplest evaluative research, it is regrettable that a broader spectrum of change criteria was not employed within the confines of the individual study.

202

TABLE 6

Number of Types of Instrument Used Per Study

TYPES OF INSTRUMENT USED	STUDIES
1	64
2	57
3	32
4	20
5	5
6	2
7	–
8	–
9	–
10 or more	10

TABLE 7

Errors in Methodology

No control for interaction between method and measuring instrument	96%
No control for subject's degree of belief in the method	89
Impossibility of distinguishing between the effect of the therapy and the effect of the therapist	59
No control for the effect of the therapist's general level of ability	59
No control for the effect of the therapist's personality	59
No control for the previous experience of the therapist	59
No control for degree of interest of the therapist	59
No control for the effect of providing experimental subjects with attention	52
No control for differential ability of therapist with different methods	41
No objective confirmation of the method tested	31
Failure to use either matching or randomization	21
Lack of experimental control with consequent impossibility of repeating the experiment	17
Statistical ambiguities (e.g., regression effects)	17
Possible measurement bias	15
Incorrect control group	15
Failure to use appropriate change criteria	5
Failure to provide an appropriate test of the method considered	1

Table 7 summarizes the frequency with which various types of methodological error occurred in the studies reviewed. The importance of this information is hard to overestimate, since the existence of error in the experimental procedure casts a reasonable doubt on the findings. The greater the amount of error, the greater the difficulty in interpreting the experiment. Table 7 indicates that the categorized errors occurred in the studies in from 1 to as much as 96 per cent of the cases.

The most frequent error was a failure to provide a control for the effect of interaction between test and method. Even in cases where such a control was attempted, it was not entirely satisfactory, so that this error existed in virtually all the studies reviewed.

The findings reported in Table 7 are extremely damaging to the cause of evaluative research. With two or three exceptions, the errors are of a major character. In other areas of research in the behavioral sciences, any of them would probably render a study unfit for publication. They are not errors within subtle experimental refinements. Rather, they reflect the abuse of basic scientific procedures. It is, therefore, surprising that a sample of the better examples of evaluative research should prove so contaminated with experimental error. These findings raise grave doubts as to whether any conclusions can be drawn from such research.

An analysis of these statistics led to several basic conclusions. First, most evaluative research uses the simplest possible experimental design, substituting simplicity for efficiency. Second, the findings of evaluative research are unrelated to the ways in which change is measured. Third, the technical proficiency of this research is at a low level. To some extent, the third conclusion undermines the second, since experimental error renders experimental findings ambiguous. While change may be demonstrated an average of 45 per cent of the time, it cannot be said that it actually occurs this often. Probably the actual percentage of change is much less, since experimental error usually leads to an overestimate of the extent of change.

Evaluative Research in Separate Content Areas

The second basic question to be investigated was the differences that existed among studies that were conducted in different content areas. Presumably, comparisons among the character and outcome of evaluative research conducted in different content areas might aid in the broader formulation of evaluative research itself and help to demonstrate areas of similarity and difference. It was, therefore, with considerable interest and expectation that the comparative analysis of these studies was undertaken.

In order to determine whether studies executed in different content areas varied with respect to the analysis categories, the data were reanalyzed. Studies in the various areas were treated as separate groups. The homogeneity of the groups in any given category was tested by means of a chi-square test. In some cases more than 20 per cent of the cells in the chi-square analysis contained expected frequencies of less than five. Here it was necessary to collapse rows and columns to reduce the number of such frequencies, so that the chi-square test could legitimately be applied. For example, in order to test whether studies in different content areas used different numbers of subjects, it was necessary to reclassify all studies on the dichotomous criterion of containing either fewer than forty-one subjects or forty-one or more subjects. The results of this comparison, given in Table 8, indicated that the data were not homogeneous. An inspection of the table suggests that fewer of the group therapy and more of the educational studies than expected had forty-one or more subjects.

However, when research in different areas was compared, no significant differences were found in any of the categories describing the

TABLE 8
Numbers of Subjects in Different Content Areas *

CONTENT AREAS	40 SUBJECTS OR LESS		41 SUBJECTS OR MORE	
Individual psychotherapy	5	(6.7)	12	(10.3)
Individual counseling	4	(6.7)	13	(10.3)
Components and analogues of therapy	8	(4.3)	3	(6.6)
Group psychotherapy	25	(15.8)	15	(24.2)
Group counseling	7	(5.9)	8	(9.1)
Group and individual therapy combined	8	(6.7)	9	(10.3)
Human-relations training	4	(6.7)	13	(10.3)
Educational procedures	6	(14.2)	30	(21.8)

* In this and all further tables, all numbers refer to number of studies; when numbers are listed in parentheses, they are the figures for expected frequencies of studies.

experimental design that was applied, the change criteria used, or the obtained findings. These startling negative conclusions suggest that evaluative research conducted in different areas is identical in both character and outcome.

A further tabulation was made in order to determine whether certain methods, regardless of the content area in which they were applied, showed differential change patterns. For this purpose, four methods were compared: the nondirective approach, role playing, psychoanalytic therapy, and eclectic therapy. Sufficient studies of each of these approaches were available to make the comparison meaningful. The results clearly indicated that all methods produced change about 45 per cent of the time, which indicated that there was no differential superiority among them and that in amount of change produced they did not differ from all other methods tested in the other studies.

In view of the fact that these content areas are usually treated as conceptually separate, utilize separate training procedures for the preparation of practitioners, serve different populations, and are derived from varying historical and social conditions, the lack of any demonstrable difference in the ability to induce change among them is remarkable.

The only area in which differences were detected concerned the types of methodological error associated with studies in different content areas. These findings are presented in Tables 9 through 12. Generally, the findings reflect the special conditions under which research in

TABLE 9
Control for the Effect of the Practitioner

CONTENT AREAS	CONTROL FOR PRACTITIONERS		NO CONTROL	
Individual psychotherapy	4	(7.4)	14	(10.5)
Individual counseling	1	(8.3)	19	(11.7)
Components and analogues of therapy	9	(4.5)	2	(6.4)
Group psychotherapy	14	(17.0)	27	(24.0)
Group counseling	4	(7.4)	14	(10.5)
Group and individual therapy combined	14	(7.0)	3	(9.9)
Human-relations training	9	(7.4)	9	(10.5)
Educational procedures	20	(15.7)	18	(22.2)

TABLE 10
Experimental Control

CONTENT AREAS	EXPERIMENTAL CONTROL		NO EXPERIMENTAL CONTROL	
Individual therapy and counseling	32	(30.8)	6	(7.2)
Group therapy and counseling	56	(47.8)	3	(11.2)
Human-relations training	12	(14.6)	6	(3.4)
Educational procedures	24	(30.8)	14	(7.2)

TABLE 11
Control for Attention

CONTENT AREAS	CONTROL FOR ATTENTION		NO CONTROL	
Individual psychotherapy	7	(8.6)	11	(9.3)
Individual counseling	0	(9.6)	20	(10.4)
Components and analogues	9	(5.3)	2	(5.7)
Group psychotherapy	18	(19.7)	23	(21.3)
Group counseling	2	(8.6)	16	(9.3)
Group and individual therapy combined	15	(8.2)	2	(8.8)
Human-relations training	8	(8.6)	10	(9.3)
Educational procedures	28	(18.3)	10	(19.7)

TABLE 12
Objective Confirmation of Method

CONTENT AREAS	OBJECTIVE CONFIRMATION		NO OBJECTIVE CONFIRMATION	
Individual psychotherapy	12	(12.5)	6	(5.5)
Individual counseling	0	(13.9)	20	(6.1)
Components and analogues of therapy	11	(7.6)	0	(3.3)
Group psychotherapy	25	(28.5)	16	(12.4)
Group counseling	10	(12.5)	8	(5.5)
Group and individual therapy combined	14	(11.8)	3	(5.2)
Human-relations training	18	(12.5)	0	(5.5)
Educational procedures	36	(26.4)	2	(11.5)

one or another area is usually conducted. Otherwise, they appear to have no general significance. For example, Table 11 provides a comparison of the content areas by the criterion of "control for attention" provided to members of the different experimental groups. Studies of both individual and group counseling have a higher amount of this error than expected. Counseling evaluations are generally nonspecific, so that it is difficult to introduce an alternate method into the experimental design to control the effect of attention.

Even these findings, relating to differential distribution of experimental error, are vitiated if content areas are compared on over-all degree of experimental error. In order to make this comparison, each study was rated for methodological adequacy by inspecting the number and nature of errors made in each study. Table 13 presents the results of this comparison.

TABLE 13
The Quality of the Methodology of Studies

| | QUALITY OF THE METHODOLOGY | | |
CONTENT AREAS	*Poor and below average*	*Average*	*Above average and good*
Individual psychotherapy	6	5	7
Individual counseling	3	7	10
Components and analogues of therapy	0	2	9
Group psychotherapy	8	14	19
Group counseling	6	6	6
Group and individual therapy combined	3	5	9
Human-relations training	7	3	8
Educational procedures	12	9	17

A chi-square test indicates that there is no difference in the average amount of error associated with studies performed in different content areas, even though the precise nature of particular errors may be unequally distributed, as demonstrated in Tables 9 through 12.

At this point in the analysis, it was clear that the findings of evaluative research could not provide any insight into relationships among the studies performed in different content areas, since all relevant findings were negative. It was still possible, however, that the lack of positive findings was due to the already demonstrated experimental error

TABLE 14

The Relation Between Demonstrated Change and Methodological Deficiency

	CHANGE DEMONSTRATED		NO CHANGE DEMONSTRATED	
Poor methodology	4	(2.7)	2	(3.3)
Below average methodology	17	(17.6)	22	(21.3)
Average methodology	19	(22.2)	30	(26.8)
Above average methodology	32	(30.8)	36	(37.2)
Good methodology	9	(7.7)	8	(9.3)

in the research rather than to the nature of evaluative research itself. In order to check this hopeful possibility the relationship between degree of experimental error and outcome of the study was determined.

Table 14 indicates that no relationship between the two exists. Positive findings of change are not associated with poorly designed research any more or less than they are associated with studies employing a relatively sophisticated design with elaborate experimental controls. In short, good and bad research obtained the same general finding: change occurs in approximately 45 per cent of the cases reviewed.

Several additional data analyses were undertaken in order to clarify the issues involved in arriving at a final assessment of the significance of evaluative research. These analyses appeared initially promising but proved to be either negative or puzzling in their outcome and do not affect the conclusions that have been drawn.

Summary of the General and Comparative Analysis of Evaluative Research

Two conclusions are suggested by the analysis: the quality of evaluative research is remarkably poor, and there is little difference in the results of evaluative studies conducted in different content areas. Specifically, there is no indication that the findings of evaluative research are influenced by the method tested, the content area in which the test is conducted, the change criteria used, or the methodological quality of the study of which the evaluation is made. The only clear positive finding is that change is demonstrated in approximately 45 per cent of the studies.

In considering the remarkably poor quality of evaluative research, it is necessary to remember the variety of technical and social difficulties that arise in the design and execution of these studies. However, regardless of the quality of the research itself, there remains the fact that it does not seem to produce any positive conclusions, except that change is consistently demonstrated in a certain fixed proportion of the studies. This is the heart of the problem. Evaluative research is intended to distinguish among methods of changing behavior, determining the most successful procedures, and to clarify the process of behavior change itself. To do this the demonstrated change must be related to other significant variables, such as the content area investigated, instruments used, and methods tested. None of these relationships can be clearly established. One is driven, therefore, to the inescapable conclusion that evaluative research shows no prospect of reaching these goals.

Such a damaging conclusion requires an explanation. The most reasonable explanation the author can offer, on the basis of his direct examination of the evidence, is that evaluative research is not undermined so much by the problem of its execution as by the methods it attempts to evaluate. The ingredients of evaluative studies are inappropriate to scientific methodology, which, like any good recipe, requires the use of specific pure elements that are combined in known proportions and in a fixed time schedule. Virtually all methods evaluated by the studies reviewed were of such complexity as to defy description in terms of a limited number of carefully specified variables. Such descriptive labels as psychoanalysis, nondirective therapy, or group-centered experience cover a multitude of operations whose precise nature and order of presentation are unknown. If the methods that are tested cannot be precisely described, then the results can never be cumulative, since no one can state what was tested.

The general conclusion of this comparative review is, therefore, that evaluative research represents a scientific blind alley. It has failed to validate itself in practice and the sooner its failure is accepted and recognized, the easier will be a transition to another approach to the same problem.

Studying the Components of Behavior-Change Procedures

In order to be able to study the problem of changing human behavior in a systematic and cumulative manner, it is only necessary to change the focus from the complex method as it is applied in practical situations to the components of the method, which can be examined with any desired degree of experimental precision in a laboratory setting. The number of such components is limited, and the huge variety of behavior-change techniques currently utilized represent, for the most part, variations on a few central themes.

A relatively superficial examination of the social and psychological research literature suggests that among such components of change procedures can be included the following:

1. The direction, amount, and quality of participation of both the subject and the practitioner
2. The nature of feedback mechanisms
3. The nature and extent of opportunity for the practice of the behavior patterns
4. Variations in power relationships
5. The operant conditioning of new behaviors
6. The elimination of undesired behaviors through negative conditioning
7. Elimination of undesirable reactions through deconditioning
8. The degree of faith which the subject has in the method
9. The involvement of the practitioner in the application of the method
10. The creation of stress
11. The opportunity for confession and catharsis
12. The concentration of the subject's attention on his own behavior

This list could be extended, but it sufficiently illustrates the point that it is possible to name a variety of components of the complex change processes. In addition, all of these components have been studied experimentally, so that it has already been demonstrated that they lend themselves to precise definition and measurement in keeping with customary standards in the behavioral sciences. What is more important, however, is that these components are, in fact, vital elements in most change processes. Virtually each method, for example, uses some specialized form of feedback—whether positive, negative, objective, or subjective. Further, each technique employs certain implicit or explicit laws of participation. In some, all interaction is directed toward the practitioner; in others, it is ignored and group members talk with each other. Further, the type of participation is usually specified; in psychotherapy, for example, particular stress is laid on emotionally toned materials rather than on extensive use of rational formulation.

Additional examples are easily provided. Some methods of therapy emphasize the creation of stress, opportunity for catharsis, and the continuous focus of the subject's attention on his own reaction. In other behavior-change techniques stress is minimized, and attention on the individual and opportunity for confession are both avoided. Even the same method may use different degrees of a given component at separate stages. For example, stress may be initially avoided, but emphasized at a later period.

The more known methods are reinterpreted in terms of specific components, the more one is struck by the fact that in studying the variations in given components, something is learned about the efficiency of a wide range of change processes, even though one does not test any one of them. Furthermore, testing of components is natural to the scientific method. The experimenter can control all relevant aspects of the social situation. Conflicts of interest with the practitioner need not occur, since the research involves testing components in the laboratory rather than evaluation of programs and treatment methods. This procedure also bypasses the practitioner's resistance to being evaluated, since he is not directly involved in the testing process. More generally, studies of separate components avoid all of the previously described social problems associated with evaluative research.

The major obstacle to the development of a program of research designed to test behavior-change components is that, despite the existence of a vast amount of research into such topics as attitude change, group dynamics, social influences on learning, and intergroup relations, this material has not been systematically and thoroughly examined to determine which components of change processes have been scientifically validated. It is crucial that such a critical examination of the experimental literatures involved should precede any actual research program so that central emphasis can be placed on the variables most likely to be of importance in producing behavior and attitude change.

So often in the behavioral sciences new areas are opened up in an opportunistic and superficial manner because of the development of a new and simple research technique; or they are developed one-sidedly due to a popular but limited theory that happens to be current at the time. Almost inevitably in such instances, with the accumulation of some research data a critical reaction sets in. Persons working in the area realize that much of the previous work has been misapplied, has ignored important variables and, in general, has been extremely inefficient in terms of a lasting return in secure scientific knowledge.

In the analysis of behavior change, much of this developmental inefficiency can be avoided, because a large body of relevant research studies already exists. A review of this literature can accomplish several purposes. It can help to establish precisely which components of behavior-change processes have been experimentally validated. And it can determine what is known about the effect of the simultaneous application of different components, each of which may have been independently validated. In such cases, it may be possible to judge whether components are additive or interactive in their effect. Moreover, it can establish which components have proved either difficult to measure or relatively weak as determinants of change. When this information has been accumulated and organized, it should be possible to develop a set of priorities that could dictate, on the basis of known experimental findings, which relationships among components ought to be tested, and in what order.

The power of experimental designs combining the simultaneous variation of a number of different components on a series of different levels has been greatly increased by recent developments in multiple statistical comparisons, which enable researchers using complex factorial designs to test not only for the effect of each component included in the design, but also for the relative effects of each unique combination of components. In addition, whether combined effects are additive or interactive can be determined.

An example of such a factorial study of behavior-change components might involve three variations in power relations (democratic, laissez-faire, and autocratic), four variations in feedback (subjective, objective, positive, and negative), and three variations in stress (strong, moderate, and weak). Such a factorial study would require the testing of thirty-six independent conditions if all possible combinations of power relations, feedback mechanisms, and stress were examined.

The significance of studying the behavior changes produced by various combinations can best be seen by examining several of them. For example, consider the case of an authoritarian power structure with objective feedback and high stress. Such a condition would appear to resemble certain types of staff meetings that occur in highly differentiated institutional structures. The complementary experimental condition would consist of a laissez-faire structure, subjective feedback, and low stress. This condition resembles a normal, friendly social gathering. Another of the thirty-six possible conditions would consist of a democratic structure with positive feedback and moderate stress, resembling certain types of volunteer action groups. Thus, many of the combined components tested in such a study would resemble behavior-change processes currently in use and cast some indirect light on their validity.

However, the greatest significance of this approach to the study of behavior change is not that the experimental conditions resemble practical methods currently in use, but in the degree and character of the information it provides for a given amount of effort.

The effect of each level of each component in the example would be tested not only for its absolute effectiveness, but also for its relative effectiveness in comparison to each level of every component. The absolute and differential effect of each of the thirty-six component combinations would be determined. This is particularly important, since it is of greater significance to determine how the elements of known potency combine than to know that they are individually potent. Components of behavior change are rarely, if ever, applied singly, except for experimental purposes. A complex experimental condition is the analogue of the practical treatment as applied by the practitioner. It would be determined whether certain combinations of conditions are more effective in producing specified behavior changes than knowledge about their individual effectiveness would lead one to predict.

In this manner, a complex factorial approach to the study of behavior-change components could efficiently accumulate much information directly relevant to the understanding and evaluation of a number of change-inducing procedures, while not directly testing any one of them. This, in turn, would help to provide the basis of a science of behavior change that was both systematic and comprehensive.

References

CHAPTER TWO

1. S. Rosenzweig, "A Dynamic Interpretation of Psychotherapy Oriented Towards Research," *Psychiatry*, I (1938), No. 4.
2. J. D. Frank, *Persuasion and Healing* (Baltimore: Johns Hopkins Press, 1961).
3. W. Schofield, *Psychotherapy: the Purchase of Friendship* (Englewood Cliffs, N. J.: Prentice-Hall, Inc., 1964).
4. P. London, *The Modes and Morals of Psychotherapy* (New York: Holt, Rinehart & Winston, Inc., 1964).
5. C. Rogers, "A Process Conception of Psychotherapy," *American Psychologist*, XIII (1958), pp. 142–149.
6. R. Lippitt, J. Watson, and B. Westley, *The Dynamics of Planned Change —A Comparative Study of Principles and Techniques* (New York: Harcourt, Brace & World, Inc., 1958).
7. D. H. Ford and H. B. Urban, *Systems of Psychotherapy: a Comparative Study* (New York: John Wiley & Sons, Inc., 1963).
8. J. Hayley, *Strategies of Psychotherapy* (New York: Grune & Stratton, Inc, 1963).
9. C. Slack, "Development of Educational and Rehabilitative Systems for Offenders on Probation" (unpublished report on a Ford Foundation project, 1962).

CHAPTER THREE

1. T. Leary, *Interpersonal Diagnosis of Personality* (New York: The Ronald Press Company, 1957).

CHAPTER FOUR

1. S. J. Van Pelt, "The Control of Heart Rate by Hypnotic Suggestion," in *Experimental Hypnosis*, ed. L. M. Lecron (New York: The Macmillan Company, 1954), pp. 268–275.
2. B. B. Raginsky, "Temporary Cardiac Arrest Induced Under Hypnosis," *International Journal of Clinical and Experimental Hypnosis*, VII (1959), pp. 53–68.
3. C. M. McClure, "Cardiac Arrest Through Volition," *California Medicine*, XC (1959), pp. 440–441.
4. A. H. C. Sinclair-Gieben and D. Chalmers, "Evaluation of Treatment of Warts by Hypnosis," *Lancet*, II (1959), pp. 480–482.
5. T. X. Barber, "Hypnosis, Analgesia, and the Placebo Effect," *Journal of the American Medical Association*, CLXXII (1960), pp. 680–683.

CHAPTER FIVE

1. C. B. Ferster and B. F. Skinner, *Schedules of Reinforcement* (New York: Appleton-Century-Crofts, 1957).
2. J. M. Grossberg, "Behavior Therapy: A Review," *Psychological Bulletin*, LXII (1964), pp. 73–88.
3. W. A. Kennedy and H. C. Willcutt, "Praise and Blame as Incentives," *Psychological Bulletin*, LXII (1964), pp. 323–332.
4. W. S. Verplanck, "The Control of the Content of Conversation: Reinforcement of Statements of Opinion," *Journal of Abnormal and Social Psychology*, LI (1955), pp. 668–676.
5. L. Krasner, "Studies of the Conditioning of Verbal Behavior," *Psychological Bulletin*, LV (1958), pp. 121–147.

CHAPTER SIX

1. F. A. Volgyesi, "School for Patients, Hypnosis Therapy, and Psycho-Prophylaxis," *British Journal of Medical Hypnotism*, Vol. V (1954), pp. 8–17.
2. L. H. Gliedman, E. H. Nash, S. D. Imber, A. R. Stone, and J. D. Frank, "Reduction of Symptoms by Pharmacologically Inert Substances and by Short-Term Psychotherapy," *American Medical Association Archives of Neurology and Psychiatry*, LXXIX (1958), pp. 345–51.
3. J. D. Ashby, D. H. Ford, B. G. Guerney, and L. F. Guerney, "Effects on Clients of a Reflective and a Leading Type of Psychotherapy," *Psychological Monographs*, LXXI (1957), No. 24, Whole No. 321.
4. J. E. Gorden, "Leading and Following Psychotherapeutic Techniques with Hypnotically Induced Repression and Hostility," *Journal of Abnormal and Social Psychology*, LIV (1957), pp. 405–410.
5. C. D. Keet, "Two Verbal Techniques in a Miniature Counseling Situation," *Psychological Monographs*, LXII (1948), Whole No. 294.
6. D. Grossman, "An Experimental Investigation of a Psychotherapeutic Technique," *Journal of Consulting Psychology*, XVI (1952), pp. 324–331.
7. W. H. Coons, "Interaction and Insight in Group Psychotherapy," *Canadian Journal of Psychology*, XI (1957), pp. 1–8.
8. N. C. Bourestom and W. L. Smith, "A Comparison between Fantasy and Social Behavior in Experimental Group Psychotherapy," *Group Psychotherapy*, VII (1954), pp. 205–214.
9. K. M. Colby, "Computer Simulation of a Neurotic Process," in S. S. Tompkins and S. Messick, eds., *Computer Simulation of Personality: Frontier of Psychological Theory* (New York: John Wiley & Sons, Inc., 1963), pp. 165–179.

REFERENCES

CHAPTER SEVEN

1. L. M. Terman, "A Preliminary Study of the Psychology and Pedagogy of Leadership," *Pedagogical Seminary*, XI (1904), pp. 413–451.
2. A. P. Hare, "A Study of Interaction and Consensus in Different Sized Groups," *American Sociological Review*, XVII (1952), pp. 261–267.
3. R. F. Bales and E. F. Borgatta, "A Study of Group Size: Size of Group as a Factor in the Interaction Profile," in A. P. Hare, E. F. Borgatta, and R. F. Bales, eds., *Small Groups* (New York: Alfred Knopf, Inc., 1955), pp. 398–413.
4. J. K. Hemphill, "Relations Between the Size of the Group and the Behavior of 'Superior' Leaders," *Journal of Social Psychology*, XXXII (1950), pp. 11–22.
5. R. Marriot, "Size of Working Group and Output," *Occupational Psychology*, XXIII (London, 1949), pp. 47–57.
6. J. R. Gibb, "The Affect of Group Size and of Threat Reduction upon Creativity in a Problem Solving Situation," *American Psychology*, VI (1951), p. 324.
7. E. B. South, "Some Psychological Aspects of Committee Work," *Journal of Applied Psychology*, XI (1927), pp. 437–464.
8. B. M. Bass and M. Fay-Taylor Norton, "Group Size and Leaderless Discussion," *Journal of Applied Psychology*, XXXV (1951), pp. 397–400.
9. T. M. Mills, "Power Relations in Three-Person Groups," *American Sociological Review*, XVIII (1953), pp. 351–57.
10. R. Heslin, "Predicting Group Task Effectiveness from Member Characteristics," *Psychological Bulletin*, LXII (1965), pp. 248–256.
11. M. G. Preston and R. K. Heintz, "Effects of Participatory versus Supervisory Leadership on Group Judgment," *Journal of Abnormal and Social Psychology*, XLIV (1949), pp. 345–355.
12. K. Lewin and R. Lippitt, "An Experimental Approach to the Study of Autocracy and Democracy: A Preliminary Note," *Sociometry*, I (1938), pp. 292–300.
13. L. G. Wispe, "Evaluating Section Teaching Methods in the Introductory Course," *Journal of Educational Research*, XLV (1951) pp. 161–186.
14. L. Berkowitz, "Sharing Leadership in Small, Decision-Making Groups," *Journal of Abnormal and Social Psychology*, XLVIII (1953), pp. 231–238.
15. H. G. McCurdy and H. W. Eber, "Democratic versus Authoritarian: A Further Investigation of Group Problem-Solving," *Journal of Personality*, XXII (1953), pp. 258–269.
16. M. Deutsch, "An Experimental Study of the Effects of Cooperation and Competition upon Group Process," *Human Relations*, II (1949), pp. 199–231.
17. F. F. Stephan and E. G. Mishler, "The Distribution of Participation in Small Groups: An Exponential Approximation," *American Sociological Review*, XVII (1952), pp. 598–608.

18. J. L. Moreno, "Contributions of Sociometry to Research Methodology in Sociology," *American Sociological Review*, XII (1947) pp. 287–292.
19. H. J. Leavitt, "Some Effects of Certain Communication Patterns on Group Performance," *Journal of Abnormal and Social Psychology*, XLVI (1951), pp. 38–50.
20. I. L. Janis and B. T. King, "The Influence of Role Playing on Opinion Change," *Journal of Abnormal and Social Psychology*, XLIX (1954), pp. 211–218.
21. S. E. Asch, "Effects of Group Pressure Upon the Modification and Distortion of Judgments," in H. Guetzkow, ed., *Groups, Leadership, and Men* (Pittsburgh: Carnegie Press, 1951).
22. V. M. Bechterew, and M. de Lange, "Die Ergebnisse des Experiments auf dem Gebiete der Kollectiven Reflexologie," *Zsch. f. angew. Psychol.*, XXIV (1924), pp. 305–344.
23. W. A. Timmons, "Decisions and Attitudes as Outcomes of the Discussion of a Social Problem," *Teachers College of Columbia University Contributions to Education*, No. 777 (1939).
24. L. Coch and J. R. P. French, Jr., "Overcoming Resistance to Change," *Human Relations*, I (1948), pp. 512–532.
25. J. Levine and J. Butler, "Lecture vs. Group Decision in Changing Behavior," *Journal of Applied Psychology*, XXXVI (1952), pp. 29–33.
26. K. Lewin, "Group Decision and Social Change," in E. Maccoby, T. M. Newcomb and E. L. Hartley, eds., *Readings in Social Psychology* (New York: Holt, Rinehart & Winston, Inc., 1958), pp. 197–211.
27. K. Lewin, *ibid.*
28. E. B. Bennett, "Discussion, Decision, Commitment and Consensus in 'Group Decision,'" *Human Relations*, VIII (1955), pp. 251–274.
29. H. H. Jennings, *Leadership and Isolation* (New York: Longmans, Green & Co., Inc., 1950).
30. R. H. Van Zelst, "An Interpersonal Relations Technique for Industry," *Personnel*, XXIX (1952), pp. 68–76.
31. E. P. Torrance, "Methods of Conducting Critiques of Group Problem-Solving Performance," *Journal of Applied Psychology*, XXXVII (1953), pp. 394–398.
32. L. Carter, in a personal communication to the author, (1958).
33. D. Cartwright, "Achieving Changes in People: Some Applications of Group Dynamics Theory," *Human Relations*, IV (1951), pp. 381–393.
34. L. P. Bradford, J. R. Gibb and K. D. Benne, eds., *T-Group Theory and Laboratory Method* (New York: John Wiley & Sons, Inc., 1964).

CHAPTER EIGHT

1. C. I. Hovland, A. A. Lumsdaine, and F. D. Sheffield, *Experiments on Mass Communication* (Princeton University Press, 1949).
2. H. I. Abelson, *Persuasion* (New York: Springer Publishing Co., Inc., 1959).

REFERENCES

3. F. Heider, "Social Perception and Phenomenal Causality," *Psychological Review*, LI (1944), pp. 358–374.
4. L. Festinger and J. M. Carlsmith, "Cognitive Consequences of Forced Compliance," *Journal of Abnormal and Social Psychology*, LVIII (1959), pp. 203–210.
5. M. J. Rosenberg and C. W. Gardner, "Case Report: Some Dynamic Aspects of Post-Hypnotic Compliance," *Journal of Abnormal and Social Psychology*, LVII (1958), pp. 351–366.

CHAPTER NINE

1. C. I. Hovland, "Reconciling Conflicting Results Derived from Experimental and Survey Studies of Attitude Change," *American Psychologist*, XIV (1959), pp. 8–17.

CHAPTER TEN

1. D. Katz and K. W. Braly, "Verbal Stereotypes and Racial Prejudice," *Journal of Abnormal and Social Psychology*, XXVIII (1933), pp. 280–290.
2. G. M. Gilbert, "Stereotype Persistence and Change Among College Students," *Journal of Abnormal and Social Psychology*, XLVI (1951), pp. 245–254.
3. J. H. Mann, "The Relationship between Cognitive, Affective and Behavioral Aspects of Racial Prejudice," *Journal of Social Psychology*, XLIX, pp. 223–228.
4. S. W. Cook and C. Selltiz, "A Multiple-Indicator Approach to Attitude Measurement," *Psychological Bulletin*, LXII (1964), pp. 36–55.
5. H. E. Kagan, *Changing the Attitude of Christians toward Jews: A Psychological Approach through Religion* (New York: Columbia University Press, 1952).
6. R. C. Peterson and L. L. Thurstone, *Motion Pictures and the Social Attitudes of Children* (New York: The Macmillan Company, 1933).
7. M. Deutsch and M. E. Collins, *Interracial Housing: A Psychological Evaluation of a Social Experiment* (Minneapolis: The University of Minnesota Press, 1951).
8. G. Allport, *The Nature of Prejudice* (Reading, Mass.: Addison-Wesley Publishing Co., Inc., 1954).
9. I. Katz, "Review of Evidence on Effects of Desegregation on the Intellectual Performance of Negroes," *American Psychologist*, XIX (1964), pp. 381–399.

CHAPTER ELEVEN

1. G. Wallas, *The Art of Thought* (New York: Harcourt, Brace and Company, Inc., 1926).
2. O. W. Taylor, W. R. Smith, and B. Ghiselin, "Analysis of Multiple Criteria of Creativity and Productivity of Scientists," in C. Taylor, ed.,

The 1959 University of Utah Research Conference on the Identification of Creative Scientific Talent (Salt Lake City: The University of Utah Press, 1959), pp. 5–28.
3. J. P. Guilford, "Traits of Creativity," in H. Anderson, ed., *Creativity and Its Cultivation* (New York: Harper & Brothers, Inc., 1959), pp. 142–161.
4. W. J. J. Gordon, *Synectics: The Development of Creative Capacity* (New York: Harper & Row, Publishers), pp. 124–126. Copyright © 1961 by William J. J. Gordon. Reprinted by permission of Harper & Row, Publishers.
5. *Ibid.*

CHAPTER TWELVE

1. A. J. Keys, J. Brozek, *et al.*, *The Biology of Human Starvation* (Minneapolis: The University of Minnesota Press, 1950).
2. E. D. Luby, C. E. Frohman, J. L. Grisell, J. E. Lenzo, and J. S. Gottlieb, "Sleep Deprivation: Effects on Behavior, Thinking, Motor Performance, and Biological Energy Transfer Systems," *Psychosomatic Medicine*, XXII (1960), pp. 182–192.

CHAPTER THIRTEEN

1. E. W. Maupin, "Zen Buddhism: A Psychological Review," *Journal of Consulting Psychology*, XXVI (1962), pp. 362–378.
2. A. Watts, *Psychotherapy: East and West* (New York: Pantheon, 1961).
3. R. O. Ballou, ed., *The Bible of the World* (New York: The Viking Press, Inc., 1939), pp. 245–246. From *The Sacred Books of the Buddhists*, T. W. and C. A. F. Rhys Davids, trans., Vol. III, Part II, pp. 328–329. Reprinted by permission of the Clarendon Press, Oxford.

CHAPTER FOURTEEN

1. M. Nicoll, *The New Man* (New York: Hermitage House, 1951).
2. A. Huxley, *The Perennial Philosophy* (New York: Harper & Row, 1945), p. 292.
3. *Ibid.*
4. *Ibid.*, pp. 112–114.
5. *Ibid.*, p. 103.
6. *Ibid.*, p. 277.

APPENDIX A

1. F. E. Fiedler, "The Concept of an Ideal Therapeutic Relationship," *Journal of Consulting Psychology*, XIV (1950), pp. 239–245.

APPENDIX B

1. J. H. Mann, "The Assessment of Efforts to Change Adult Personality," Russell Sage Project No. 8-8548-131.

Glossary

Alpha wave pattern, an electrical pattern produced by the neural activity of the brain producing approximately ten fluctuations a second when the subject is in a relaxed state.

Behavioral sciences, the sciences devoted to the study of human behavior, including psychology, sociology, and cultural anthropology.

Change agent, a professional who administers a procedure that is designed to produce behavioral, attitudinal, and personality change. Two essential criteria must be satisfied for the change agent: the individual must be acting in a professional rather than personal capacity; and the impact of his actions must be directed toward producing change in others with whom he is working.

Classical conditioning, a learning procedure in which the unconditioned stimulus follows the conditioned stimulus. *See* conditioned stimulus and unconditioned stimulus.

Cognitive dissonance, an attitude-change theory based on the principle that an individual finds it uncomfortable to hold inconsistent attitudes; he therefore alters them so that they become consonant with each other. The theory states when and how such attitude modifications will occur.

Communications analysis, a study of the process and content of communication.

Communications network, the set of channels employed by a group of individuals when communicating with each other.

Communications theory, the theory describing and analyzing how messages are sent from a sender to a receiver over a communications channel.

Conceptual model, an abstract set of relationships designed to represent the underlying basic processes of a particular series of objective events. Such models perform the vital function of directing research efforts in a coordinated manner. Each investigation that is conducted on any aspect indirectly tests the efficacy of the whole model itself, since it is designed to be logically consistent.

Conditioned stimulus, a stimulus, such as a bell, that, when presented for a period of time together with another stimulus naturally arousing a certain response, such as food, itself comes to arouse the same response.

Conditioning, the process through which conditioned responses are acquired.

Control, the specification of certain conditions in experimental studies designed to limit or eliminate the action of certain variables.

Control group, in an experiment, a group of subjects that does not receive the experimental treatment. The control group is a vital aspect of any evaluative research effort. Without it, one cannot determine whether change is produced by the experimental treatment or by other concurrent circumstances, such as normal routine activities.

Congruity model, an attitude-change model based on the general concept that an individual attempts to keep his attitude structure in a state of balance. The basic principle of this model is that when the equilibrium is disturbed an attitude change will occur that is inversely proportional to the strength of the original opinion and in the opposite direction from the force that upset the previous equilibrium.

Creativity, the ability to perceive familiar materials in an unusual manner. Creativity has been defined as anything from the ability to think of unfamiliar word associations to the ability to produce great artistic or scientific works. The latter definition confounds creativity and success, while the former sacrifices significance of definition for purity. Creativity must be viewed in the context of the type of measurement employed to detect, or a series of apparently contradictory findings is likely to emerge.

Cortex, the outer layer of a bodily organ, such as the adrenal cortex or the cerebral cortex.

Directive therapy, a form of therapy in which the practitioner tells the patient how he ought to behave.

Evaluative research, a study designed to determine the effectiveness of a particular procedure.

Ex-post facto design, a study that depends on a respondent's recollections in order to determine how he felt at a certain time in the past about an issue under investigation.

Factor analysis, a statistical procedure for reducing a complex set of relationships into simpler form. Factor analysis supplies an exact method for drawing general conclusions from a set of data that otherwise might be difficult to interpret in a coherent and meaningful manner. It is perhaps the outstanding example of a method of multivariant analysis, that is, the simultaneous study of a large group of variables.

Feedback, the channeling or directing of communications to a control center from which future communications output can be regulated.

Group dynamics, the name of a scientific movement devoted to the dual objectives of studying small-group processes and the utilization of such research for the production of behavior change in members of such groups.

Group therapy, the treatment of mentally ill persons in a group setting.

Human-relations trainer, a change agent who works with normal individuals usually in a group setting. The trainer's objectives are most often to increase the diagnostic skills and behavioral effectiveness of the trainees and to foster their leadership abilities. *See* change agent.

Homeostasis, the maintenance of a physiological system within narrow limits of tolerance through an appropriate system of controls.

Hypnosis, an artificially induced state characterized by trance and extreme suggestibility.

Hypnotic trance, the state of semisleep that is typically induced by hypnotism. *See* hypnosis.

Intelligence quotient (IQ), the relation between an individual's mental age and his chronological age.

Instrumental conditioning, conditioning produced by rewarding the performance of a behavior pattern that one seeks to establish. *See* conditioning.

Interaction, the behavior persons direct toward each other.

Interaction process analysis, a set of 12 categories for analyzing individual behavior in small group situations.

LSD, an abbreviated name for the hallucinogenic drug lysergic acid diethylamide.

Mantrum, a sacred East Indian chant.

Matrix of probabilities, a table showing the relationship of a set of variables to each other.

Model, see conceptual model.

Naturalistic experiment, a study conducted in normal social circumstances that do not lend themselves to precise experimental control.

Nondirective therapy, therapy in which an affort is made to avoid any direct attempt to influence the patient as he formulates his own problems and slowly works out appropriate solutions.

Objective feedback, feedback of information to a subject obtained from standard sources, such as tests or independent observations.

Operant conditioning, see instrumental conditioning.

Personality psychologist, a practitioner who specializes in the study of human personality.

Persuasibility, the characteristic of being persuaded. This trait has been widely studied as a personality correlate of attitude change.

Placebo, a physiologically nonactive substance, such as a sugar pill or distilled water, that is used as a control for the effects of a presumably active physiological agent, such as a drug or a hormone. The placebo is designed to duplicate the active substance in appearance. Ideally, neither the subject nor the physician are aware of whether or not the placebo is being used. In this way, the beliefs of the practitioner and the patient about the effectiveness of the treatment are controlled.

Placebo effect, the influence exerted by the belief the subject has in the treatment he receives.

Practitioner, see change agent.

Primacy effect, the influence related to being exposed to one message before another. If the order of presentation has a demonstrable effect on the relative impact of the messages, then a primacy effect can be said to exist.

Primary group, a small group with which the individual has frequent, informal contact.

Primary motivation, physiologically determined needs, such as hunger and sleep.

Process analysis, the study of patterns of communication.

Process variable, a variable that is studied in a process analysis.

Program, a set of steps that controls the operation of a machine, such as a teaching machine or an electronic computer.

Projective test, a set of standardized, ambiguous stimuli to which the subject is asked to respond. Since the stimuli have no actual meaning, any meaning the subject ascribes to them is presumed to reflect his personality. Responses to the test can, therefore, be used as a basis for analyzing personality.

Psychiatrist, a practitioner with a medical specialization in the treatment of the mentally ill.

Psychoanalyst, a practitioner who uses the method of treating mentally disturbed individuals originated by Sigmund Freud.

Psychotherapist, a practitioner who specializes in the psychological treatment of mentally disturbed persons.

Role playing, a procedure that employs improvisational techniques to train individuals to understand and perform new social roles.

Satori, a Japanese term meaning enlightenment.

Sensory deprivation, the elimination of various kinds of sensory stimuli for experimental purposes.

Simulation, the abstract re-creation of a complex natural event. Simulation provides the final test of scientific understanding since, it can only approximate reality when all important aspects of the natural event are fully understood, not only in their own right, but also in relationship to each other.

Sleeper effect, an unexpected attitude change that occurs long after the attempt to influence the attitude has ceased.

Social psychology, the study of the impact of social influences on individual behavior.

Socialization, the process of educating the young in the basic expectations and process of social living.

Sociometry, the science of measuring social relationships.

Sociometric reassignment, the placement of individuals in groups that they themselves chose.

Sociometric status, the level of popularity of the individual in a group.

Stimulus, any event that produced a reaction on the part of an individual.

Sufism, a form of Mohammedan mysticism in which God is described and approached as a beloved.

Survey research, research utilizing a large sample of persons selected to represent a known population.

Synectics, a method of enhancing creative capacity through the use of a specialized type of small-group experience.

Syndrome, a set of presenting symptoms.

Taoism, a form of Chinese mysticism that emphasizes the importance of simplicity and naturalness of action and the conception that all things come from and are manifestations of one universal principle, "Tao."

GLOSSARY

Teaching machine, a machine designed to present information to the student and to test whether he has mastered the material.

T-group, a training group employed by group-dynamics experts.

Therapist, see psychotherapist.

Trauma, a psychological or physiological injury.

Unconditioned stimulus, the stimulus in classical conditioning, such as food, that produced a specific response before the conditioning was undertaken. *See* classical conditioning.

Yoga, a general term for a number of different types of Indian systems of physical, religious, and philosophic training.

Zen Buddhism, a Japanese form of Buddhism characterized by an attempt to attain direct insight into the basic nature of the world and the self without recourse to sacred scriptures or other intellectual activities.

Suggestions for Further Reading

Bennis, W. G., Benne, K. D., and Chin, R. (eds.). *The Planning of Change*. New York: Holt, Rinehart & Winston, Inc., 1961.

Bennis, W. G., Schein, E. H., Berlew, D. E., and Steele, F. I. (eds.). *Interpersonal Dynamics*. Homewood, Ill.: Dorsey Press, 1964.

Biderman, A. D., and Zimmer, H. (eds.). *The Manipulation of Human Behavior*. New York: John Wiley & Sons, Inc., 1961.

Bradford, L. P., Gibb, J. R., and Benne, K. D. (eds.). *T-Group Theory and Laboratory Method*. New York: John Wiley & Sons, Inc., 1964.

Brown, R. "Models of Attitude Change." In *New Directions in Psychology*. New York: Holt, Rinehart & Winston, Inc., 1962.

Ford, D. H., and Urban, H. E. *Systems of Psychotherapy*. New York: John Wiley & Sons, Inc., 1963.

Frank, J. D. *Persuasion and Healing*. Baltimore, Md.: The Johns Hopkins Press, 1961.

Halacy, D. S., Jr. *Cyborg*. New York: Harper & Row, 1965.

Hayley, J. *Strategies of Psychotherapy*. New York: Grune & Stratton, Inc., 1963.

Krasner, L., and Ullmann, L. P. (eds.). *Research in Behavior Modification: New Developments and Implications*. New York: Holt, Rinehart & Winston, Inc., 1965.

Lippitt, R., Watson, J., and Westley, B. *The Dynamics of Planned Change*. New York: Harcourt, Brace & World, Inc., 1958.

Matarazzo, J. D. "Prescribed Behavior Therapy: Suggestions from Interview Research." In Bachrach, A. J. (ed.). *Experimental Foundations of Clinical Psychology*. New York: 1962.

Taylor, C. W., and Barron, F. (eds.). *Scientific Creativity: Its Recognition and Development*. New York: John Wiley & Sons, Inc., 1963.

Worschel, P., and Byrne, D. (eds.). *Personality Change*. New York: John Wiley & Sons, Inc., 1964.

Zollschan, G. K., and Hirsch, W. (eds.). *Explorations in Social Change*. Boston: Houghton Mifflin Company, 1965.

Index

model, 16–31, 67, 68, 76, 79, 81, 101,
103, 129, 177
  balance, 105
  congruity, 103, 105
  of influence processes, 103–106
*Modes and Morals of Psychotherapy,
The,* 21
Mohammed, 143
Mohammedanism, 156
Moreno, Jacob, 88
multifamily transcendent living, 36
mushrooms, containing hallucenogenic
drugs, 35
mystical experience, through drugs,
35
mystics, 127, 156, 157, 158, 160, 161,
163

needs, deprivation of, 140
nervous system, 33
neurologists, 33
New Man, The, 157
Nicoll, Maurice, 157
nondirective therapist, 12, 65
nondirective therapy, 26, 62, 68, 70,
166, 170, 206

Old Testament, 157

pain relief
  with drugs, 40
  with hypnosis, 43
paradox, in psychotherapy, 27 ff, 53–
54
parapsychology, 2
patients, 27, 28 ff, 32–33, 37, 40, 50 ff,
62, 65, 74, 75, 76, 79, 173
Pavlov, Ivan, 56
perception
  alteration of, 33
  faulty, 23, 45
permissiveness, in psychotherapy, 28
personality, description of, 3
personality psychologist, 111
persuader; *see* communicator
persuasibility, 100, 102
Persuasion, 99
Persuasion and Healing, 19
physicists, 3
physiological change, produced by
hypnosis; *see* hypnosis
physiological psychiatrist, 4

placebo, 37, 39, 50, 69
placebo effect, 180
practitioners, 9, 15 ff, 22–24, 43, 67,
69, 70, 74, 75, 78, 87, 171, 179,
181, 182, 183, 186, 200, 211, 212
  authority of, 19
  commitment to patient, 19
  as educator, 23–24
  effect of, 179–180
  as mediator, 19–20, 23
  number of, in experimental studies,
185–186
  relation to researchers, 183–184
prejudice, 118, 119, 120, 121, 123, 124
  components of, 119, 120, 123
  effects of education on, 120–122
  against Jews, 121
  against Negroes, 123
Preston, Malcolm G., 86
primacy effect, 116
Princeton University, 118
printed matter, 108, 109, 113, 115, 122
process analysis, 72
programming, of computers, 69, 77, 79
projective tests, 72, 73, 131, 141
psychiatrists, 2, 3, 9, 33, 173
psychoanalysis, 11, 152, 154, 206
psychoanalysts, 9, 24, 152
Psychological Corporation (New York
City), 169
psychologists, 2, 3, 25, 56, 62, 63, 81,
111, 112, 124, 140
psychopharmacology; *see* drugs, to
change behavior
Psychopharmacology Service Center
(National Institute for Mental
Health, Bethesda, Md.), 37
psychosocial change produced by
hypnosis; *see* hypnosis
psychotherapeutic process, 68, 70,
79–80
psychotherapeutic techniques, 75
psychotherapists, 4, 9, 20 ff, 24, 25,
26, 27, 28 ff, 60, 65, 68, 70, 71,
72, 73, 74, 75, 76, 78, 150, 172,
173, 179
psychotherapy, 5, 9, 10, 17, 18, 22,
24 ff, 37, 60, 61–62, 65, 74, 75,
77 ff, 124, 142, 150, 158, 165,
166, 167, 170, 171, 179, 192, 206
  evaluative statements in, 26

ABOUT THE AUTHOR

John Mann is an Associate Professor in the Graduate School of Arts and Sciences, New York University. Dr. Mann, whose area of specialization is social psychology, is interested in both the theoretical and applied aspects of modern psychology. He has acted as principal investigator for projects sponsored by the National Institute of Mental Health, the Russell Sage Foundation, and the Vocational Rehabilitation Administration and the Children's Bureau (U.S. Department of Health, Education, and Welfare).

Changing Human Behavior is the culmination of investigations that he has conducted during the last decade in intergroup relations, group dynamics, psychotherapy, and attitude and behavior change under the auspices of New York University, St. Vincent's Hospital, the Jewish Board of Guardians, the Retarded Infants Services, and the Child Study Association of America. The author of numerous technical articles in his field, Dr. Mann has also written, for the lay reader, *Frontiers of Psychology*.